PATISSERIE

REVOLUTION

Library and Archives Canada Cataloguing in Publication
Title: Patisserie revolution: the healthy baking bible / Johanna Le Pape, world champion of confectionary arts; Mélanie Frechon, dietitian.
Other titles: Révolution pâtisserie. English
Names: Le Pape, Johanna, author. | Frechon, Mélanie, contributor. | Mahoney, Anne Louise, translator.
Description: Translation of: Révolution pâtisserie. | "Translator: Anne Louise Mahoney" — Copyright page. | Includes index. | In English, translated from the French.
Identifiers: Canadiana 20240351533 | ISBN 9780778807247 (hardcover)
Subjects: LCSH: Pastry. | LCGFT: Cookbooks.
Classification: LCC TX773 .L413 2024 | DDC 641.86/5—dc23

Editor: Merel Elsinga
Translator: Anne Louise Mahoney
Indexer: Gillian Watts
Graphic design and illustrations: Coralie Chaffanjon
Layout and Production: PageWave Graphics Inc.
Photography: Nicolas Bouriette

We acknowledge the support of the Government of Canada.
Canadä

Published by Robert Rose Inc.
120 Eglinton Avenue East, Suite 800, Toronto, Ontario, Canada M4P 1E2
Tel: (416) 322-6552 Fax: (416) 322-6936
www.robertrose.ca

Printed and bound in China

1 2 3 4 5 6 7 8 9 ESP 32 31 30 29 28 27 26 25 24

PATISSERIE

REVOLUTION

The Healthy Baking Bible

A complete ingredient reference for
gluten-free, low-GI, dairy-free & vegan pastry

JOHANNA LE PAPE

World Champion of Confectionary Arts

Mélanie Frechon, Dietitian

Robert
ROSE

Contents

INTRODUCTION

Our world is faced with an opportunity for evolution and transformation. The time we are living in is pushing us to question how we act, how we approach life and work, and how we consume.

As we all seek to find our raison d'être, we must also consider the raison d'être of our professions to accompany this change.

Pastry lovers and professionals, what would you say to continuing to push the boundaries to bring together pastry making and current health, social and environmental issues? Listening, learning and constantly trying new things, being curious, getting informed and sharing our findings are essential if we are going to evolve. There is nothing more powerful than working in a particular way that gives meaning to our actions.

And what if we use our creativity to serve a much larger purpose? Healthy pastry making can be more than just a culinary trend.

It is a way of expressing our commitment to our own well-being and that of our planet. By using natural ingredients that are aligned with the seasons, choosing sustainable production methods and minimizing waste, we can offer sweet treats that support all these issues.

This book about making healthy pastry is a call to action. Through innovative, balanced recipes, I hope to inspire chefs, pastry fans and all those who seek to eat in a conscious way.

Together, let's explore the flavors, textures and techniques that allow us to make delicious and nutritious desserts while taking care of ourselves and our world.

A book created by a committed chef

Early on, I was drawn to pastry. Its elegance and deliciousness make birthdays a delight, and pastries are often displayed artfully on a sideboard or become small guilty pleasures.

Paris, the capital of this very French art, was a gold mine for learning the fundamentals of this haute couture pastry making that I dreamed of. I spent my early years learning with top chefs before competing at the Mondial des arts sucrés (a global confectionary arts competition), where I earned the title of World Champion, Arts Sucrés, with my partner, Gaëtan.

Wanting to create pastries that were more my personal style, I have been seeking a new approach at a time when the pastry making profession is getting more exposure on social media. Although the trend is toward what is visually stunning, with every glaze shinier than the one before, I tackled it from a different angle. Would it be possible to imagine healthy pastries that are just as delicious? Which ingredients would be used in these new, more nutritious recipes? Could I revise all the basic recipes, which took so many years to be developed by my peers who are all great pastry chefs? So many questions led me to read widely and speak with a number of experts. Nutrition, naturopathy, Chinese medicine... These subject areas revealed my scope of analysis and allowed me to approach my profession from a different angle, combining the health aspect with flavor and aesthetics.

It's a revolution!

In recent years, a movement has taken shape. Both professionals and non-professionals have demonstrated their commitment to

> choosing select local producers

> producing flour

> returning to the source of the chocolate bean, promoted by the Bean-to-bar movement

> creating pastries with a low glycemic index

> creating vegan pastries

Gluten-free, raw, vegan pastries... there's something for everyone. These new pastries are possible in part thanks to consumers' interest in a diet that suits them. There's no judgment: it is above all pastry that is wide ranging, diverse and with which everyone can identify. The pastry scene revolves around some great traditions and chefs. What a pleasure to be able, in keeping with one's own desires, to rediscover the hallmarks of these chefs, each of whom has a story and values to share.

A book for *your* revolution

This book is the result of eight years of work and research. With more than 250 ingredients included, I offer you a guide to using them in bold, delicious and balanced recipes, whether they are gluten-free, low glycemic index or vegan.

Along the way, you will discover, for example, more than 30 types of flour with distinct characteristics and a variety of sugars and syrups with a low glycemic index. It is a combination of sensory experiences, working on textures and balancing to meet an objective that is dear to my heart: making pastry healthier. That is how "well-being pastry," as I call it, was born. It is built on five main pillars.

The 5 pillars of healthy and committed baking

Diversify

using a wide range of ingredients: flours, sugars, vegetables, seeds.

Balance

sugars, combining them with fiber, to get a low glycemic index.

Source

quality raw materials from producers who care about the environment.

Innovate

constantly, testing new ingredients and "gentle" processing methods, with the aim of preserving the nutritional values of the recipe.

Recycle

by reusing waste to make new raw materials.

To all those who love pastries, I offer this wish: What if we dared to imagine a new future? It's up to you to start your own revolution!

Ingredient families

Flours

INTRODUCTION
THE STORY OF FLOUR

We know that flour is an essential ingredient in cooking, especially for pastry making and baking.

What we may not realize is how long humans have been using it! This powdered grain was bringing joy to Egyptian cooks more than 5,000 years ago. All they needed was a mortar and pestle to crush emmer or barley grains to make bread.

Today, production methods have evolved, and there are many more types of grains. Although wheat flour is the one most consumed in Europe and North America, corn flour is popular in South America and rice flour is a staple in Asia, the family of flours has gradually expanded due to variants made from millet, spelt, chickpea, lentil, buckwheat and lupin. Now, flour is available in more forms than ever: we can find flour that is gluten-free, with a low glycemic index, high in fiber, made from seeds, fruits or tubers... Each variety has specific properties: flavor, technical qualities and/or nutritional values.

In this chapter, you will discover all the flour alternatives and their characteristics, which will help you use them in the best way, add them to your recipes and vary them from day to day. Don't forget: our bodies are like nature; they like biodiversity!

⸝ HOW DO FLOURS WORK? ⸜

GI = The speed at which a food raises glucose levels in the blood

Cereal, fruit, legume or vegetable

Glycemic index (GI)

Source

Aromatic note

Color

Cereal, herbaceous, sweet, roasted ...

White, cream, yellow, brown ...

Gluten

With or without

WHAT IS GLUTEN?

Gluten (from *glu*, Latin for "glue") is a blend of different proteins. It is not present as such in cereals. Gluten is a viscoelastic material that is made of protein linked to a watery element. For gluten to form, two insoluble proteins, such as gliadin and glutenin, found in wheat, need to connect with water through kneading.

Wheat flour

THE GREAT HISTORY OF WHEAT FLOUR

Over the centuries, the production of wheat flour has greatly evolved: the yield and the physicochemical characteristics have been improved.

This was especially the case following the Second World War, where the aim was to feed populations that had known shortages and famine. This was the time of developing "industrial" production, as the volume had to be sizable to meet demand.

FROM WILD WHEAT TO MODERN WHEAT

Ever since wheat has been grown, humans have not stopped studying it to understand which variety had the best yield. To keep producing more and more, hybridization (the crossing of several species) was accelerated in the 1960s.

A classification of different varieties was established based on the number of chromosomes in wheat. Some crosses made it possible to increase this number from 14 to more than 42.

These hybridizations had an impact on the proportion of gluten in the grain as well as on the nature of the proteins modified, making it possible to obtain a "baking strength"[1] that is more favorable for baking.

Ancient wheat > baking strength = 90 → the dough was supple and not very sticky.

Modern wheat > baking strength = 202 → the dough does not tend to lose its shape, has high resistance, is easily worked, and the result is more aesthetically pleasing.

NEW PRODUCTS IN THE FIELDS

In this quest for high yields, we have also taken up the habit of spraying cereal crops with pesticides. As a result, chemical particles (inputs) are added to the grain and therefore into the flour it makes.

EVOLUTION OF THE CHANGES

FROM THE MILL...
Before the advent of industrialization, the only method for producing flour was to use a millstone. This technique gently crushed the whole grain, leaving some of the germ and the bran in the flour. Through the milling process, the grain was neither heated nor oxidized: this preserved its nutritional qualities, which remained in the flour. It was at the mill, at the end of the production process, that additives began to be used to improve the quality of the flour and/or to preserve it.

...TO THE FACTORY
With modern production techniques (use of cylinders), yields soared but the quality of the flour suffered, as the wheat was now missing its bran and its germ – the two components that offer nutritional benefits. The speed at which the grain is processed heats it, which increases its oxidation, and it loses some nutrients.

[1] The baking strength of a given wheat variety corresponds to the elasticity and stretchability ("viscoelasticity") levels of the dough that it will give.

MORE INFO

However, if we choose organic whole-grain or whole wheat flour that is stone-milled without additives, we can eat it more readily, as long as there are no risks of intolerance. Hence the importance of carefully choosing your mill, or brand of flour, but also your baker.

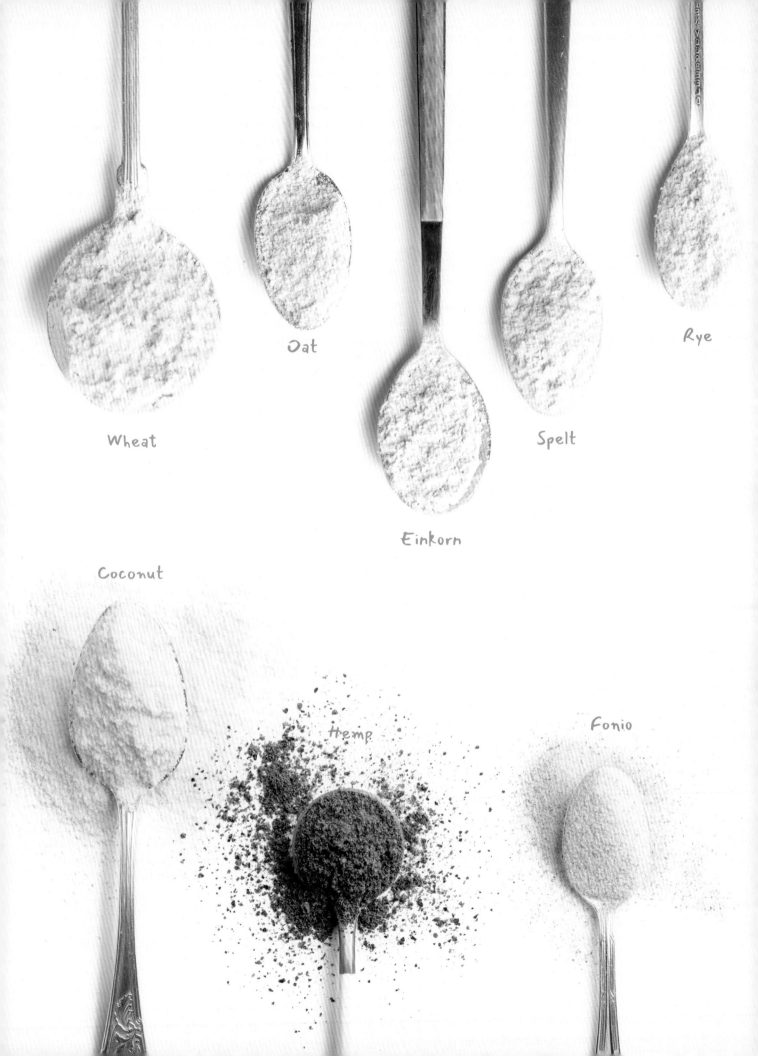

Wheat

Oat

Einkorn

Spelt

Rye

Coconut

Hemp

Fonio

Amaranth

Almond

Peanut

Green banana

Carob

Green
lentil

Cocoa

Kamut

Flax

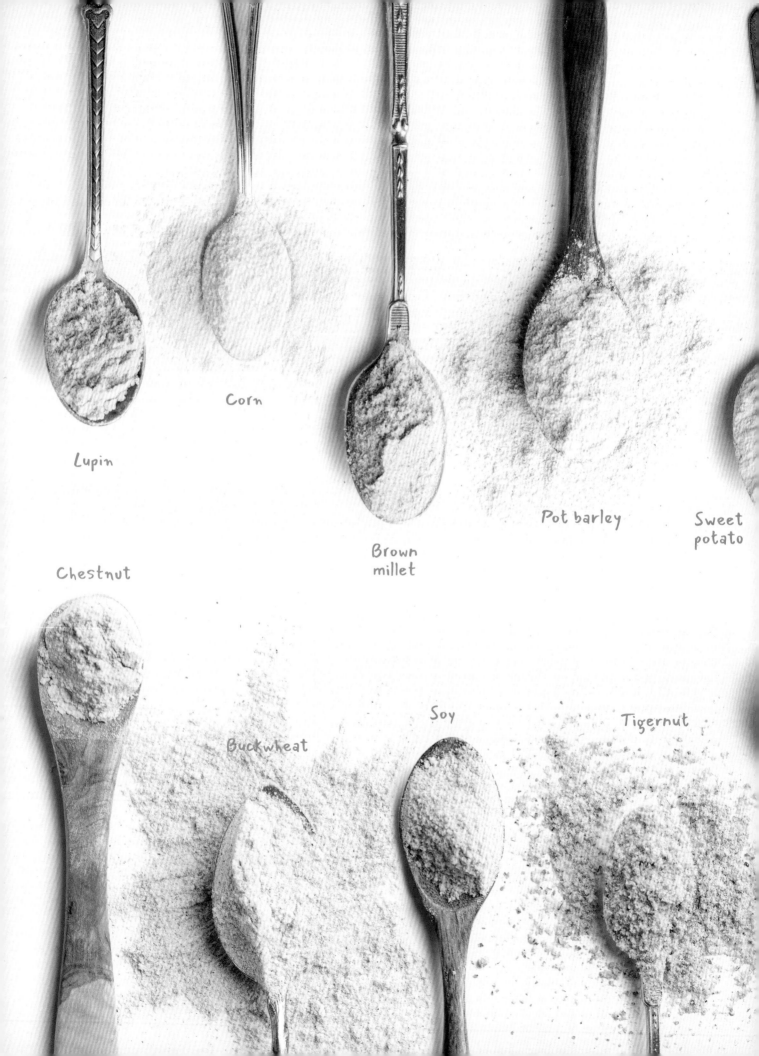

Corn

Lupin

Brown
millet

Pot barley

Sweet
potato

Chestnut

Buckwheat

Soy

Tigernut

Grape seed

Chickpea

Quinoa

Rice

White teff

Arrowroot
starch

Tapioca
starch

Potato
starch

Cornstarch

Rice
starch

Alternatives to wheat flour

⸰⸱

Legend

Origin	Color	Aromatic note	Absorption	Gluten	GI (raw)

ALMOND FLOUR: VERY LIGHT

Nut	◯	Light almond note, mild	+	⊗🍃	▯ 20

Source > Almond flour is made of dried almonds, ground and cold pressed to remove the oil; the residue is dried then ground finely.

Nutrients > This flour is of interest because it is made from raw almonds, whose skin contains significant nutritional qualities. Compared to ground almonds, the flour contains very little fat. It is known for being rich in essential amino acids and fiber (12 g/100 g). Low in carbohydrates, this flour has a low GI of around 20. It is rich in antioxidants, calcium and magnesium.

Use > Almond flour has a round, sweet flavor. It is finer than ground almonds and white in color. It brings a velvety texture to baking.

AMARANTH FLOUR: THE MOST COMPLETE

Cereal	◯	Earthy, beet	+	⊗🍃	▯ 40

Source > This flour comes from amaranth (called "the grain of the Incas"), a plant native to South America that is related to quinoa. It is obtained from crushing the seeds. There are about 100 varieties of amaranth plants. Some are used for their leaves and others for their seeds.

Nutrients > It is rich in protein, with its 9 essential amino acids (including lysine, which is rare in a grain). It contains fiber, iron, magnesium, antioxidants and folic acid (vitamin B9), an essential vitamin for healthy development of the fetal nervous system.

Use > Amaranth flour brings a viscous, even sticky, texture. It is important to mix it with another type of flour, such as rice or corn, to get softer cookies or crumbly shortbread. Its flavor, with earthy notes, is pronounced, and its color is light.

BARLEY FLOUR: THE BEST DETOXER

🌿 Cereal ⚪ Neutral +++ ⊗ ▮▯ 30

Source > This flour is made from a cereal and is found in two forms: pot barley and pearl barley. Pot barley still has the germ and the bran; only its cellulosic casing has been removed to make it edible. Pearl barley is more refined and contains fewer nutrients and less fiber, as its bran coating has been removed and the barley has been polished like a pearl.

Nutrients > Barley flour has been known for centuries for its detoxifying properties. This allows it to work for intestinal problems. Made of a molecule called "inositol," it also helps to regulate cholesterol. It contains plenty of vitamins B and K as well as minerals such as iron, copper and zinc and has high amounts of soluble fiber and carbohydrates and a low amount of gluten.

Use > It is white in color, has a sweet flavor and blends easily with wheat for making bread.

BROWN MILLET FLOUR: THE MOST ENERGETIC

🌿 Cereal ◐ Walnut, roasted note +++ ⊗ ▮▯ 70

Source > This flour comes from a cereal of the grass family. It is the result of milling wild unhusked brown millet grains (unlike yellow millet). Bonus: better nutrients.

Nutrients > Brown millet is a gluten-free cereal. As it is rich in starch, it is a source of fiber and vegetable protein. This makes it a small energy bomb that is considered to be a superfood because of its high vitamin B, silica and mineral content that is found in its husk.

Use > Brown millet flour has a grayish color and a nutty flavor. It can easily be combined with a neutral flour or a starch to give cakes a velvety texture.

BUCKWHEAT FLOUR: A ONE-OF-A-KIND FLAVOR

🌿 Cereal ◐ Roasted, earthy ++ ⊗ ▮▯ 40

Source > Buckwheat is the flour used in Breton galettes (a type of crepe). It is made not from wheat but from buckwheat, a plant grown mainly for its seeds.

Nutrients > It is rich in fiber and protein and is gluten-free. Its GI is medium and its caloric value is fairly high, thanks to its starch content.

Use > Buckwheat flour is gray in color. It gives mixtures a very dense texture and has a pronounced flavor. For these reasons, it is often used with another, lighter flour, or even a starch.

CAROB FLOUR: PACKED WITH BENEFITS

Fruit   Sweet and a caramel note   ++   15

Source > Carob flour is made from the fruit of the carob tree. It grows in a long pod, turning from green to brown when it is ripe. The seeds are removed to make carob bean gum. The fruit peel with pulp is turned into flour, after being dried and ground. It is often mentioned as a superfood because of its nutritional richness.

Nutrients > It is one of the most fiber-rich foods (40%): an ideal partner for helping move waste out of the body. Its richness in vitamins A, E, B2 and D2 add to its winning profile. Its low GI (15) is also an asset.

Use > It has a high capacity for absorption, allowing it to quickly thicken doughs and creams. With its slightly sweet chocolate notes, it can replace chocolate in a drink or a cake, for example.

CHESTNUT FLOUR: PACKED WITH ENERGY

Fruit   Sweet chestnut   ++   65

Source > After being shelled, chestnuts are dried and ground. Today we can identify dozens of different varieties of chestnuts that can be used as flour.

Nutrients > This gluten-free flour is rich in fiber and very high in carbohydrates, with a medium GI. This winning trio makes it a high-energy flour.

Use > Chestnut flour has a cream color and a strong, slightly sweet taste. It brings a dense texture to savory or sweet mixtures. It is often combined with rice flour.

CHICKPEA FLOUR: THE GOOD STUDENT

Legume   Mild, roasted chickpea   ++   35

Source > The production process is similar to that of other flours. Chickpeas are dried, then ground to get a powder.

Nutrients > Its richness in fiber and vegetable protein is a real plus, especially for bowel health. Chickpea flour has a satiating effect and is an excellent source of protein. It also contains many vitamins (primarily B) and minerals, such as magnesium and potassium.

Use > This pale-yellow flour is a fairly dense powder. Its flavor is rather pronounced in recipes, which is why it blends easily with other, more neutral flours.

COCOA POD FLOUR: THE NEW KID ON THE BLOCK!

Cocoa pod (fruit)   ●   Bitter, acidic   ++   ⊗

Source > This new product on the market is made of ground cocoa pods. In the past, it was used in garden beds as mulch or used for pig feed. Today, the trend is to upcycle: we make new raw materials out of "waste," and that works really well with cocoa pods!

Nutrients > This flour is very rich in fiber and trace elements such as potassium, magnesium, calcium and phosphorus.

Use > This flour has a strong, bitter flavor and is dark in color. It can give bread dough elasticity and moistness with an airy crumb after baking. Ideally, mix it with 50% whole wheat flour for optimal flavor and texture.

COCONUT FLOUR: NATURALLY SWEET

Fruit   ○   Sweet coconut   ++++   ⊗   ▮▯ 35

Source > This flour is made from the flesh of dried coconut, which is cold pressed to extract the oil. The dry extract is dried and ground until it forms flour.

Nutrients > It is rich in fiber and in protein, containing the 9 essential amino acids. In contrast, it is low in carbohydrates with a low GI, which is an asset for people with diabetes.

Use > With its slightly sweet flavor and subtle coconut notes, this is a real treat! As it is gluten-free, it does not have elastic properties but it does have a strong capacity for absorption. As a result, it can thicken a drink or a cream very easily or can be added in small quantities to a cake

CORN FLOUR: CARBS TO BURN

Cereal   ○   Neutral   ++   ⊗   ▮▯ 70

Source > Corn was being grown in Mexico at the time of the Incas and the Mayas. After it was exported to Europe during the 20th century, it became extensively hybridized. This whole-grain flour is made by milling whole corn kernels.

Nutrients > This gluten-free flour is very high in carbohydrates and has a high GI of 70. It also has a significant amount of potassium, phosphorus and magnesium.

Use > Corn flour has a slightly sweet flavor. Because of its yellow color, it gives baked goods a golden hue. Its high starch content allows it to soften the texture of baked goods and thicken creams or sauces.

MORE INFO

For people who are sensitive to gluten, this is a very good alternative to wheat flour or spelt flour.

EINKORN FLOUR: THE OLDEST ONE

 Cereal   Nutty, tangy   +   40

Source > Einkorn, occasionally also called small spelt, is sometimes compared to spelt. It belongs to the wheat family and is one of the oldest cereals cultivated by humans. Its résumé doesn't mention any genetic modification, as it has not undergone any crossbreeding. Before being made into flour, einkorn is husked, then ground.

Nutrients > Einkorn contains 7% gluten, compared to 12% for wheat. It is very nutritionally rich, with the highest levels of calcium, phosphorus and zinc. A bonus: it contains the 9 essential amino acids.

Use > Einkorn has a lightly golden color and a subtly roasted flavor. This flour is good for baking; it offers bread with a denser crumb.

FLAXSEED FLOUR: FIBER RICH

 Plant   Almond, walnut   +++   40

Source > This flour is made from the seeds of flax, an herbaceous plant. The seeds are ground to make powder.

Nutrients > Flax seeds are known for being rich in omega-3. Also, the fiber they bring is not to be overlooked, as 1 cup (100 g) of flaxseed flour covers almost the total daily requirement. Its low carbohydrate content is popular in low-GI recipes.

Use > Flaxseed flour has a high capacity for absorption and notes of pumpkin seed. It can be used in all pastries in combination with other flours. After being combined with water, its thick consistency and high fat content allow it to replace eggs and butter in certain recipes.

FONIO FLOUR: THE MOST FUTURISTIC

 Cereal   Slightly bitter   ++++   55

Source > This flour is made from fonio, a traditional grain native to Africa, where this tasty flour is used to make festive meals. The fonio plant has tiny seeds. Once they are husked, they are ground to make flour. In 2019, the World Wildlife Fund chose fonio flour as one of 50 foods of the future, for both well-being and the planet.

Nutrients > This gluten-free flour is an excellent source of protein and carbohydrates (starch). This exotic flour also offers a multitude of nutritional benefits: it is rich in vitamin B, calcium and zinc, and it has a medium glycemic index.

Use > It is a light brown color, has a woody flavor and has a high capacity for absorption.

GRAPE SEED FLOUR: CONCENTRATED FIBER

| | Fruit | | Earthy, bitter | ++++ | ⊗ | | 55 |

Source > This flour is obtained after several steps: first, the grapes are pressed to remove the liquid (must), then the resulting pulp is dried before being separated to collect the grape seeds. Everything in the grape is good!

Nutrients > This is one of the richest flours with 58% fiber. It contains many minerals, including precious selenium, which is essential for our bodies.

Use > Its dark brown color and strong aromas make it a distinctive flour marked by slightly bitter grape notes.

GREEN BANANA FLOUR: THE DIABETIC'S FRIEND

| | Fruit | | Bitter, green banana | ++++ | ⊗ | | 15 |

Source > Green banana flour has been used for centuries in some African countries. It is made from bananas when they are still green. Its flesh is firmer, less sweet and starchier than that of yellow bananas. The fruit is peeled, dried, then ground into a fine powder.

Nutrients > Nutrients become more concentrated during the dehydration process, and the amount of potassium and magnesium rises. This flour is very rich in carbohydrates, especially starch, and contains a significant amount of fiber (8 g/100 g). Also, its GI is low, making it a great ally for people with diabetes.

Use > This flour, which has a beige to gray color, has a light, slightly bitter flavor, with light notes of unsweetened banana. It brings a soft texture to baking and helps to bind and thicken creams. Its high starch content makes it a dense flour, with a high capacity for absorption.

MY ADVICE

Because bananas are chemically treated, make sure the flour comes only from the fruit without the skin.

GREEN LENTIL FLOUR: AN IRON CONSTITUTION

| | Legume | | Herbaceous flavor | + | ⊗ | | 30 |

Source > Lentils are part of the legume family. They are ground to make flour. Although lentils have been cultivated and eaten for more than 10,000 years, using them in the form of flour is very recent in the West. India, for example, is much more advanced on this culinary front, with many specialties using this flour. Note that you can also get flour from red, blond, brown or black lentils.

Nutrients > Legume flours have the advantage of having higher protein, carbohydrate and fiber content. This is also the legume that is richest in iron.

Use > This flour is green in color. It gives a sweet flavor, with lightly herbaceous notes. It is used to thicken sauces and can be used to make breads and cakes, blended with other flours.

HEMP FLOUR: THE MOST DIGESTIBLE

 Plant   Hazelnut and herbaceous +++   45

Source > Don't panic: although hemp flour is part of the cannabis family, its THC level is very low and therefore has no psychotropic effect. Hemp seeds are first pressed to extract the oil, then dried and ground.

Nutrients > It is extremely rich in complete protein, as it contains the 9 essential amino acids. Fiber makes up 25% of its composition, which makes it very digestible and easy to absorb. It is also rich in omega-3 and -6, as well as potassium and phosphorus. This makes it a superfood.

Use > This dark green flour with an herbaceous flavor must be used in small quantities in recipes because of its strong flavor.

JACKFRUIT FLOUR: A TREASURE FROM THE EAST

 Fruit   Acidic, fermented, sweet ++++   35

Source > This flour comes from the fruit of the jackfruit tree, native to India and widely grown in South-East Asia. Its fresh seeds are dried then reduced to powder.

Nutrients > It is an excellent source of protein, fiber and carbohydrates. Its assets: a low GI and a large amount of antioxidants.

Use > This flour has an acidic, woody flavor and is brown in color. Because of its powerful aroma, it can easily be used with another more neutral flour, such as rice flour.

KAMUT FLOUR: A HINT OF SWEETNESS

 Cereal   Sweet flacor, lightly roasted note +   45

Source > This flour is made from kamut, also called Khorasan wheat, a grain that belongs to the durum wheat family and has not been hybridized.

Nutrients > It is very rich in carbohydrates, protein and fiber, and it has a good concentration of magnesium, zinc and potassium. Like all flours in the family of wheat that has not been hybridized, it is easier to digest than wheat flour.

Use > Its gentle flavor is similar to brown butter. Although its gluten content is lower than that of wheat, it has a denser texture. When it is used to make bread, it brings a lot of elasticity to the dough.

LUPIN FLOUR: VERY DIGESTIBLE

◯ Legume	◯ Bitter	++++	⊗	▮▯ 15

Source > This legume has been eaten for thousands of years. Another gluten-free alternative! Lupin flour is made from seeds of the lupine flower that are toasted. The toasting involves heating the seeds, which increases the amount of protein that can be digested in the intestines.

Nutrients > This flour contains neither gluten nor starch, has a very low GI and is high in fiber. This cocktail of benefits makes a very digestible flour, which helps to stabilize blood sugar and improve bowel function.

Use > Its yellowness adds color to dough and baked goods. This flour has aromatic notes of hazelnut and a slightly bitter flavor. These attributes make it easily blendable, and it can replace eggs or butter in sweet dough and shortcrust.

OAT FLOUR: THE ATHLETE'S FRIEND

◯ Cereal	◯ Neutral	+++	✓	▮▯ 40

Source > This flour is a product of milled oat grains and may contain a small amount of gluten; if it only represents a small proportion in a recipe, there may be almost none, depending on the variety. Oat protein is called avenin; its structure is very different from that of wheat. It is found in the form of whole wheat and whole-grain flour.

Nutrients > Because oat flour is very rich in carbohydrates and more precisely in starch (68%), it is a good energy reservoir. It contains 8 of the 9 essential amino acids, with lysine being the only one missing, making oat flour a great source of protein. Oats were used mainly for animal feed for a long time, but today oat flour is very popular, especially with athletes, as it brings carbohydrates while maintaining a low GI.

Use > Because it is fairly fine, it blends well into a mixture. It has a neutral flavor and can replace wheat flour in cakes and other baked goods.

PEANUT FLOUR: OMEGAS AND VITAMINS, THE WINNING COMBO

◯ Nut	◯ Roasted peanut	++	⊗	▮▯ 15

Source > Peanuts are the seed of a legume. The shell is removed and the seeds are cold pressed to remove the oil. The resulting dry extract is further dried and ground. This flour, often used in North America and Africa, arrived in Europe recently.

Nutrients > With its low GI of 15, it is one of the flours that is richest in protein (45 g/100 g). It contains all 20 amino acids. Although the oil has been removed, peanut flour still contains 15% fatty acids, with a significant amount of oleic acid (omega-9).

Use > It has a pronounced peanut flavor and caramel color. To get a soft texture in a mixture, it is best to blend peanut flour with another flour, such as corn or rice flour, as peanut flour on its own brings a dense or very crumbly texture.

QUINOA FLOUR: YOUR BOWELS WILL THANK YOU

| 🌿 Cereal | ⬤ | Bitter, earthy | + | ⊗🌾 | ▭ 40 |

Source > Do you think quinoa is a cereal? Wrong! Called "rice of the Incas," it is a pseudo-cereal from a plant that looks like a feather. This terrific gluten-free alternative is obtained from grinding the quinoa seeds.

Nutrients > It is digestible, rich in protein and carbohydrates, and has all the essential amino acids. It is also a good source of fiber.

Use > Quinoa flour is slightly bitter. It has notes of hazelnut and a high capacity for absorption, which allows it to thicken a mixture quickly. Note: use in moderation if you don't want the dough to be too dense.

RICE FLOUR: THE GLUTEN-FREE STAR

| 🌿 Cereal | ◯ | Neutral | +++ | ⊗🌾 | ▭ 75 |

Source > Rice flour is one of the most commonly used gluten-free flours. There are 3 main types of rice flour: white (refined), whole wheat and brown.

Nutrients > Because it is rich in carbohydrates, it has a high GI and is an excellent source of energy.

Use > This very fine, light powder has a neutral flavor. It brings a crumbly quality after cooking and works well with all flours with strong aromatic notes and those with a high capacity for absorption.

RYE FLOUR: BAKERS' OTHER FAVORITE

| 🌿 Cereal | ⬤ | Strong toasted cereal note, rustic flavor | ++ | ✓🌾 | ▭ 40 |

Source > Rye flour contains gluten, which makes it good for bread. It is therefore mainly used in bakeries. Like wheat flour, different rye flours are determined by how much of the rye kernel is present; the more kernel, the darker the flour.

Nutrients > Rye flour is rich in fiber and vegetable protein, and it contains many minerals, such as potassium and magnesium.

Use > It can replace wheat flour up to 100% in breads and can be mixed with other flours in baked goods or sweet dough. In mixtures, it offers fragrant rustic notes.

SOY FLOUR: FULL OF PROTEIN

| 🫘 Legume | ⬤ | Light, nutty flavor | +++ | ⊗🌾 | ▭ 25 |

Source > Soy flour is made from a legume, soybeans, that has been grown in China for millennia. Two versions exist: toasted and untoasted (defatted). The flour is made from previously deoiled beans that are then ground.

Nutrients > It contains all the essential amino acids.

Use > This cream-colored flour has a slightly sweet flavor and is very fine. It has emulsifying properties, which sometimes make it a substitute for eggs and butter. As it is related to a starch, it can replace wheat flour in gluten-free baba or brioche recipes.

SPELT FLOUR OR LARGE SPELT: THE VERSATILE ONE

Cereal   ◯   Neutral   +   ✓   45

Source > Here is a grain akin to soft wheat! Nicknamed "wheat of the Gauls," it is one of the oldest grains. Forgotten for a long time, it has become popular among consumers for its nutritional makeup, which is richer than wheat's. Unlike einkorn, it has been crossbred with wheat to increase its yield.

Nutrients > This flour is rich in carbohydrates and protein (19% compared to 12% for wheat), phosphorus and potassium. It also contains the 9 essential amino acids.

Use > Spelt flour is suitable for bread thanks to its high amount of protein. It has properties similar to those of wheat and therefore can easily stand in for it.

SWEET POTATO FLOUR: MINERALS GALORE

Vegetable   ◯   Earthy   ++   ⊗   50

Source > This root vegetable from South America is peeled, cut into pieces and dried. Then it is turned into flour using a very simple production method: after the flesh is dehydrated, it is ground. Because sweet potatoes are more than 80% water, dehydrating the flesh allows the nutrients to be concentrated.

Nutrients > Sweet potato flour is low in sugar and fat, and rich in minerals and fiber (8%). This flour is also high in potassium and full of beta-carotene, which is a powerful antioxidant.

Use > This flour ranges in color from white to orange and has a naturally sweet flavor. It is often used to replace starch.

TIGERNUT FLOUR: A GLUTEN-FREE ALLY

 Vegetable   ◯   Mild, with hazelnut notes, sweet   +   ⊗   35

Source > The tiger nut tuber has a round, slightly wrinkled shape. The tuber appears to be related to a grain... but it's not. Tiger nut is an herbaceous plant whose tuber is dried, then ground to make flour.

Nutrients > Tigernut flour is rich in fiber, trace elements and minerals, such as potassium, calcium and magnesium. Tiger nut has antioxidant properties thanks to the vitamins E and C it contains.

Use > The flour is slightly granular and a light brown color; it resembles ground almonds. With its sweet, natural flavor note, it is an easy substitute for wheat flour in doughs or baked goods. It's best to blend it with another flour because of its slightly granular texture.

WHEAT FLOUR: THE ESSENTIAL STAPLE!

 Cereal   ◯   Neutral   Reference value   75

Source > We could have called this section "Wheat flours," in the plural, as there are so many varieties. All are made by grinding grains of wheat exclusively. Durum wheat, for instance, is used to make dry pasta, semolina and bulgur. Wheat flour is good for baking, even though it is often criticized, especially for its gluten content.[1] There are many types of wheat flour, from the most refined to the most complete (whole grain). The more complete the flour is, the darker it is, and the richer it is in fiber, vitamins and minerals. Since the 1960s, wheat has undergone a major mutation because of its numerous hybridizations. The change in its original organic structure and the fact that large amounts of it are consumed daily are responsible for growing intolerance to wheat.

Nutrients > Wheat flour is rich in carbohydrates and contains a small amount of protein. The inhibitors of digestive enzymes in raw flour are destroyed during cooking. It is a good source of energy because of its high starch concentration. Although it contains essential amino acids, its protein content is relatively low.

Use > Wheat flour is the most commonly used flour in baking. And for good reason: it works well in anything from bread to brioche, from sweet dough to fruitcake. It develops a certain "baker's strength" (elasticity and extendibility) when kneaded with a certain amount of water. If you add yeast to the kneaded dough, the gases formed during fermentation create an airy texture after cooking.

MORE INFO

Baking strength is the relationship between elasticity (ability to stretch and return to its original state) and extendibility (ability to stretch as much as possible without breaking).

WHITE TEFF FLOUR: A LITTLE CHAMPION

 Cereal   Mild, slightly toasted flavor   +   45

Source > Teff is considered one of the smallest grains in the world. The grains are ground to make flour.

Nutrients > Teff is rich in protein and fiber and is one of the richest grains when it comes to calcium, phosphorus and iron.

Use > Its color ranges from white to brown, depending on the variety. It has a hazelnut flavor and sweet notes, and also the ability to provide dough with elasticity to be used in breadmaking due to its rising effect.

---

[1] Thanks to its gluten content, it can be used to make bread and yeast doughs.

The various starches

Starch is a powder obtained from roots, rhizomes or tubers (potato starch, tapioca…) or from the seeds of grains (cornstarch, rice starch). This essential ingredient binds creams and sauces and aerates pastries. Another advantage is that it suits people with gluten intolerance because it is gluten-free.

WELLNESS TIP
The glycemic index of starches is medium to high. It is important to add fiber to recipes that use starches to maintain the lowest GI possible.

ARROWROOT STARCH

Rhizome   Neutral   ⊗   90

Source > Arrowroot starch is made from the rhizome of arrowroot, a tropical plant, which is plunged into hot water, peeled, then ground to remove the pulp, which is then dried and ground.

Nutrients > This rhizome is rich in starch (85%) and gluten-free, and it plays an active role in digestion thanks to its prebiotics. It has many other medicinal properties, especially because of its high concentration in minerals such as calcium, magnesium and phosphorus.

Use > Arrowroot starch binds sauces and creams and has a strong elasticity. Its flavor is neutral and its color remains light after binding.

CORNSTARCH

Cereal   Neutral   ⊗   85

Source > The grain is soaked in water to remove the germ, protein and fiber more easily. The starch is then dried and pulverized.

Nutrients > One of cornstarch's great qualities is that it is naturally gluten-free, which makes it a non-allergenic ingredient. It is rich in carbohydrates (note: its GI is fairly high at 85), which gives the body the fuel it needs to handle days filled with adventures. Also, cornstarch is very digestible.

Use > This is a less elastic starch. When it is heated in a liquid, it swells, thickens and forms a gel. Each grain increases to up to 30 times its volume at 70 °C. It remains opaque after cooking.

POTATO STARCH

 Tuber   Neutral   95

Source > Potato starch is made from potatoes. First, they are crushed to release the starch granules, which are then dried and processed.

Nutrients > Potato starch is very rich in carbohydrates (86%); it is an excellent source of energy.

Use > Ideal for giving cakes and other baked goods a light, soft texture. Once cooked, its color is white.

RICE STARCH

 Cereal   Neutral

Source > This is the starch from rice.

Nutrients > Like the other starches, it is a very good source of energy. It is an incredible and light ingredient with remarkable nutritional properties: naturally gluten-free, rich in carbohydrates and low in fat. It is perfect for a varied diet.

Use > It is used in the same way as tapioca.

TAPIOCA

 Root   Neutral   80

Source > Tapioca, discovered in Brazil, is made from the cassava root. The root is grated and washed to separate the fiber from the starch. It is ground after being dried.

Nutrients > Tapioca is rich in carbohydrates. It is a good source of iron and calcium. This starch also contains fiber and is naturally gluten-free.

Use > It is used as a thickener in creams. It is able to inflate, giving dough elasticity. Its flavor is neutral and it is white in color.

⋗ PAIRING FLOURS ⋖

Use this table of equivalents to combine various flours by their weights.
These suggestions are useful when you are making a sweet dough and replacing wheat flour.

40% almond flour + 40% brown rice flour
+ 20% corn flour

20% amaranth flour + 80% einkorn flour

40% oat flour + 60% brown rice flour

30% peanut flour + 70% brown rice flour

20% green banana flour + 80% einkorn flour

20% cocoa flour + 80% spelt flour

20% hemp flour + 80% brown rice flour

30% chestnut flour + 40% rice flour
+ 30% corn flour

20% coconut flour + 40% brown rice flour
+ 40% starch

100% einkorn flour

100% spelt flour

30% fonio flour + 70% spelt flour

30% soy flour + 70% brown rice flour

50% kamut flour + 50% einkorn flour

20% jackfruit flour + 80% einkorn flour

20% green lentil flour + 40% brown rice flour +
40% corn flour

40% flaxseed flour + 60% einkorn flour

30% lupin flower + 70% rice flour

20% pot barley flour + 80% einkorn flour

30% millet flour + 70% brown rice flour

30% pot barley flour + 40% brown rice flour
+ 30% corn flour

40% sweet potato flour + 60% einkorn flour

20% grape seed flour + 80% brown rice flour

20% chickpea flour + 40% rice flour
+ 40% corn flour

50% quinoa flour + 50% brown rice flour

50% brown rice flour + 50% soy flour

30% buckwheat flour + 40% cornstarch
+ 30% brown rice flour

40% rye flour + 40% spelt flour
+ 20% quinoa flour

30% soy flour + 40% brown rice flour
+ 30% corn flour

40% tigernut flour + 30% brown rice flour
+ 30% corn flour

30% teff flour + 70% brown rice flour

How to choose your flour?

❡

1 > Choose the characteristics of your flour(s) based on your recipe

2 > Choose the type(s) of organic flour(s): refined, whole wheat, or whole-grain (ideally stone ground)

3 > Choose the flour based on the desired quality

Making your own flour at home

❡

Make your own flour? Good idea! The benefits can't be beat...

Today, there are many ways to make your own flour. Choose the method based on what you want to make. The nutritional benefits of a flour made just before use are far superior compared with flours that are ground months or even years before being used.

Method	Type	Technique
Powerful blender or grain mill	All grains and cereals	Mix everything until you get a fine powder.
Drying then grinding	Chestnut, jackfruit, green banana or sweet potato	Peel, wash, cut into pieces and dry in the oven. Once the flesh is dry, process until you get a fine powder.

Note: some flours, such as those that need to be deoiled beforehand (coconut flour, peanut flour, soy flour, hemp flour and almond flour), cannot be made at home.

CHAPTER 2

Sugars

INTRODUCTION

✦

Sugar is often criticized, but it's not all bad!

Sugar is part of the family of carbohydrates, which are essential for keeping our bodies functioning properly as they provide energy to our cells and organs. The brain, for example, depends on glucose: it needs carbohydrates to perform its role well.

In baking and pastry making, sugar has many purposes. It provides a sweet taste, of course; brings out flavors; helps products stay fresh longer; colors dough and batter during baking; and adds a crisp texture. It's easy to see why it is a key player on a pastry maker's team.

In recent years, many studies have looked at the impact of sugar, showing that consuming too much of it is harmful for the body. In this chapter, we will talk about the glycemic index and look at which sugars and sweeteners are better for healthy pastries. There are alternatives to reduce the glycemic index of your desserts... and promote the well-being of your cells!

With sugar, it's all a question of balance – as one of the five pillars of healthy baking, in the introduction to this book, reminds us.

You must adjust the amount of sugar in a dessert, learn about the alternatives and round it off with a "miracle ingredient" from the same family: fiber.

The challenge? Maintaining a glycemic index that is as low as possible and saving our body from regular insulin shots!

Here, I chose natural sugars and sweeteners that will allow you to "sweeten" your pastries in light of your expectations, your allergies or your intolerances.

By the end of this chapter, you will be a pro when it comes to sugars!

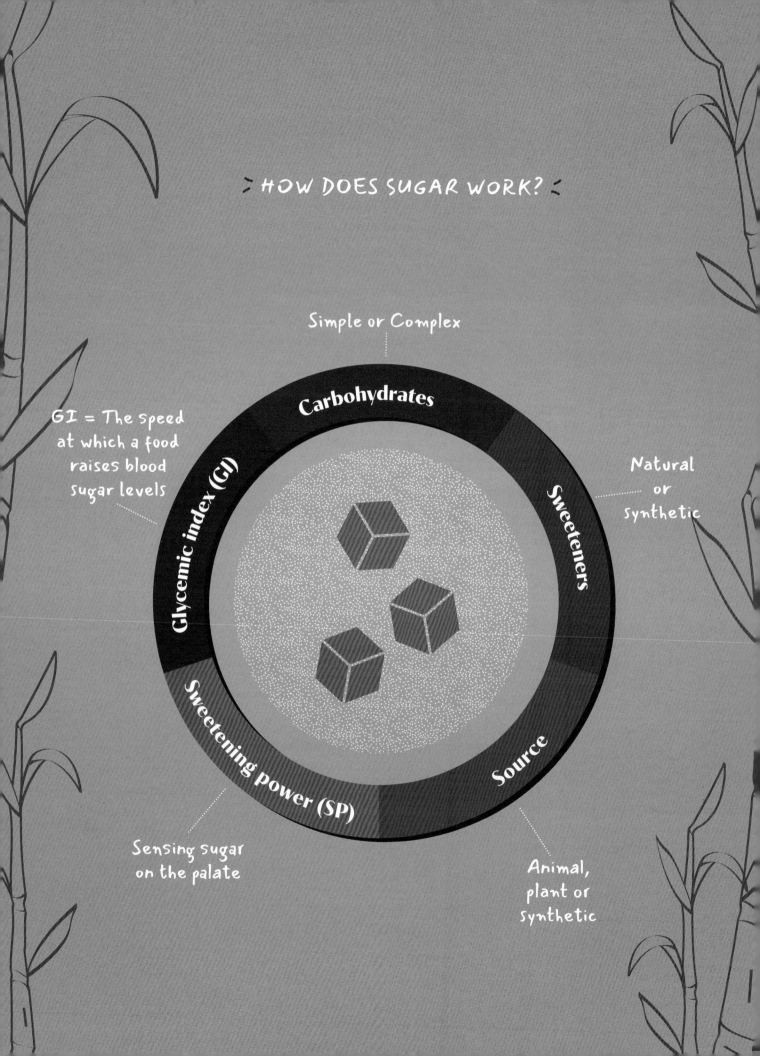

⋛ HOW DOES SUGAR WORK? ⋛

Simple or Complex

Carbohydrates

GI = The speed
at which a food
raises blood
sugar levels

Glycemic index (GI)

Natural
or
synthetic

Sweeteners

Sweetening Power (SP)

Source

Sensing sugar
on the palate

Animal,
plant or
synthetic

Everything you need to know about sugar!

WHERE DOES SUGAR COME FROM?

Let's go back to the 18th century. A major discovery had just been made – the principles of photosynthesis, or how to create energy naturally, with three magic ingredients: water, carbon dioxide (CO_2) and sun. This potent cocktail allows a plant to make glucose, a simple and agile molecule, for its own growth, from the stem to the fruit, by way of the roots.

The plant will either use the glucose for its immediate needs or store it as a starch, giving it a permanent source of energy. In the latter case, what happens exactly? The simple glucose molecules get together to form two types of "sugars" that the plant will keep in reserve:

> **starch**, a complex carbohydrate that can be used when the sun or water is not available. Seeds, roots and tubers are full of starch.

> **fiber**, which is found throughout the plant and allows it to consolidate its structure. It is found more specifically in the stem, branches and leaves.

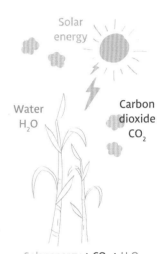

Solar energy + CO_2 + H_2O are the raw materials needed for photosynthesis. Thanks to them, the plant produces sugars that are sent from the leaves to the rest of the plant.

THE PRODUCTION OF FRUCTOSE

REPRODUCTION: THE OTHER MAGIC TRICK

When it's time for the plant to reproduce, it draws on a foolproof asset for a successful courtship: turning glucose into fructose, which is twice as sweet. What could be better for the plant than offering delicious fruits to charm birds or other animals and encourage them to scatter its seeds? Clever, right?

Note that this process was enhanced due to crossing varieties by humans, which made it possible to get plants whose fruits are increasingly sweet.

To complete the picture, fructose combines with glucose to make saccharose, the main form of carbohydrate in sap (this nourishes the whole plant with organic matter).

The moral of the story: plants are the source of all natural sugars – a gift of nature that allows humans to refill their energy tank!

THE CARBOHYDRATES FAMILY

This family is divided into two categories: simple carbohydrates and complex carbohydrates. Within this energy-filled family are eight main forms of sugars, which we find in their natural state in the plant world.

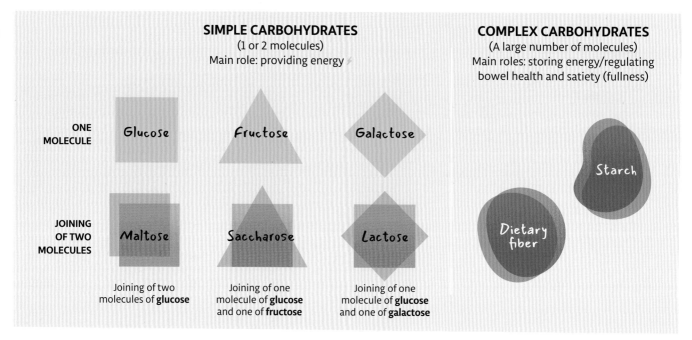

SIMPLE CARBOHYDRATES
(1 or 2 molecules)
Main role: providing energy

COMPLEX CARBOHYDRATES
(A large number of molecules)
Main roles: storing energy/regulating bowel health and satiety (fullness)

ONE MOLECULE

Glucose · Fructose · Galactose

JOINING OF TWO MOLECULES

Maltose · Saccharose · Lactose

Starch · Dietary fiber

Joining of two molecules of **glucose**

Joining of one molecule of **glucose** and one of **fructose**

Joining of one molecule of **glucose** and one of **galactose**

SWEETENERS

Sweeteners are sweet substances used in food to replace white sugar. They have a more or less high sweetening power. Note: they are not necessarily artificial: for example, honey is a natural sweetener.

Here is an overview:

	High-intensity sweetener	Bulk sweetener
Source	Synthetic, or a refined natural product	Natural
Sweetening power[1]	Very high, up to 300, or even higher in industrial products	0.5 to 1
Calories	0	Low-calorie
Glycemic index	0	Low

GOOD TO KNOW
The use of sweeteners should be guided by a daily dose to be respected.

[1] Based on saccharose, with a sweetening power of 1.

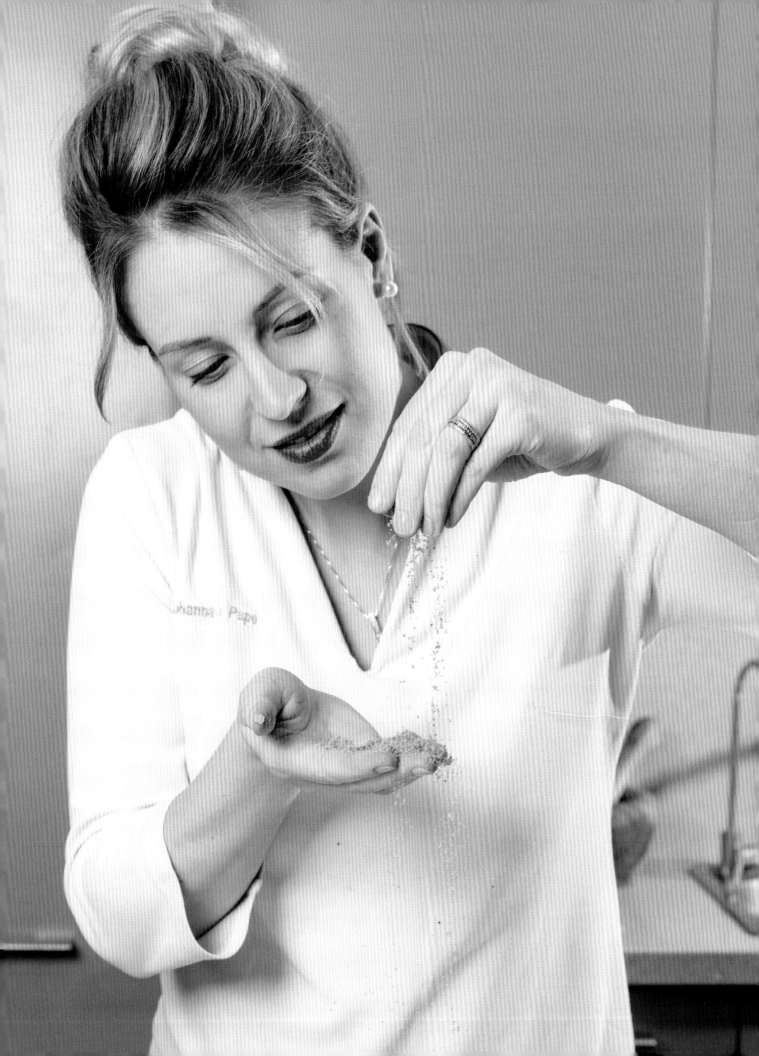

Whole
cane sugar

Yacon
Syrup

Agave
Syrup

Palm
Sugar

Date
Sugar

Erythritol

Lucuma

Maple
Syrup

Coconut
Sugar

Beet
Sugar

Rice
Syrup

Date
Syrup

Kithul
Syrup

Xylitol

Honey

Stevia
powder

Grape
Sugar

Sugar and its alternatives

AGAVE SYRUP: A MULTIFACETED SUGAR

Source > Agave syrup comes from the blue agave plant, found mainly in Mexico. The juice (sap) is extracted from the core of the plant. It is heated to concentrate it and develop the sugars, then filtered.

Nutrients > Although the agave plant is rich in fiber, agave syrup doesn't contain much fiber. The syrup contains mostly fructose (+60%), which can cause adverse effects, especially to the liver.

Use > Agave syrup is a light-colored liquid with a neutral flavor. Its sweetening power is 30% higher than that of white sugar (100 g sugar = 70 g agave syrup).

BEET SUGAR: A JACK OF ALL TRADES

Source > Beet sugar is obtained from crushing sugar beets. The juice is filtered and concentrated through evaporation until the sugar crystallizes.

Nutrients > Its GI is high and allows for a quick burst of sugar in the blood. Despite what is commonly stated, it is an unrefined sugar and is low in nutrients.

Use > The sweetening power of beet sugar is 1. It serves as a reference point as it is the most commonly used sugar. This sugar, which is naturally white, comes in powder form. It can be used in various types of pastry making and helps to preserve foods. It melts at 100 °C and caramelizes.

> **GOOD TO KNOW**
> Two other types of sugar derived from beet sugar are available:
> - Vergeoise is a kind of brown sugar.
> - Confectionary sugar is made from finely ground crystallized white sugar, to which starch is added (anti-caking agent).

CANE SUGAR

Source > Cane sugar is made from the juice of the sugar cane plant, which is then filtered, concentrated and centrifuged until saccharose crystals form. Once cane sugar starts to crystallize, depending on its extraction level, its color will change: from dark whole cane sugar to brown sugar, then white sugar (all molasses removed = refined sugar).

Nutrients > The GI is high in all cases, identical to white sugar.

Use > Like beet sugar, cane sugar can generally be used in all kinds of pastry making. Whole cane sugar has a more pronounced color. Its sweetening power is similar to beet sugar.

BLACK SUGAR
Source > Japan.
Production > Juice is cold pressed, reduced over a wood fire then left to decant for 5 days.
Nutrients > Mineral salts (potassium, calcium and magnesium).
Characteristics > Very dark color, licorice flavor.

MUSCOVADO

Source > Philippines or Mauritius.
Production > Cane juice is pressed, then heated and dried.
Nutrients > Mineral salts (potassium, calcium and magnesium).
Characteristics > Caramel flavor.

RAPADURA OR PANELA

Source > South America.
Production > Cane juice is cold pressed and air dried.
Nutrients > Mineral salts (potassium, calcium and magnesium).
Characteristics > Amber color, moist texture with a licorice flavor.

GOOD TO KNOW
Behind the name "brown sugar" are several very different processes. It can be obtained naturally following the first extractions of "unrefined sugar" or be made from cane sugar to which molasses is added. To find out, check with the manufacturer which method they used.

COCONUT SUGAR: INCREDIBLY RICH

Source > Coconut sugar comes from the sap of the coconut palm tree. Unrefined, it is heated until the water evaporates completely. Another product is coconut sugar paste; it is partially evaporated, which preserves the nutritional qualities.

Nutrients > Coconut sugar is rich in polyphenols and potassium and contains inulin (fiber). Inulin is a prebiotic that plays an important role in the intestinal flora. Its caloric input is the same as sugar, and its GI is low to medium, depending on the production process.

Use > Coconut sugar is dark and aromatic and has the same characteristics as whole cane sugar. Due to its high mineral content, this sugar is not suitable for making a caramel. Its sweetening power is 20% higher than that of white sugar (100 g white sugar = 80 g coconut sugar).

DATE SUGAR, A STRONG SWEETENER FROM THE EAST

Source > The dates are pitted, dehydrated, then finely ground to get date sugar.

Nutrients > Date sugar contains potassium, magnesium and iron. It is very rich in trace elements compared to other sugars. Its GI is high.

Use > Date sugar has caramel notes and a light caramel color. It is very fine, therefore, it replaces white sugar perfectly in recipes. Its sweetening power is higher than that of white sugar (100 g white sugar = 60 g date syrup).

ERYTHRITOL: THE FRIEND OF THOSE WITH DIABETES

Source > Erythritol is naturally present in seaweed, wine and aged cheeses. We can also get this sweetener by fermenting rice or wheat starch using enzymes and yeasts (the syrup obtained will be sterilized, filtered, purified and crystallized).

Nutrients > Low in calories and with a glycemic index (GI) of zero, it is ideal for people with diabetes and others who are monitoring their blood sugar.

Use > Erythritol melts at 250 °F (120 °C), is water soluble and has a refreshing flavor. As a result, its behavior is similar to that of white sugar. Erythritol can therefore easily substitute for white sugar, even though its sweetening power is lower (100 g sugar = 130 g erythritol).

HONEY: UNRIVALED RICHNESS

Source > The honeybee collects flower nectar, which it carries in its honey sac. Back at the hive, it regurgitates the nectar into the sacs of other bees. The processing begins. As the nectar is transferred from bee to bee within the hive, they add new enzymes, and the nectar turns into fructose and glucose. Due to the heat of the hive and the ventilation created by the bees, the humidity in the nectar evaporates until the water content is perfect. This allows the honey to be stored in the honeycomb, which the bees cap with wax. There are as many kinds of honey as there are flowers to forage in the fields.

Nutrients > Honey is a sweetener that is nutritionally rich. The composition varies widely from one honey to another. We must be vigilant when it comes to honey and how it is made: some products sold as honey have been mixed with glucose or other syrups.

Use > Just as the nutrients vary from one honey to the next, its flavor and texture vary enormously. The GI of honey is high, and its sweetening power is 30% greater than that of white sugar (100 g sugar = 70 g honey).

MORE INFO

Watch out for "fake honey" that is in fact honey with added sweeteners. Be vigilant: check the label carefully for the ingredients.

Honey crystallizes over time. The more fructose honey contains, the longer it will take to crystallize. The higher its glucose content, the faster it will crystallize.

Here are the characteristics of 5 types of honey:

ACACIA HONEY
Nutrients > High in mineral salts and amino acids.
Therapeutic effects > Soothes and calms pain; used for respiratory infections.
Aspect and flavor > Transparent, light yellow color, smooth and mild flavor.

CHESTNUT HONEY
Nutrients > High in iron, minerals and vitamins.
Therapeutic effects > Calms the nerves; stimulates the immune system.
Aspect and flavor > Yellow-orange color, intense, strong flavor with woody notes.

FIR TREE HONEY
Nutrients > Rich in trace elements, potassium, phosphorus, sulfur, calcium.
Therapeutic effects > Combats respiratory disorders.
Aspect and flavor > Very dark color, woody flavor.

LAVENDER HONEY
Nutrients > Rich in potassium and calcium.
Therapeutic effects > Antiseptic and anti-inflammatory; soothes colds and treats wounds.
Aspect and flavor > White in color, creamy texture, delicate flavor.

MANUKA HONEY
Nutrients > High concentration of methylglyoxal, which gives it strong antibacterial properties. Rich in flavonoids.
Therapeutic effects > Great antibacterial properties; promotes radiance of the skin and hair.
Aspect and flavor > Dark color and pronounced flavor.

KITHUL SYRUP: AN EXOTIC FLOWER

Source > Kithul syrup is made from the sap of the flower of the kithul tree, a palm tree found in Sri Lanka. It is filtered and then heated and boiled at a temperature reaching around 230 °F (110 °C), until a syrup forms.

Nutrients > It has slightly fewer calories than sugar, and its glycemic index is low, especially owing to the presence of fructose. It is rich in minerals such as calcium and iron.

Use > Kithul syrup is smooth and has an amber color. It has fine caramel, spicy, woody, deliciously amber notes and its scent is mild and subtly smoky. Its sweetening power is equal to that of white sugar.

LUCUMA: THE GOLD OF THE INCAS

Source > Lucuma is the fruit of the lucuma tree. Its shape resembles that of an avocado, and its orange flesh is very sweet. The fruit is dried, then reduced to powder.

Nutrients > Lucuma is very rich in fiber and has a low GI (25). Lucuma is a superfood because it is high in iron, potassium and zinc. It is also rich in antioxidants because it contains a lot of beta-carotene.

Use > The powder has a sandy (light yellow) color, is very fine and blends easily into a mixture. Its sweetening power is 50% lower than that of white sugar.

MAPLE SYRUP: FOR PAMPERING YOUR CELLS!

Source > Maple syrup comes from the sap of maple trees, collected in the spring and then concentrated through boiling. It is mainly produced in Canada. Its flavor and composition vary depending on when it was collected, and its color can be amber to a darker brown.

Nutrients > This syrup is rich in polyphenols and antioxidants. Many research studies show that it has therapeutic benefits. It contains significant amounts of manganese, riboflavin, copper and calcium.

Use > This is a darker syrup with a caramel flavor. Its sweetening power is 50% higher than that of white sugar (100 g sugar = 50 g maple syrup).

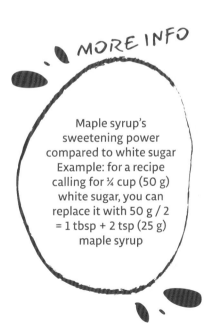

MORE INFO

Maple syrup's sweetening power compared to white sugar Example: for a recipe calling for ¼ cup (50 g) white sugar, you can replace it with 50 g / 2 = 1 tbsp + 2 tsp (25 g) maple syrup

PALM SUGAR: THE MOST DELICATE

Source > Palm sugar comes from the flower sap of the sugar palm tree. An incision is made at the flower stem to collect the juice in bamboo containers. The juice is filtered and heated for several hours, then poured to cool it down.

Nutrients > Its GI is low and therefore has little effect on blood sugar. It is an unrefined sugar, rich in nutrients like potassium and magnesium.

Use > Palm sugar has a golden color and is used in recipes like classic sugar. Its flavor is mild and slightly spicy with honey notes. Its sweetening power is 10% higher than that of sugar (100 g sugar = 90 g palm sugar).

GOOD TO KNOW
Palm sugar has nothing to do with palm oil, which comes from the oil palm tree. Growing palm sugar is ethical, doesn't require pesticides or fertilizers and uses very little water.

RICE SYRUP: THE MARATHON GLUCOSE

Source > Rice syrup is made from fermenting rice grains with enzymes and yeasts. Next, the mixture is filtered and concentrated through evaporation.

Nutrients > This syrup is made of 2 types of simple and complex carbohydrates. It contains potassium and magnesium and makes glucose available to the body for up to 3 hours. This is a great advantage for athletes.

Use > Rice syrup has a mild flavor with an almost honey-like consistency. It has a high sweetening power, 50% higher than that of white sugar (100 g sugar = 50 g rice syrup).

STEVIA LEAF POWDER: A GREEN MIRACLE POWDER

Source > Here, I am talking about stevia leaf powder and not the sugar obtained after several stages of processing. It comes from the plant *Stevia rebaudiana*, found in the Amazon rain forest. The leaves are picked, dried and blended in a processor.

Nutrients > The calorie content and glycemic index of stevia leaf powder are both zero. It is very high in fiber (24/100 g).

Use > Stevia leaf powder is green in color and has licorice notes. It cannot be heated above 100 °C. It has a strong sweetening power, 15 times more than white sugar (100 g white sugar = 6.5 g stevia leaf powder).

What are the differences between stevia leaf powder and stevia powder?

STEVIA LEAF POWDER
Composition > 100% stevia leaf
Production > **Natural sweetener.** The leaf is dried and ground.
Sweetening power > 15

WHITE STEVIA POWDER

Composition > Rebaudioside A

Production > **Refined high-intensity sweetener.** The leaf is dried and ground. Water is added to make an infusion. This mixture is microfiltered to select certain molecules which are then refined (turning the mixture from green to white). The resulting juice is mixed with ethanol and then centrifuged to extract only the powder.

Sweetening power > +300

XYLITOL

Source > Xylitol, also called birch sugar, is extracted from birch bark or sometimes from corn. The birch bark or corn is crushed, then water is added to release the hemicellulose molecules into the solution. Enzymes are added to break down the molecules through hydrolysis. The molecule of interest, called D-xylose, is then selected. The solution containing the D-xylose will then be hydrogenated once again and concentrated to crystalize it.

Nutrients > With its low GI, this sugar has a low impact on blood sugar. It is an ideal sugar for people with diabetes.

Use > Xylitol has the same sweetening power as saccharose. It is used in the same way as beet sugar, down to how it is caramelized.

YACON SYRUP: THE CHAMPION THAT WINS ALL THE TROPHIES

Source > Yacon syrup comes from the yacon plant; a yacon is a South American tuber. Juice is obtained after crushing the flesh then evaporating the liquid at a low temperature (below 170 °F/80 °C).

Nutrients > Yacon syrup is the sugar with the highest fiber content. Owing to its fiber, the syrup has a prebiotic role in the intestinal flora. Below 200 °F/100 °C, this sugar maintains its glycemic index of 1, which is good news for people with diabetes.

Use > The color of yacon syrup is dark and it is thick, like molasses. The flavor is fruity and caramelized. Its sweetening power is 50% higher than that of white sugar (100 g sugar = 50 g yacon syrup).

MAKE THE RIGHT CHOICE!

Do you want...	Use
Sugar adapted for people with diabetes?	Stevia leaf, xylitol or erythritol
A sugar with flavor and a low GI?	Kithul syrup or yacon syrup
A sugar with high sweetening power and a low GI?	Stevia leaf
A sugar with therapeutic qualities?	Maple syrup or honey

What is the role of carbohydrates in our bodies?

WHY DO WE NEED CARBOHYDRATES?

Carbohydrates (which turn into glucose once they are in the body) are a major source of energy for our cells. Through their energy generators, called mitochondria, cells spend their time burning glucose and carrying out the role for which they were designed: heartbeat, activation of the cardiovascular system, movement...

Although glucose is important for our body to function, the body can also metabolize it from fats and protein, which means we don't need to eat carbohydrates to have glucose!

HOW DOES THE DIGESTIVE PROCESS WORK?

Understanding the effects of sugar on the body means first understanding how the body reacts after digesting sugar. We also must of course keep in mind the crucial role of fiber.

1. FROM THE MOUTH TO THE SMALL INTESTINE: After being swallowed, carbohydrates break down into simple glucose molecules, which enter the wall of the small intestine via the blood; this increases the level of sugar in the blood.

2. FROM THE SMALL INTESTINE TO THE BLOOD: The pancreas is alerted to the concentration of sugar in the blood. It can release insulin as a result to allow the glucose to enter the cells that need it. Excess glucose will be stored in the cells of the liver and the muscles in the form of glycogen. It will act as an energy reserve that can be used by all cells to address new needs.

3. FROM SUGAR TO FAT: If the glycogen reserves are full, the body turns the surplus of glucose into fatty acids, which will be stored in fat tissues.

Note that in the case of excess glucose, the cell, and especially its energy generators (mitochondria), will produce free radicals. These are harmful to the life of the cell: they can cause it to malfunction or even die. This accumulation of oxidative stress is responsible for diseases such as type 2 diabetes, heart disease and premature aging. Luckily, cells have antioxidant systems to counteract these effects... whenever possible!

4. AT THE INTESTINAL LEVEL:

> Insoluble fiber can inflate and can slow digestion. It increases the weight and volume of stools, which helps the body evacuate them.
> Soluble fiber can dissolve on contact with liquids. It makes a gel that, in slowing down the speed at which carbohydrates are absorbed, reduces blood sugar spikes. It reduces the absorption of fat and cholesterol and helps with the sensation of satiety. It stimulates bowel activity less than insoluble fiber.

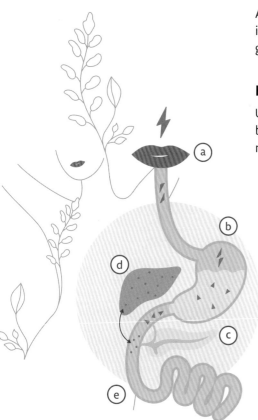

(a) **Mouth** – Carbohydrates break down into simple molecules

(b) **Stomach** – Simple molecules are broken down by gastric juices

(c) **Pancreas** – Pancreatic amylase turns carbohydrates into glucose

(d) **Liver** – As a crossroad for the metabolism, it releases glucose into the bloodstream, is a glucose reservoir and makes it available to the body

(e) **Small intestine** – Glucose is absorbed by the blood and carried to the liver

WHY IS SUGAR ADDICTIVE?

All sugars have this superpower of pleasing our taste buds, ever since we were born and had mother's milk. This leads to the secretion of dopamine, the happiness hormone. We love this flavor so much that in agriculture, choosing species through crossing was for centuries done based on the sweet flavor obtained.

WHAT IS A BLOOD SUGAR SPIKE?

When we talk about sugar, we tend to think about fast sugar and slow sugar, and we classify them this way: fast sugar = simple carbohydrate; slow sugar = complex carbohydrate. In reality, it's a little more subtle.

A blood sugar spike is a bit like a roller coaster at an amusement park: it goes up fast and it goes down faster! This happens when we eat foods that are rich in carbohydrates that then break down into glucose and are absorbed by the blood. If we eat too much all at once, our blood sugar level can skyrocket.

This spells trouble: we can feel tired, irritable, thirsty and hungry. But don't panic! To avoid these emotional roller coasters, all you need to do is eat foods that are rich in fiber, protein and healthy fats, which are digested more slowly and avoid blood sugar spikes.

As a bonus, doing regular physical activity helps to regulate our blood sugar level by increasing our insulin sensitivity. Insulin is a hormone that helps to regulate blood sugar. It's a little like having a superhero in our body to help us maintain a stable energy level all day long!

So, to avoid these ups and downs and stay on a gentle and pleasant track, you just need to eat healthy foods, move your body and keep an eye on your blood sugar level. Then you can enjoy life without worrying about the blood sugar roller coaster!

MORE INFO

Nutritionist Michel Montignac introduced the idea of the glycemic index. In the 1980s, he discovered the secret for losing weight by making the connection between consuming high-GI foods and heart disease, obesity and diabetes.

WHAT IS THE GLYCEMIC INDEX?

> It is a food's ability to release sugar into the blood quickly. The higher a food's GI, the more it releases a large amount of "sugar" (glucose) into the blood in a short time. That is our "fast" sugar.

Insulin's role is to immediately accompany the excess blood sugar to the liver and muscles, storing it there until needed.

GOOD TO KNOW
Several actions can help to vary a food's glycemic index. It can change if it is cooked or processed. The order in which foods are eaten can significantly reduce blood sugar levels, too. Adding fat and fiber also help the glycemic index to change.

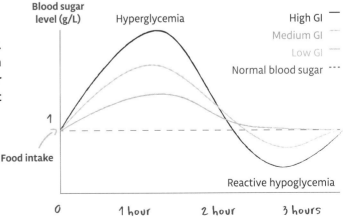

WHAT ARE THE DOWNSIDES OF SUGAR?

We have to admit it: a series of blood sugar spikes and crashes is not conducive to excellent health. In the **short term**, these variations will cause constant hunger, chronic fatigue, a fragile immune system, hot flashes, migraines or memory problems. In the **long term**, they can lead to weight gain, recurring skin problems, accelerated aging, a higher risk of cancer, depression or type 2 diabetes.

Throughout these glycemic ups and downs, the body takes a serious beating. Luckily, there are solutions...

HOW CAN YOU MAINTAIN A LOW GLYCEMIC INDEX?

Although sugar is often criticized for its harmful effects on the body, there are many solutions to avoid these:

SOLUTION 1: REDUCE THE AMOUNT OF SUGAR IN YOUR RECIPES

SOLUTION 2: ADD FIBER

Fiber is our best ally for balancing our blood sugar. It is part of the same family as sugar but is its more virtuous cousin. You will soon understand why... When simple carbohydrates and starch cause blood sugar to rise, leading to a roller coaster effect on the body, we just need to call a cousin to the rescue. There is always a caring ally in every family: here, it's fiber.

Fiber is not digested or absorbed by the body and has no nutritional value, but it plays several major roles (later in this book, we will highlight how it works with "sugar," depending on the type).

Where can you find it? In vegetables, fruit, whole-grain flours and some food supplements, such as psyllium. We can enhance our recipes with all these ingredients!

SOLUTION 3: VARY THE SUGARS YOU USE

As we have seen, there is a great variety of sugars, with different nutrients and a glycemic index ranging from 0 to 100.

When we use a variety of sugars and choose those with a low or medium GI, our metabolism will thank us. This golden rule also applies to our environment: it is good to support a diversified agriculture that is not based on a single product.

SOLUTION 4: CHOOSE GENTLE COOKING METHODS

The glycemic index varies based on processing and cooking. When possible, why not use low temperatures, steam or opt for raw pastry making?

⋝ SUGAR BY THE NUMBERS ⋜

Glycemic index, carbohydrate levels, aromatic notes...
This table presents the different types of sugars at a glance!

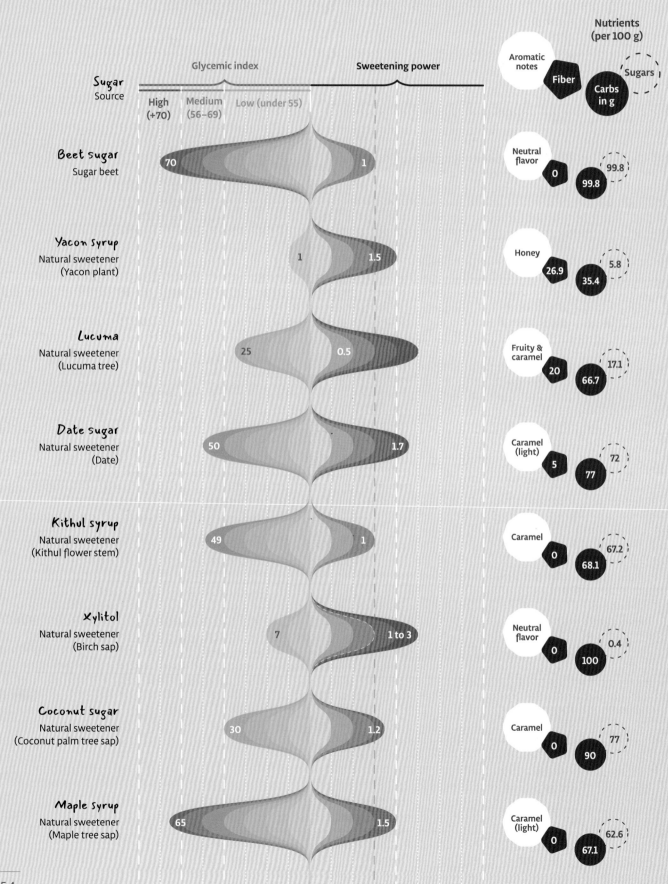

Sugar Source	Glycemic index			Sweetening power	Aromatic notes	Nutrients (per 100 g)		
	High (+70)	Medium (56–69)	Low (under 55)			Fiber	Carbs in g	Sugars
Beet sugar Sugar beet	70			1	Neutral flavor	0	99.8	99.8
Yacon syrup Natural sweetener (Yacon plant)			1	1.5	Honey	26.9	35.4	5.8
Lucuma Natural sweetener (Lucuma tree)			25	0.5	Fruity & caramel	20	66.7	17.1
Date sugar Natural sweetener (Date)			50	1.7	Caramel (light)	5	77	72
Kithul syrup Natural sweetener (Kithul flower stem)			49	1	Caramel	0	68.1	67.2
Xylitol Natural sweetener (Birch sap)			7	1 to 3	Neutral flavor	0	100	0.4
Coconut sugar Natural sweetener (Coconut palm tree sap)			30	1.2	Caramel	0	90	77
Maple syrup Natural sweetener (Maple tree sap)		65		1.5	Caramel (light)	0	67.1	62.6

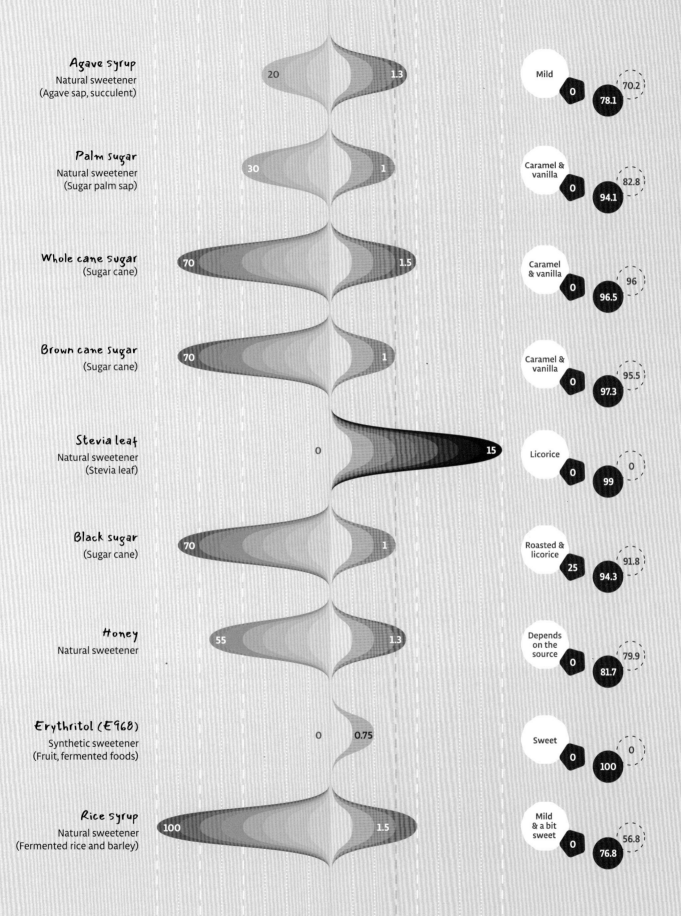

Agave syrup
Natural sweetener
(Agave sap, succulent)

20   1.3

Mild   0   78.1   70.2

Palm sugar
Natural sweetener
(Sugar palm sap)

30   1

Caramel & vanilla   0   94.1   82.8

Whole cane sugar
(Sugar cane)

70   1.5

Caramel & vanilla   0   96.5   96

Brown cane sugar
(Sugar cane)

70   1

Caramel & vanilla   0   97.3   95.5

Stevia leaf
Natural sweetener
(Stevia leaf)

0   15

Licorice   0   99   0

Black sugar
(Sugar cane)

70   1

Roasted & licorice   25   94.3   91.8

Honey
Natural sweetener

55   1.3

Depends on the source   0   81.7   79.9

Erythritol (E968)
Synthetic sweetener
(Fruit, fermented foods)

0   0.75

Sweet   0   100   0

Rice syrup
Natural sweetener
(Fermented rice and barley)

100   1.5

Mild & a bit sweet   0   76.8   56.8

CHAPTER 3

Milks, yogurts and creams

INTRODUCTION

٭

Milk and cream! These two ingredients have been used in pastry recipes since the beginning.

Although it is difficult to date the first creations made from these dairy products, we do know that the consumption of animal milk goes back to the early days of livestock breeding, when hunter-gatherers settled down and began domesticating animals. This happened in the Neolithic age (6000 to 2200 BCE).

Although milk and cream are still enjoyed in pastries, there are now some new plant-based versions on the block. Coconut milk, oat-based beverage, soy-based cream and almond-based yogurt have made inroads in recipes. This emerging market is supported by demand from consumers who are lactose intolerant or who have chosen a plant-based diet.

What do these various products bring to pastry making? What do they offer in terms of taste? What are their technical characteristics? What is their nutritional value?

So many questions that we will explore in this chapter...

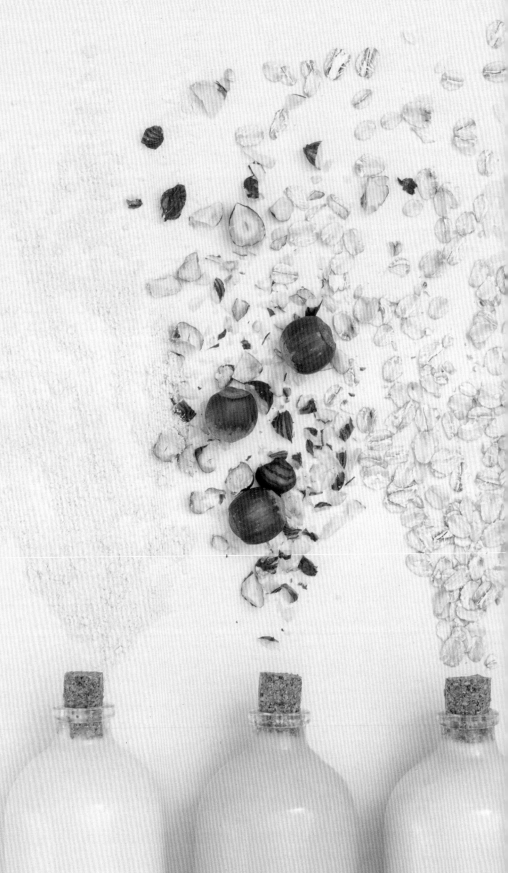

Spelt
beverage

Hazelnut
beverage

Oat
beverage

Rice
beverage

Almond
beverage

Milks

Although cow's milk is traditionally used in pastry making, today it can easily be combined with plant-based beverages in a recipe and even be replaced by them. Note that although the water content of these milk alternatives is almost the same, their nutritional value is very different.

Milk from animals

NUTRITIONAL VALUE OF WHOLE COW'S MILK

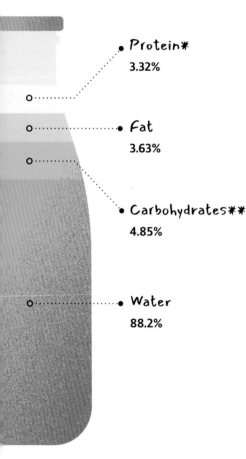

Protein*
3.32%

Fat
3.63%

Carbohydrates**
4.85%

Water
88.2%

* Mostly casein.
** Mostly lactose (milk sugar).
The nutritional makeup of other milks described is similar, but with varying levels.

GOOD TO KNOW
Here we will look at whole milk, and not skim or semi-skimmed milks, which contain less fat but also fewer vitamins and minerals...

WHOLE COW'S MILK: USED MOST OFTEN

Nutrients > Cow's milk is rich in protein (casein) and is more or less well tolerated. Its levels of saturated fatty acids are significant, while its levels of unsaturated fatty acids are lower. Their quality and quantity vary depending on what cows eat (proportion of grains, grass...). This milk is rich in calcium, phosphorus, potassium and magnesium. It also contains lactose, which doesn't work for people who are intolerant of or allergic to it.

Use > Milk contains a lot of water. In pastry making, it moistens creams, doughs or ice cream. Its flavor is sweet and mild.

WHOLE GOAT'S MILK: THE TASTIEST

Nutrients > Goat's milk contains vitamins A, B and C. It contains more minerals (calcium, phosphorus and magnesium) than cow's milk but has the same amount of protein.

Use > Goat's milk can be used in ice creams, cakes or creams. Its flavor is very pronounced.

WHOLE SHEEP'S MILK: THE RICHEST

Nutrients > Sheep's milk contains vitamins and minerals, such as calcium and vitamin C. It has more protein and fat than other milks.

Use > Its flavor is milder than that of goat's milk. It is used in the same way as other milks (in the same types of recipes).

Plant-based beverages

Given the wide variety of plant-based beverages, here we will look at the nutrients in beverages composed of 10% grains, oleaginous fruits or oilseeds or legumes, and 90% water.

HOW ARE THEY USED?

All plant-based "milks," except coconut milk, can replace cow's milk. Coconut milk must be blended with a more watery milk chosen from those presented below.

GOOD TO KNOW

In some countries, the designation "milk" is reserved for animal milk. In that case, the law requires companies to call their products "juice" or "beverage."

ALMOND BEVERAGE: THE MOST COMMON

Nutrients > This plant-based beverage is low in calories and sugar. Its few fats are monounsaturated and polyunsaturated fatty acids. Almond milk is not as rich in calcium as whole almonds.

Characteristics > White in color, slightly translucent, with brown pigments due to the almond skin, this beverage has a mild flavor.

BUCKWHEAT BEVERAGE: BENEFITS GALORE

Nutrients > Buckwheat beverage is a good source of protein. It is rich in antioxidants and contains carbohydrates, especially starch and fiber.

Characteristics > This cream-colored beverage has hazelnut notes with a roasted flavor.

CHESTNUT BEVERAGE: THE RIGHT BALANCE

Nutrients > Chestnut beverage is rich in monounsaturated fatty acids. It is also a good source of calcium, fiber, minerals, trace elements and vitamins.

Characteristics > The color is brown and translucent. It gives fullness to mixtures, with a pronounced chestnut flavor.

COCONUT MILK: THE SMOOTHEST

Nutrients > Coconut milk contains a notable amount of minerals and vitamins, such as iron, phosphorus, calcium, magnesium and potassium – nutrients that are essential for the body to function properly. Like cow's milk, it is high in saturated fatty acids.

Characteristics > Coconut milk is an opaque white color and has a thicker texture than cow's milk. It has a coconut flavor.

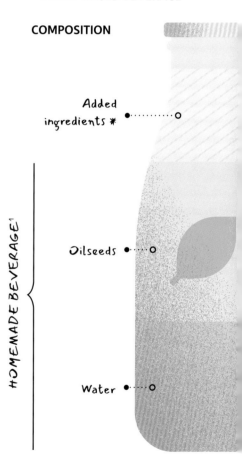

NUTRITIONAL VALUE OF A
PLANT-BASED BEVERAGE

COMPOSITION

Added ingredients *

HOMEMADE BEVERAGE[1]

Oilseeds

Water

* **Only in commercial products.** You can find sugar (in different forms), oil, salt, additives (sunflower lecithin, carrageenan, agar agar, guar gum...).

[1] See the recipe in the "Basic Recipes" section of this book.

HAZELNUT BEVERAGE: AN ANTIOXIDANT BOMBSHELL

Nutrients > Hazelnut beverage is rich in monounsaturated and polyunsaturated omega-3 fatty acids. It also contains antioxidant vitamins, such as A and E, as well as calcium and phosphorus.

Characteristics > Hazelnut beverage has a light brown opaque color and is fragrant, with a slightly roasted flavor.

OAT BEVERAGE: THE MILDEST

Nutrients > Like almond beverage, this drink lacks calcium and vitamin D. That is why many manufacturers enrich their oat beverage with these two elements. Oat beverage contains very little fat. However, it is sweeter than many other milks and most plant-based beverages. It also contains a small amount of gluten.

Characteristics > With a flavor similar to cow's milk, this cream-colored beverage has a creamier texture than almond milk.

QUINOA BEVERAGE: THE MOST COMPLETE

Nutrients > Quinoa beverage contains a significant amount of protein. It also has all the essential amino acids! As well, this plant-based beverage is low in calories and has many benefits. It contains fiber, minerals and fatty acids that are essential for our bodies.

Characteristics > It is white in color and has light earthy notes that are not pleasing to all palates.

RICE BEVERAGE: SLIGHTLY SWEET

Nutrients > Once rice is turned into a beverage, its makeup is very high in simple carbohydrates (fast sugar). Like soy beverage, rice beverage contains a small amount of fiber.

Characteristics > It is white, translucent and has a very liquid texture. It is slightly sweet.

SOY BEVERAGE: PROTEIN AND FIBER

Nutrients > Soy beverage has a level of protein somewhat like cow's milk. Unlike most plant-based beverages, it also contains a small amount of fiber. On top of that, it is rich in monounsaturated and polyunsaturated fatty acids.

Characteristics > Soy beverage is white in color. Due to its very high protein content, it is popular in vegan recipes as an emulsifier, which is why it is also often used in creams. Its distinct flavor is noticeable in mixtures.

SPELT BEVERAGE: THE TASTIEST

Nutrients > This beverage is low in saturated fatty acids. Note to those who are sensitive to gluten: spelt contains a small amount of it.

Characteristics > It is a light brown color, and its mild flavor has aromatic notes of lightly roasted grain.

Yogurts

Yogurt has a place in pastry making. It is used in baked goods to achieve a soft texture, in ice cream for a creamy texture, and in mousses, to which it brings an acidic, milky flavor, linked to the addition of enzymes.

Plant-based alternatives contain starch, or another thickener is added to stabilize the texture. Just as beverages have diversified, yogurt has followed suit, to meet a growing demand for lactose-free or vegan products.

BACTERIA

Yogurt is made with two types of ingredients: milk and lactic acid bacteria called *Streptococcus thermophilus* and *Lactobacillus bulgaricus*. Consuming these bacteria increases "good" cholesterol (HDL cholesterol). And as these "benefactors" are also probiotics, they contribute to the proper functioning of our intestinal microbiota. They therefore promote good digestion, help us avoid bloating and strengthen our immune system!

Yogurt made from animal products

PLAIN YOGURT

Composition > Yogurt is a form of curdled milk (skimmed, liquid, concentrated, powdered) that has undergone heat treatment (pasteurization) during which bacteria are added. It can be made from cow's, goat's or sheep's milk.

Nutrients > Yogurt is a source of very good quality animal protein, with a small amount of fat and simple carbohydrates. It is also an excellent source of calcium.

Use > Ranging from stirred to firm depending on the fermentation process, yogurt gives cakes and cookies a smooth texture. It is also found in recipes for mousses, flans, cheesecake and yogurt cake.

FROMAGE BLANC (QUARK)

Composition > Fromage blanc, also called quark, is made from curdling milk with lactic acid bacteria, including an enzyme called rennet. It is then strained and beaten.

Nutrients > It is rich in protein, contains all the essential amino acids and therefore is easily digestible by the body. It also has a significant amount of calcium and vitamins A, B and D. It contains more protein but fewer probiotics than yogurt.

Use > Fromage blanc has a thicker texture and a more acidic flavor than yogurt. It can be used in the same types of recipes as yogurt.

COMPOSITION OF YOGURT MADE FROM ANIMAL MILK

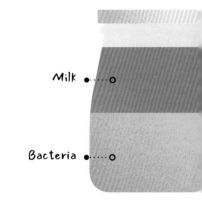

Milk •·····o

Bacteria •·····o

Plant-based yogurts

Also called "yogurt alternatives," their texture resembles that of stirred yogurt, and they are a light cream color. They can be used in the same recipes as yogurt made from animal milk. A final feature they share: the bacteria give them a slightly acidic flavor. All are good alternatives to classic yogurt.

ALMOND MILK YOGURT

Nutrients > It has numerous benefits. It has fewer calories than yogurt made from cow's milk. Also, it contains more fat, which comes from the fat of the raw ingredient, almonds.

COCONUT MILK YOGURT

Nutrients > It is much higher in saturated fat but has less protein and calcium than plain cow's milk yogurt. However, it contains a fair amount of iron, phosphorus, magnesium and potassium. Like yogurts made from animal milk, it contains good bacteria, which are added during production: probiotics.

SILKEN TOFU

Composition > Silken tofu is made of soy milk curdled with nigari, a natural crystal of magnesium chloride from seawater. It is neither strained nor pressed, which gives it a soft gelatinous, moist texture.

Nutrients > Silken tofu is an excellent source of plant protein but also of iron, phosphorus, calcium and vitamin B. As well, it contains no cholesterol and almost no fat or saturated fatty acids.

Use > Its texture is like that of panna cotta. It can replace eggs and can bind creams, cakes or ice creams while offering a lot of texture. Its flavor is neutral.

SOY BEVERAGE YOGURT

Nutrients > It contains plant protein, unsaturated fatty acids and fiber. Soy protein can be well absorbed by the body as it brings all the essential amino acids.

> **TIP**
> It is recommended not to consume more than two servings of soy products per day. Scientific studies are still under way, but the isoflavones in soy are thought to be endocrine disruptors. As a precautionary measure and as we await new recommendations, it is best to limit daily soy intake, especially for pregnant women, infants and children under three.

COMPOSITION OF A PLANT-BASED YOGURT

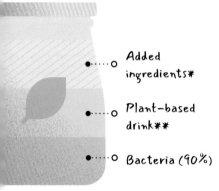

• ····o Added ingredients*

• ····o Plant-based drink**

• ····o Bacteria (90%)

* You can find sugar (in various forms), oil, salt, additives (sunflower lecithin, carrageenan, agar agar, guar gum...).

** Made from oilseeds, cereals and legumes

Creams

What would pastry be without whipped cream, used with babas, ganache, ice cream or gateau Saint-Honoré? Cream is a key ingredient in the trade; it is everywhere. Thanks to its fluffy qualities, it allows us to make fancy decorations, wonderful new shapes or cakes with multiple layers. Vegan "creams" have also appeared on the market. Let's learn more about the various creams...

Creams made from animal milk

WHIPPING CREAM

Composition > This is a cream that has undergone only one type of treatment: pasteurization (not sterilization, inoculation or aging). It must contain at least 30% fat from milk itself.

Nutrients > It contains a significant amount of vitamin A. The product is not highly processed, which preserves most vitamins and minerals (but fewer than in raw cream). It is one third fat, with saturated fatty acids being the majority.

Use > Its texture is liquid, and it has a slightly acidic and milky flavor. It can be used in all types of pastry recipes.

CRÈME FRAÎCHE

Composition > It has not had any heat treatment except pasteurization. After being inoculated with lactic acid bacteria, the cream undergoes a fermentation phase that gives it a creamy texture.

Nutrients > Like whipping cream, crème fraiche has significant amounts of vitamin A, magnesium, phosphorus, calcium and potassium. This cream is 30% fat with mostly saturated fatty acids, like whipping cream.

Use > Crème fraîche, which has a thick texture, has an acidic, milky flavor and is used in cake batter to add moistness. It can be found in ice cream, be eaten with cake, such as tarte Tatin, or used in creams.

Plant-based creams

These are found in stores with the name "alternative" to or "substitute" for dairy creams.

They don't have the same nutritional composition as cream from animal milk. Although it's easy to substitute them in a ganache or a cream, it is more difficult to get a stable whipped texture.

To learn more about additives and consuming them, see chapter 8.

ALMOND "CREAM"

Nutrients > This cream has plant protein but also unsaturated fatty acids: omega-3, -6 and -9.

Use > It is white in color and has a creamy texture. Its flavor has light almond notes. It serves as a binder or thickener in the same way in recipes that usually contain classic cream.

COCONUT CREAM

Nutrients > Its nutrients are similar to those of coconut milk: magnesium, calcium and phosphorus. It also contains saturated fatty acids, similar to those in crème fraîche made from animal milk.

Use > It is white in color, with a thick texture. It has a pronounced coconut flavor, at times slightly bitter. Thanks to its high fat content, it can be used to make whipped cream. The texture remains pliable, however.

OAT "CREAM"

Nutrients > It brings fiber and essential minerals, such as magnesium. Also, it contains carbohydrates. In most cases, this cream does not contain gluten.

Use > With its creamy texture, it is used in the same mixtures as cream. However, it does not whip up like whipping cream. Its neutral flavor allows it to work with other flavors.

RICE "CREAM"

Nutrients > It has less fat than classic crème fraîche and is high in carbohydrates, especially starch. It therefore provides a lot of energy.

Use > Rice cream is white in color and has a creamy texture and a neutral flavor. Unlike its peers, it does not have rich mouth feel. It is used as a replacement for classic cream.

SOY "CREAM"

Nutrients > Soy cream is a very good source of protein and omega-3. Soy cream has significant amounts of magnesium, calcium, potassium and vitamins B1 and B9.

Use > It is a creamy color with a creamy texture. It is used in all recipes calling for cream. Its flavor is neutral but slightly acidic.

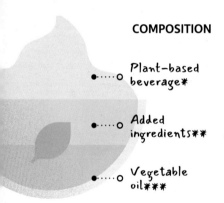

COMPOSITION

● · · · · ○ Plant-based beverage*

● · · · · ○ Added ingredients**

● · · · · ○ Vegetable oil***

* Made from oleaginous fruits or oilseeds, cereals or legumes.

** Depends on the brand: Thickeners: lecithin, guar gum, xanthan gum, carrageenan
Emulsifiers: lecithin
Other: salt, cane sugar, agave syrup, wheat syrup

*** Sunflower or canola oil.

CHAPTER 4

Fats

INTRODUCTION

·

**Fats, also called lipids, are essential
ingredients in pastry making.**

Solids or liquids at room temperature, fats have very different
nutritional properties and techniques once they are mixed or
heated. Butter, margarine, oil… Each has its own properties!
Fats also play a key role in how the body functions.

Owing to their nutritional makeup, which is high in fatty
acids (omega-3, -6 and -9) and vitamins (mainly E and K1),
they have many health benefits. This chapter will show you
how best to use them.

Grape seed
oil

Sunflower oil

Macadamia
oil

Olive
oil

Canola
oil

Hazelnut
oil

Pumpkin seed
oil

Flaxseed
oil

Fatty acids

Fats are lipids made up of fatty acids. Although there are many fatty acids, we will focus on three: saturated fatty acids, unsaturated fatty acids and naturally occurring trans fatty acids.

> **Saturated fatty acids (SFA)** are naturally synthesized by the body but are also found in butter and coconut oil. They are more stable than unsaturated fatty acids and less sensitive to oxidation. Although they provide energy, eating too much of them promotes the risk of cardiovascular disease. A distinctive feature is that they crystallize at room temperature.

> **Unsaturated fatty acids (UFA)** get good press as they help the body fight against risks of cardiovascular disease. They are, so to speak, the best members of the family. You will recognize their names: omega-3, omega-6 and omega-9. In pastry making, we mainly find them in oleaginous fruits and oilseeds.

Omega-3

Our current diet is significantly lacking in omega-3 fatty acids, which is a shame as they have many benefits! They boost "good" cholesterol, have an anti-inflammatory role in the body and help to prevent many cardiovascular, neurodegenerative and psychiatric diseases[1]

Omega-3s are part of the family of essential fatty acids as they are not made by the body. It is therefore essential to get them through diet. They help to lower cholesterol levels, play a role in immune and inflammation response, and help to keep skin healthy.

Omega-6

Omega-6 fatty acids, like omega-3s, belong to the family of essential fatty acids, which must be obtained through food. Unlike omega-3s, they tend to be overconsumed in our modern diet. They therefore become pro-inflammatory and dangerous to our health.

Omega-9

Omega-9 fatty acids can be made by the body from other fatty acids, but consuming them is recommended. They lower LDL ("bad") cholesterol levels and help to maintain or increase HDL ("good") cholesterol levels. They therefore play a positive role in the functioning of the heart and the blood vessels.

> **Trans fatty acids (TFA)**

Trans fatty acids are unsaturated hydrogenated fatty acids. Oil is combined with hydrogen molecules, turning a liquid oil into a solid, or at least a firmer oil, which means it keeps longer.

As a result, these fatty acids are found in many industrially made products and in some margarines.

---

[1] Cleveland Clinic, "Omega-3 Fatty Acids," https://my.clevelandclinic.org/health/articles/17290-omega-3-fatty-acids/.

Oils

Olive, argan, canola, virgin, hydrogenated, first press... There are many varieties, designations and production methods to get to know!

The quality of an oil depends on the raw material used (fruit, dried fruit, seeds, cereals...), how it is grown, how the oil is extracted and how it is stored. These factors determine the quality of its micronutrients and its functional fatty acids.

Regarding the nutrients of oils, they are 100% fat. What distinguishes them from each other is their omega-3, -6 and -9 content. Oils contain very few vitamins and minerals: the only ones they can contain are vitamins E and K1 (in different amounts from one oil to another).

HOW BEST TO CHOOSE AND STORE OIL

Here are the steps for the best way to choose and use oil.

1 - EVERYTHING IS ON THE LABEL!
Where it comes from
• Type of fruit/seed/grain used
• Where it was harvested
• Where it was processed

PROCESSING METHOD
The following three appellations guarantee that an oil is rich in vitamins, antioxidants and unsaturated fatty acids:

> **"First cold pressed":** Certifies that an oil was produced in the traditional way, through crushing fruits and seeds on a millstone at room temperature (80 °F / <27 °C), without added chemicals. This technique allows the "juice" to be extracted: it is then decanted and filtered to separate the water from the oil.

> **Cold extraction":** Fruits and seeds are turned into a paste which is then placed in a centrifuge to separate the oil from the water and organic matter. The oil must also be extracted at a temperature below 80 °F (27 °C).

> **Virgin" or "extra virgin":** The term "virgin" indicates that the oil has not been heated. This is a first guarantee of quality. The oleic acidity of an extra virgin oil must not exceed 0.8%, while that of virgin oil can be up to 2% of the oil's total composition. The level of oleic acidity of an oil corresponds to its oxidation level – a high rate of oxidation is caused by fruit that is overripe or damaged during processing. "Virgin" or "extra virgin" appellations are given to the best olive oils.

What is oxidation? It is an unavoidable chemical process for organic products that can happen more or less quickly and that can be slowed down. Here are the signs of oxidation of oil: it becomes rancid, its odor goes off, its color changes and it forms compounds that are harmful to health (ketones, peroxide, hydrocarbons).

COMPOSITION OF OILS

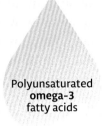

Polyunsaturated **omega-3** fatty acids

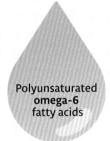

Polyunsaturated **omega-6** fatty acids

Monounsaturated **omega-9** fatty acids

Vitamin E

Vitamin K1

> **Refined oil:** Seeds and fruits are heated, and the oil is extracted while hot. The resulting paste (pulp) is mixed with a chemical solvent to collect the residual oil. The mixture is distilled to remove the solvent and obtain the raw oil, which is then refined with a hot water treatment. Next comes washing and drying. The color is then removed over activated carbon or caustic soda and, finally, deodorized and filtered by steam injection at 350 °F (180 °C) sous vide. At the end of this process, no vitamins remain; compounds such as trans fatty acids appear, giving the oil high stability over time. These are called hydrogenated oils.

2 - STORING: A MAJOR CHALLENGE

The precautions to take to store oils vary depending on the fatty acids they contain:

> **Oils rich in omega-3 and -6** are stored in the fridge, as they are very sensitive to rancidity and oxidation. Storing these oils in a cool temperature slows down this process and helps the oil keep better.

> **Oils rich in omega-9 and refined oils** are stored at room temperature.

In all cases, choose opaque containers, which protect the oil from the light.

As you have seen, although oils potentially have a good nutritional makeup, it is important to know how to choose them, store them and use them with care.

FUNCTIONS OF OIL IN PASTRY MAKING

Pastry product	Technical contributions of the oil
Brioche	texturing agent (softener), texturing agent (binder)
Cookie	texturing agent (softener), texturing agent (binder)
Cake	texturing agent (softener), keeps a spongy texture longer, texturing agent (binder), flavoring agent (flavor)
Shortbread	flavoring agent (flavor), texturing agent (binder)
Cream	flavoring agent (flavor), texturing agent (emulsifier)
Mousse	flavoring agent (flavor), texturing agent (emulsifier)

The different oils[2]

ᛘ

All the oils presented here are of organic origin and are extracted by either "first cold pressed" or "cold extraction" methods. Guidance on using them is related to their nutritional qualities.

Oils from seeds

CAMELINA OIL: HIGH IN OMEGA-3

Source > Camelina is a plant that was overlooked for a long time. It is being cultivated again for its seeds, which are rich in fatty acids.

Nutrients > It is the richest oil in omega-3 after flaxseed oil and has two advantages compared to the latter: it oxidizes more slowly and has a neutral flavor. It has strong antioxidant properties thanks to its vitamin E content and is rich in phytosterols and beta-carotene.

Use > Camelina oil's flavor is mild, with aromatic notes similar to hazelnut and sesame. It is used cold and works well with chocolate, honey and citrus fruit.

CANOLA OIL: MULTIPURPOSE

Source > This oil is made from seeds of the canola plant. It is an oilseed because of its high fat content.

Nutrients > It is rich in antioxidants thanks to the presence of vitamin E and canolol, a powerful antioxidant in canola.

This oil is composed of saturated and unsaturated fatty acids, including omega-9, omega-6 and omega-3.

Use > It has a slightly fruity flavor. It pairs with all ingredients as it remains relatively neutral once it is added to a mixture. It is only used cold.

GRAPE SEED OIL: ADORED BY PASTRY CHEFS!

Source > This oil comes from the residue (dregs) of wine production. The story goes that King Ferdinand IV of Spain called it royal oil. It is widely used in cooking and pastry making.

Nutrients > This oil contains saturated and unsaturated fatty acids, including omega-3, -6 and -9.

It contains a small amount of potassium, which is fairly rare for oils.[1] (See the effects of potassium on the body at the end of the chapter.)

Use > This oil is popular with pastry chefs. Since it is a neutral oil, it can be used in any recipe. It can be heated up to 325 °F (160 °C) or used cold. Like sunflower oil, it is used in all types of mixtures.

---

[2] For all the cited nutritional values, see Table Ciqual, ANSES (2022): https://ciqual.anses.fr/ (information is in English) or https://www.nutritionvalue.org/

NUTRIENTS OF OILS PER 100 G

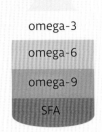

omega-3
omega-6
omega-9
SFA

35–45 g ⋯⋯ omega-3

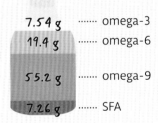

7.54 g ⋯⋯ omega-3
19.4 g ⋯⋯ omega-6
55.2 g ⋯⋯ omega-9
7.26 g ⋯⋯ SFA

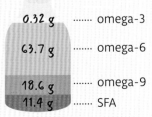

0.32 g ⋯⋯ omega-3
63.7 g ⋯⋯ omega-6
18.6 g ⋯⋯ omega-9
11.4 g ⋯⋯ SFA

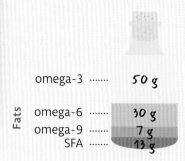

omega-3 .... 50 g

omega-6 .... 30 g
omega-9 .... 7 g
SFA .... 13 g

Fats

INCA INCHI (OR SACHA INCHI) OIL: AN OIL WORTH KNOWING!

Source > Inca inchi is a plant found in the Amazonian rainforest. This oil is obtained by cold pressing the seeds from its star-shaped fruits.

Nutrients > Here is an oil that is not well known but contains significant amounts of omega-3 and -6. It also has strong antioxidant properties, especially owing to its high concentration of vitamin E.

Use > Its flavor is mild and herbaceous. It goes well with dried fruit, coffee and chocolate.

NIGELLA OIL: ASIAN NOTES

Source > The nigella or black cumin flower's seeds are used to make the oil. They are cold pressed to extract the oil.

Nutrients > It has high amounts of omega-6 and -9 and strong antioxidant properties, especially due to nigellicine, a substance found in black cumin seeds.

Use > It has a strong, spicy flavor. It is used in recipes for Asian pastries or pastries with spicy notes. It can be mixed with a neutral oil to mellow it. It goes with stone fruits such as apricot, Mirabelle plums or peaches, and berries. It is used cold.

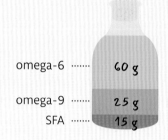

omega-6 .... 60 g

omega-9 .... 25 g
SFA .... 15 g

PEANUT OIL: THE GOURMET

Source > It is made from peanuts, which grow in South America, the southern United States and tropical regions. Its fruits bury themselves in the ground to produce their seeds; they are harvested in the shell that contains the seed.

Nutrients > This oil is made up of saturated fatty acids and unsaturated fatty acids, with a very significant amount of omega-9. Like most oils, it has antioxidant properties due to its vitamin E content.

Use > It has a mild flavor, with notes typical of peanuts. It pairs very well with chocolate, dried fruit and citrus fruit. It can be used cold or hot, up to 350 °F (180 °C).

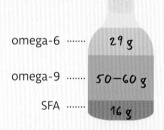

omega-6 .... 29 g

omega-9 .... 50–60 g

SFA .... 16 g

POPPYSEED OIL: THE THERAPEUTIC OIL

Source > Poppyseed oil comes from the poppy, a popular plant in Ayurvedic medicine. It is found in the Himalayas and in Tibet. It is not to be confused with the opium poppy (*Papaver somniferum*), which is used to make opium and contains an alkaloid similar to morphine.

Nutrients > Poppyseed oil is made of saturated and unsaturated fatty acids, including omega-9, omega-6 and omega-3.

Use > This oil has a subtle flavor between pine nut and hazelnut. It pairs very well with lemon and other fruits. It is only used cold.

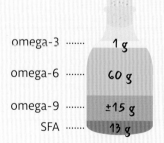

omega-3 .... 1 g

omega-6 .... 60 g

omega-9 .... ±15 g
SFA .... 13 g

SAFFLOWER OIL: SUNFLOWER OIL'S COUSIN

Source > This oil comes from a plant similar to the thistle. The seeds are harvested for their high omega-9 content.

Nutrients > This oil is made up of saturated and unsaturated fatty acids, including a large proportion of omega-9 and omega-6. Like most oils, it contains significant amounts of vitamins E (antioxidant) and K1.

Use > It has a mild flavor and is related to sunflower oil. It pairs with all flavors in pastry making and is only used cold.

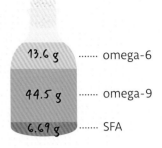

13.6 g ······· omega-6

44.5 g ······· omega-9

6.69 g ······· SFA

SESAME OIL: THE MOST EXOTIC

Source > Sesame oil comes from an aromatic plant that grows in tropical areas in Africa and Asia. Although the seeds are sometimes toasted before the oil is extracted, it is better to choose an oil with non-toasted seeds, which still has all its nutritional benefits.

Nutrients > This oil contains saturated and unsaturated fatty acids, including omega-9. It also contains omega-3 and omega-6.

Sesame oil contains very little vitamin E, unlike most oils.

Use > With its pronounced flavor, it pairs very well with chocolate, caramel, lemon and nuts. It is only used cold.

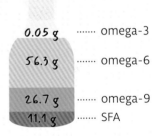

0.38 g ······· omega-3

39.6 g ······· omega-6

38.5 g ······· omega-9

14.9 g ······· SFA

SUNFLOWER OIL: THE MOST COMMON

Source > Sunflower oil is made from seeds of the sunflower plant. It is used widely in cooking.

Nutrients > It contains saturated and unsaturated fatty acids, including omega-9, -6 and -3.

A little bonus for people who don't want to add salt to their recipes: sunflower oil has the most sodium of all those presented in this book.[3]

Use > Like grape seed oil, it is often used in pastry making. However, its mild and fruity flavor is not neutral when cold pressed. It can only be used cold. It pairs with all ingredients as it becomes neutral once it is added to a mixture.

0.05 g ······· omega-3

56.3 g ······· omega-6

26.7 g ······· omega-9

11.1 g ······· SFA

[3] Table Ciqual, ANSES (2022). https://ciqual.anses.fr/

Oils from fruits and nuts

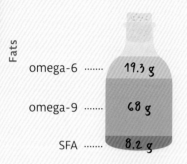

omega-6 ········ 19.3 g

omega-9 ········ 68 g

SFA ········ 8.2 g

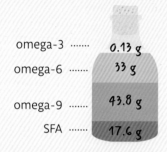

omega-3 ········ 0.13 g

omega-6 ········ 33 g

omega-9 ········ 43.8 g

SFA ········ 17.6 g

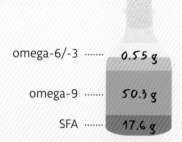

omega-6/-3 ········ 0.55 g

omega-9 ········ 50.3 g

SFA ········ 17.6 g

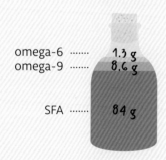

omega-6 ········ 1.3 g
omega-9 ········ 8.6 g

SFA ········ 84 g

ALMOND OIL: DRIED FRUIT'S BEST FRIEND

Source > Almond oil is made from sweet ripe almonds. It has long been widely used in cosmetics. Now it is also used in pastry making and cooking.

Nutrients > This oil contains saturated and unsaturated fatty acids, including omega-9. It has strong antioxidant properties thanks to vitamin E (which is present in most oils).

Use > It has a sweet flavor, round and buttery. It is only used cold. It goes with all dried fruit, vanilla and berries.

ARGAN OIL: A GEM FROM MOROCCO

Source > Argan oil is produced from the fruit of the argan tree. Morocco's production of this oil is recognized by the European Union as a "protected geographical indication" (PGI).

Nutrients > This oil contains saturated and unsaturated fatty acids, including omega-9, -6 and -3. This oil also contains polyphenols, which are antioxidant molecules.

Use > It has a typical flavor, close to toasted hazelnut, that lingers in the mouth. It is used cold, like almond oil, as it does not tolerate heat. It pairs with coffee, honey and citrus fruit.

AVOCADO OIL: CHOCOLATE'S FRIEND

Source > Avocado oil is made from the fruit of the avocado tree, which grows in sub-tropical regions (in Mexico, for example).

Nutrients > This oil contains saturated and unsaturated fatty acids, including significant amounts of omega-9, and smaller amounts of omega-6 and -3.

Use > It has a sweet flavor, slightly herbaceous, and adapts to all uses. It can be used at the end of cooking or cold. It pairs perfectly with chocolate, almond and citrus fruit.

COCONUT OIL: AN ENHANCER OF EXOTIC FRUITS

Source > Coconut oil is made by cold pressing coconut pulp.

Nutrients > This oil contains a lot of saturated fatty acids compared to the other oils mentioned and a smaller amount of unsaturated fatty acids, including omega-9 and -6.

Use > Coconut oil can replace butter in a recipe and is often used in vegan pastry making for its ability to crystallize. Depending on whether it is deodorized, its flavor ranges from coconut to neutral. Its melting point is lower than butter's, which means that dough containing it is more pliable than if butter were used. It pairs very well with exotic fruits, chocolate and dried fruit. It can be heated to 475 °F (240 °C).

HAZELNUT OIL: FRAGRANT AND ELEGANT

Source > This oil is made from the fruit of the hazel tree. Hazelnuts have been eaten for many thousands of years in the Piedmont region in Italy. At that time, it was the main source of dietary fat.

Nutrients > It contains saturated and unsaturated fatty acids, including omega-9, -6 and -3.

Use > It is only used cold. It pairs with pastries made with nuts, chocolate and fruit, such as apples.

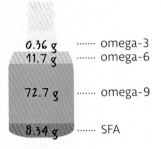

0.36 g omega-3
11.7 g omega-6
72.7 g omega-9
8.34 g .... SFA

MACADAMIA OIL: THE MILDEST

Source > This oil is made from dried macadamia nuts. It has been used for more than 5,000 years by Indigenous peoples in Australia. It is often found in cosmetics.

Nutrients > This oil contains saturated and unsaturated fatty acids, with mostly omega-9 and -6 and a little omega-3.

Use > Its flavor is mild, close to walnut. It can be used at the end of cooking or cold. It pairs with nuts such as almond and hazelnut or with chocolate and vanilla.

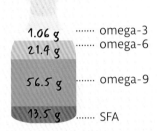

1.06 g omega-3
21.4 g omega-6
56.5 g omega-9
13.5 g .... SFA

OLIVE OIL: THE INTERNATIONAL STAR

Source > This oil is made from olives, the fruit of the olive tree. It has been part of Mediterranean history for more than 6,000 years: for example, it was used in sacred rites in Egypt at the time of the pharaohs.

Nutrients > It contains saturated and unsaturated fatty acids, including omega-9, -6 and -3.

It is the second-richest oil in omega-9 after hazelnut oil.[4] Also, it contains a small amount of beta-carotene (an antioxidant) and, like corn oil, a small amount of iodine.

Use > With its subtle, round olive notes, it can be used with many flavors in pastry making, such as lemon, chocolate and nuts. It can be heated to 350 °F (180 °C) or used cold.

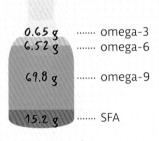

0.65 g omega-3
6.52 g omega-6
69.8 g omega-9
15.2 g .... SFA

WALNUT OIL: POWER AND BENEFITS

Source > This oil is made from walnuts from the walnut tree. In Périgord (France), the land of walnuts, it was considered a kind of gold in the 18th century. It was used for money, for painting and in soap.

Nutrients > It contains saturated and unsaturated fatty acids, including omega-9, -6 and -3. Its strong antioxidant properties are due to the presence of polyphenols and a small amount of vitamin E.

Use > Its nutty notes are strong. It is used cold, like hazelnut oil. It pairs well with chocolate, nuts and chestnuts.

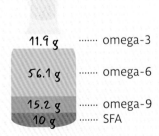

11.9 g omega-3
56.1 g omega-6
15.2 g omega-9
10 g .... SFA

---

4 Table Ciqual, ANSES (2022). https://ciqual.anses.fr/

In this table, you will find only first cold pressed organic oils (refined oils are better able to tolerate being heated, and their use is therefore different).

Oil	Use cold	For cooking	Maximum cooking temperature	Ways to use cold	Ways to use heated
Almond	YES	NO	–	praline, crispy, frosting/glaze for a cake, mousse, cream, moistening, flavoring	–
Avocado	YES	NO	–	praline, crispy, frosting/glaze for a cake, mousse, cream, moistening, flavoring	–
Argan oil	YES	NO	–	praline, crispy, frosting/glaze for a cake, mousse, cream, moistening, flavoring	–
Camelina	YES	NO	–	praline, crispy, frosting/glaze or a cake, mousse, cream, moistening	–
Canola	YES	NO	–	praline, crispy, glaze for a cake, mousse, cream, moistening	–
Coconut	YES	YES	475 °F / 240 °C	whipped cream, praline, crispy, frosting/glaze for a cake, mousse, cream, moistening	cake, sponge cake, shortbread, greasing a pan, cooking a pancake or crepe, brioche, sweet dough
Grape seed	YES	YES	325 °F / 160 °C	praline, crispy, frosting/glaze for a cake, mousse, cream, moistening	cake, sponge cake, shortbread, greasing a pan, cooking a pancake or crepe, brioche, sweet dough
Hazelnut	YES	NO	–	praline, crispy, frosting/glaze for a cake, mousse, cream, moistening, flavoring	–
Inca inchi	YES	YES	325 °F / 160 °C	praline, crispy, frosting/glaze for a cake, mousse, cream, moistening, flavoring	cake, sponge cake, shortbread, greasing a pan, cooking a pancake or crepe, brioche, sweet dough
Macadamia	YES	NO	–	praline, crispy, frosting/glaze for a cake, mousse, cream, moistening, flavoring	–
Nigella	YES	NO	–	praline, crispy, frosting/glaze for a cake, mousse, cream, moistening, flavoring	–
Olive	YES	YES	350 °F / 180 °C	praline, crispy, frosting/glaze for a cake, mousse, cream, moistening, flavoring	cake, sponge cake, shortbread, greasing a pan, cooking a pancake or crepe, brioche, sweet dough
Peanut	YES	YES	350 °F / 180 °C	praline, crispy, frosting/glaze for a cake, mousse, cream, moistening, flavoring	cake, sponge cake, shortbread, greasing a pan, cooking a pancake or crepe, brioche, sweet dough
Poppyseed	YES	NO	–	praline, crispy, frosting/glaze for a cake, mousse, cream, moistening	–
Safflower	YES	NO	–	praline, crispy, frosting/glaze or a cake, mousse, cream, moistening	–
Sesame	YES	NO	–	praline, crispy, frosting/glaze for a cake, mousse, cream, moistening, flavoring	
Sunflower	YES	NO	–	praline, crispy, frosting/glaze for a cake, mousse, cream, moistening	–
Walnut	YES	NO	–	praline, crispy, frosting/glaze for a cake, mousse, cream, moistening, flavoring	–

Butters and margarines

Butter and margarine play a key role in the most iconic pastries.

Butter

Butter is made from the cream of cow's milk, after being vigorously churned.

1 > Butter is an animal product derived from cow's milk, and more specifically cream, which is beaten for a long time. This gives buttermilk, which becomes butter after churning. This production process (the only one authorized) gives certain butters in Europe the appellation "churned butters" (which is not official).

2 > Butter contains saturated fatty acids: it should be eaten in moderation to limit an increase in bad cholesterol.

3 > Butter doesn't react well to heat. It is best to eat it uncooked or not to heat it above 275 °F (140 °C): beyond that temperature, it forms carcinogenic compounds.

4 > There are different types of butter (unsalted, salted...). Salt can be added if a salted or semi-salted butter is desired.

5 > To have the right to be considered "butter," it must contain at least 82% fat (Europe) or 80% fat (North America).

6 > For pasteurized butter, the cream has been pasteurized, which means heated for 15 to 20 seconds at 165 °F (75 °C) to increase its shelf life by eliminating certain bacteria.

THE DIFFERENT BUTTERS

DRY BUTTER (BEURRE DE TOURAGE)

Source > This butter is recombined with selected fats so its melting point is higher. This makes it possible to work dough more easily and to get a good quality of tourage (repeated folding into thirds and rolling the dough) when making pastry.

Nutrients > Its main difference is that it has more fat (84%) than classic North American butter (80%). This higher fat content is what makes it a firmer butter.

Use > It is used to make puff pastry. Its texture is firmer than classic butter.

COMPOSITION OF BUTTER

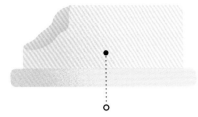

From the cream of cow's milk

COCOA BUTTER

Source > This is the fat in cocoa paste, which is removed by separating it from pure cocoa paste. It's a fat that is often used in pastry making.

Nutrients > Its saturated fatty acid content is slightly higher than that of classic butter. However, it contains twice as much omega-9. This is a very good vegetarian and lactose-free alternative to butter made from cow's milk.

Use > This butter replaces classic butter in creams. It blends well with chocolate in ganaches, is used in cream and vegan dough recipes and is a texturing agent. It has a greasy taste; that is why it is important to adjust the quantity to avoid having too strong an aftertaste and texture.

GHEE

Source > Ghee is made from butter. The butter is melted, then clarified: the casein (protein), lactose (carbohydrate) and water (whey) are removed. Ghee is widely used in Ayurvedic medicine, as it is very digestible. Made only of fat, it helps regulate bowel function. During cooking, the smoke point of ghee can be up to 400 °F (200 °C) (for butter, it is around 300 °F / 150 °C).

It is easy to make: in a saucepan, melt the butter over low heat until a fine foam forms on the top. Remove from heat (this is when the three compounds mentioned above become concentrated). Strain the clarified butter once or twice to get the purest ghee possible.

Nutrients > Its distinctive feature is that it contains neither lactose nor cow's milk protein; using it to replace "classic" butter allows for a great reduction in the risk of digestive disorders. But that's not all: it also contains less cholesterol than classic butter.

Use > Ghee replaces butter in recipes and can be used for all types of cooking. It allows you to make lactose-free and casein-free recipes. Its flavor is very close to butter, with light hazelnut notes.

SHEA BUTTER

Source > It is made from the nuts of the shea tree, which grows in the African savannah. Renowned in cosmetic products, this butter has also been used for a long time in African cuisine. Once the nuts have been picked, the meat is removed from the shell (the discarded shells are used for fuel). The nuts are dried and ground into a paste. This is mixed with water to remove impurities. The paste is then heated at a low temperature, then filtered (the excess water is removed). The butter is then conditioned.

Nutrients > This butter's composition is close to that of cocoa butter: it is also rich in omega-9 (around 40 to 45 g/100 g).

Note: Even with an organic label on the packaging, shea butter could have been refined.

Use > It is mainly used in cooking and as a replacement for butter in recipes. Its flavor is fairly pronounced, and it is yellow in color.

MORE INFO

Note: if shea butter is white, odorless and granular when rubbed on your skin, that means it has been refined; chemical products have been added during processing and it has lost 50% to 80% of its benefits.

Margarine

Unlike butter, margarine is a plant-based product. Margarines are emulsions containing 50 to 80% plant fat. They are generally a mixture of oils, water and emulsifiers. Margarine is vegan, and it contains almost no saturated fatty acids compared to traditional butter. However, you must be vigilant about the ingredients. See page 160 for the recipe for homemade margarine.

COMPARATIVE TABLE: BUTTER AND MARGARINE

	Check the label	Smoke point
Butter	Check its source and whether it's organic	250 to 300 °F (120 to 150 °C)
Margarine	Make sure it is non-hydrogenated and does not contain palm oil	Depends on the quality and characteristics of the oils used

NOTE
You are strongly encouraged to check the ingredients in margarine as, even if it is plant based, it can be very harmful to human health because of the additives it contains.

GOOD AND BAD ADDITIVES MAY BE PRESENT IN MARGARINE

HARMLESS ADDITIVES

Gellan gum (E418) > Presents no major risks

ACCEPTABLE ADDITIVES

Calcium carbonate (E170) > Do not consume large amounts (lack of current scientific studies)

Seaweed (lithothamnium calcareum) > Except in cases of kidney problems

Guar gum (E412) > Do not consume large amounts: causes digestive disorders

Xanthan gum (E415) > Do not consume large amounts: risk of digestive disorders

Carrageenan (E407a) > Risk of digestive disorders and potential risk of developing colon cancer

Soy lecithin (E322) > Possible contamination by soy protein fractions

ADDITIVES TO AVOID COMPLETELY

Calcium phosphate (E341) > Potentially harmful as it would constitute a cardiovascular risk factor, especially in cases of kidney failure

Potassium phosphate (E340) > Potentially harmful as it is a cardiovascular risk factor, especially in cases of kidney failure

Tricalcium phosphate > Can promote cardiovascular disease

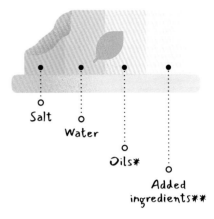

COMPOSITION OF INDUSTRIAL MARGARINE

Salt

Water

Oils*

Added ingredients**

* Sometimes vegetable fats.

** Added ingredients are dyes, preservatives, flavors and emulsifiers.

MORE INFO

Napoleon III held a competition to develop an "economic butter," margarine, that was cheaper than butter and would keep longer

CHAPTER 5

Eggs

INTRODUCTION

❖

Eggs are an essential ingredient in pastry making. They help create the texture of a cooked cream, the lightness of an airy mousse or the color of a dough.

They are also known for their excellent nutritional value. Be careful when you buy: choosing a producer that respects the animal is key to getting eggs that are both "ethical" and good quality.

Choosing eggs well

When buying eggs, choose a producer that respects the animal, which always goes hand in hand with the nutritional quality of the product. You are therefore encouraged to choose eggs from an organic farmer or, at least, free-range chickens.

Don't rely on the marketing images on the carton, showing beautiful chickens outdoors, as the image is not legally binding and they are not necessarily raised in these conditions.

Note: the egg doesn't have a good omega-6 to -3 ratio (which is essential to our health) unless the hen is fed with a high-quality natural diet and raised in the open air in an environment where it can peck whatever it wants off the ground. If the hen is fed exclusively with cornstarch and raised in a battery cage, the proportion of omega-6 is higher, at the expense of omega-3.

DECIPHERING THE FRESHNESS CODE

EXP MAR0224
P-1234 032

① **EXPIRY DATE**
mmm/dd/yy

② **PRODUCER**
The production plant's registration number—only for USDA-graded eggs*.

③ **DATE OF PACKAGING**
The 3-digit number represents the number of the day in that calendar year. You can store the eggs in the refrigerator for 4 weeks after this date.

THE THREE GRADES OF EGGS

There are three commercial grades for eggs:

> **Grade AA:** the freshest and highest-quality eggs.

> **Grade A:** very high quality of eggs.

> **Grade B:** the eggs are usually used for liquid eggs and baking. The foods that contain these eggs need to reach 325 °F (160 °C) on a food thermometer during the production process.

MORE INFO

USDA grading of shell eggs is a voluntary service paid for by shell egg producers. Eggs sold to consumers must be labeled with a grade. Egg packers who do not use the USDA grading service may put terms such as "Grade AA" or "Grade A" on their cartons, but they may not use the USDA Grade Shield.

THE ROLE OF EGGS IN PASTRY MAKING

Eggs play many roles in pastry making. That's why it's not always easy to replace them.

Composed of two elements, the yolk and the white, which have different nutritional makeups, eggs are essential to many recipes.

Egg white, made of 90% water and 10% protein:

> moistens a mixture

> adds lightness to mousses, baked goods or meringues thanks to its ability to increase in volume by up to 8 times, as its structure allows air to be incorporated by whipping

> gives structure to batter or dough, when heated, by binding

Egg yolk, very high in lipids (34%), contains 50% water and 15% protein, including 10% lipoprotein (particles made of lipids and proteins):

> binds dough and batter while giving a soft texture

> thickens cream and gives shape to batter or dough, when heated, by binding

> colors dough, batter or cream

PLANT EQUIVALENTS FOR EGGS IN PASTRY MAKING

Item	Role of the egg	Plant equivalent
Cake	Eggs moisten the dough and help give structure during baking	Hydration and structure: fruit or vegetable fiber (apple, zucchini, grated carrot...)
Mousse	The white adds volume and gives an airy texture to mousse	Volume: aquafaba* (chickpea water, for example)
Pastry cream	The yolk thickens and colors the cream	Thickener: starch Coloring: turmeric
Sponge cake	The white adds volume and gives a soft texture	Volume: aquafaba (chickpea water)*
Sweet dough	The yolk hydrates and colors the dough	Hydration: water Coloring: turmeric

MORE INFO

Legumes such as white beans and kidney beans contain the same protein as chickpeas and so have the same qualities needed for adding volume.

*RECIPE FOR AQUAFABA MADE FROM CHICKPEAS

• Soak 1 cup (200 g) dried chickpeas for 12 hours in a large bowl filled with water to remove the phytic acid (the part that makes digestion difficult).

• Rinse, then cook in 3 times their volume of water.

• Once they are cooked, remove from heat and reduce the cooking water by half to concentrate the tensio-active proteins (proteins similar to those found in eggs, allowing the bonding of air and water during whipping) that the chickpeas released into the water.

• Refrigerate. When cooled, whip the aquafaba.

• It whips up the same way as egg white.

COMPOSITION OF AN EGG

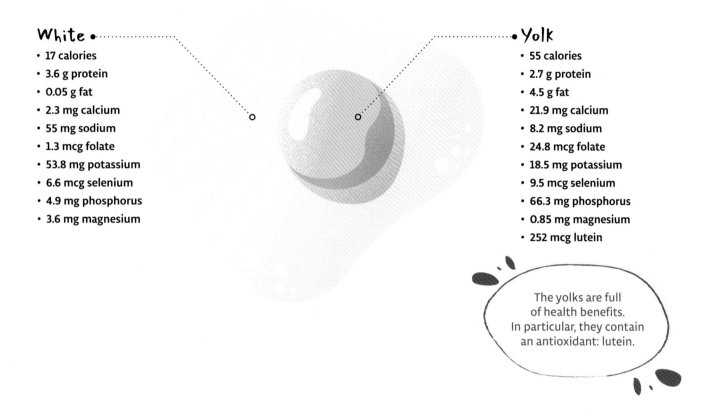

White
- 17 calories
- 3.6 g protein
- 0.05 g fat
- 2.3 mg calcium
- 55 mg sodium
- 1.3 mcg folate
- 53.8 mg potassium
- 6.6 mcg selenium
- 4.9 mg phosphorus
- 3.6 mg magnesium

Yolk
- 55 calories
- 2.7 g protein
- 4.5 g fat
- 21.9 mg calcium
- 8.2 mg sodium
- 24.8 mcg folate
- 18.5 mg potassium
- 9.5 mcg selenium
- 66.3 mg phosphorus
- 0.85 mg magnesium
- 252 mcg lutein

The yolks are full of health benefits. In particular, they contain an antioxidant: lutein.

HOW DO YOU KNOW IF AN EGG IS STILL GOOD?

Immerse the egg in a jar filled with water: if the egg sinks, it's still good; if it floats, it could make you sick.

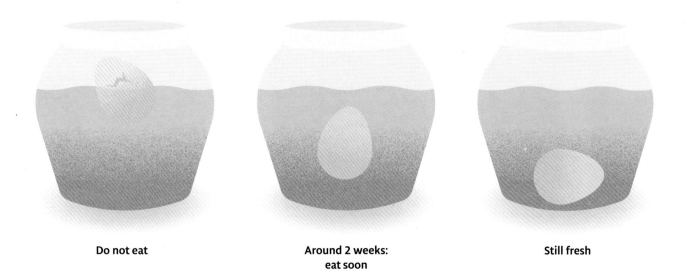

Do not eat

Around 2 weeks: eat soon

Still fresh

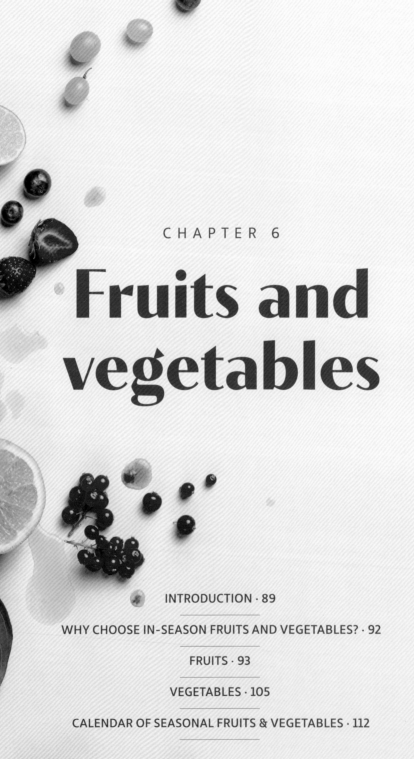

CHAPTER 6

Fruits and vegetables

INTRODUCTION

∗

You can probably picture the classic pastry buffets of the past, displaying fruit in all kinds of forms – fresh, preserves, jams, jellies...

Fruit has always been prized for its sweet flavor, the result of a wonderful plan by Mother Nature: it is with this sugar that fruit attracts pollinators (insects, birds...) to ensure that the plant reproduces by distributing its seeds. Humans then gave nature a hand, crossing species so they would produce increasingly sweet fruit.

In pastry making, we use fruit in all sorts of ways, with recipes and techniques expanding through chefs' creativity.

Vegetables arrived fairly late to pastry making, where they have recently taken center stage in innovative recipes through combinations that surprise and delight our taste buds.

In light of the new challenge that has emerged today – pastry that is both delicious and healthy – fruits and vegetables, which are incredible sources of fiber, antioxidants and minerals, have become indispensable in the realm of desserts!

Why choose in-season fruits and vegetables?

We often hear that it's important to eat fruits and vegetables in season, but do you know why?

BECAUSE THAT'S WHEN WE NEED THEM MOST

Nature is well designed: each season offers us its own variety of fruits and vegetables, which match our needs of the moment. In spring, welcome to plums and spinach! In summer, let's hear it for berries! In fall, we indulge in grapes. And in winter, citrus fruits and squash appear on store shelves. Vegetables and fruits are filled with water in summer to hydrate us and rich in vitamin C in winter to boost our immunity. When they are in season, they are packed with vitamins and minerals.

BECAUSE THAT'S WHEN THEY HAVE THE MOST FLAVOR

In-season fruits and vegetables are those that are picked when they are fully ripe (except for some fruits, such as bananas and avocados, which ripen after picking), with full flavor potential. It is at this exact moment that fruits and vegetables teem with flavor and nutrients.

BECAUSE SHOPPING LOCALLY IS GOOD FOR US!

Enjoying the fruits and vegetables of your own region means first of all knowing that the products are fresh. This is a result of the proximity of where the product was harvested and the distribution channels: this is not the case for exotic imported fruits, for example, which must be picked before they are ripe and whose flavor is therefore not ideal. The best part is that by choosing local products, we create more local resilience and at the same time limit our carbon footprint. Why wait to embrace these causes?

Depending on where you live on the planet, there may be two or four seasons, or even just one, if you're near the equator. In that case, the same fruits and vegetables are available all year long.

Fruits

Fruits are generally classified as follows:

> **Fruits with pits** (plums, peaches, cherries, apricots…)

> **Fruits with seeds** (apples, pears, grapes, quince…)

> **Berries and red fruits** (strawberries, redcurrants, blackcurrants…)

> **Citrus fruits** (lemons, grapefruits, oranges, clementines…)

> **Exotic fruits** (lychees, pineapples, mangoes, papayas…)

APPLES

Source > Apples, fruit of the apple tree, are the most commonly eaten fruits in the world. There are so many varieties (created by grafting and hybridization), it is difficult to know where they originated.

Nutrients > Apples are especially high in fiber. They also contain high levels of antioxidants, which, along with vitamin C, makes them a powerhouse. Also, apples contain vitamins B, C, E and A as well as a variety of minerals, including potassium.

Use > See the table below, which shows possible uses for four different varieties.

Apple variety	Characteristics	Best uses
Cripp's Pink	Reddish-pink, delicate and juicy flesh, sweet flavor	In compote, clafoutis, fruit salad, apple pie, tarte Tatin
Gala	Reddish-orange (striped), sweet flavor, slightly bitter, juicy and crisp	In compote, clafoutis, fruit salad, apple pie, tarte Tatin, baked apple
Golden	Yellow, juicy flesh, sweet flavor, slightly acidic, crisp	In compote, clafoutis, fruit salad, apple pie, tarte Tatin
Granny Smith	Green, acidic flavor, crisp	In fruit salad, granita, sorbet, jellied

APRICOTS

Source > Apricots are the fruit of the apricot tree, which is originally from China (where it has been known for more than 5,000 years) and has grown in the Mediterranean region since Antiquity. It wasn't until the late 1800s that the tree became popular in North America. The fruit is picked in summer.

Nutrients > When apricots are ripe, their flesh is high in fiber. Their orange color is linked to the fruit's high levels of beta-carotene, an antioxidant, and vitamin A. This fruit is also a source of minerals, including considerable amounts of iron, copper and magnesium. Dried apricots are high in calcium.

Use > Apricot flesh is sweet, slightly acidic and meaty. It's delicious roasted with thyme, poached with rosemary or fried with ginger juice and cardamom. Dried, puréed or simply raw, it makes a great energy-boosting snack, cake filling or addition to a dessert plate.

BANANAS

Source > Bananas are an exotic fruit of the banana tree that originated in Southeast Asia. Today, they are grown in all countries with a tropical climate. They have been eaten by humans for more than 7,000 years! There are countless varieties, flavors, shapes and sizes.

Although plantains are used in cooking, and baby bananas (called Fressinette in France) are loved in Europe for their sweet flavor and delicate flesh, pastry chefs mostly use Cavendish bananas. They are picked when green and ripen during shipping.

Nutrients > Bananas are nutritionally dense, which means they pack a lot of nutrients into a small amount of fruit. Also, they are filling! This fruit is rich in fiber and contains significant amounts of dopamine and vitamin C, two powerful antioxidants. It is high in potassium and magnesium. Its levels of vitamin B6 and tryptophan, an amino acid that is a forerunner of serotonin, give it relaxing properties.

Use > See the table below.

MORE INFO

Dried banana is richer in nutrients than fresh banana, but it is also higher in calories.

Banana variety	Uses	Flavor	What it pairs with
Baby banana (Fressinette)	Raw, cooked, stewed, marinated, flambéed	Tender, very sweet yellow flesh	Exotic fruits, cardamom, cinnamon, pear, chocolate
Cavendish		Soft white flesh, sweet	
Plantain	As flour, to make dough and baked goods	Not sweet, slightly bitter	Everything, as its flavor is neutral enough in a mixture

BILBERRIES (EUROPEAN BLUEBERRIES)

Source > Bilberries come from the bilberry bush, which grows mainly in the mountains. They are picked in summer. They are easily confused with blueberries, which are similar. Bilberries have great therapeutic properties: they were originally used to treat diarrhea and improve vision.

Nutrients > Bilberries protect the body against oxidative stress. They are rich in vitamin C and fiber.

Use > In pastry making, bilberries are used in the same way as blackberries. With their sweet, slightly bitter flavor, they go well with almond, peach, lemon and cinnamon.

BLACKBERRIES

Source > Wild blackberries come from bramble bushes, which grow by the side of the road. From summer to fall, the berries turn from red to black, at which point they are picked. Traditionally, they are made into jam or cordial. Eaten since the Neolithic era (6000 to 2200 BCE), they have been credited with many therapeutic properties, making them a good health-enhancing food.

Nutrients > Blackberries are very rich in antioxidants, in minerals, including potassium, calcium, phosphorus and magnesium, in vitamins, especially vitamins B, C and E, as well as pigments and tannins. They also contain fiber.

Use > Blackberries can be used in all sorts of ways in pastry making: raw, cooked or puréed. They are used in mousse or as a filling in a layer cake, baked in a cake, in sorbet, stewed or raw in a pie. Although their notes are sour and slightly sweet, they can have a very different flavor, with secondary notes of spices, rose or mint. They pair with vanilla, apple, almond and peach. They turn pastries a deep purple.

BLACKCURRANTS

Source > This is the berry of the blackcurrant bush, native to Europe and North Asia, which grows wild in mountainous areas. Blackcurrants grow in clusters and ripen during summer. They have been eaten for millennia as they are seen to have various medicinal properties. It is only recently that we've started using them as an ingredient in a cordial and then in cooking to make savory and sweet dishes.

Nutrients > Blackcurrants are rich in fiber as well as polyphenols and antioxidants such as vitamin C. They also are full of minerals such as potassium, magnesium and iron.

Use > This very sour berry colors all mixtures due to its dark pigments. Fresh, in a compote, in jelly or in jam, blackcurrants are found in cakes, cake fillings, sorbets and pies. Blackcurrant pairs very well with chestnut, almond, coffee and apple.

BUDDHA'S HAND

Source > Buddha's hand is a citrus fruit from the citron tree. It is native to Southeast Asia. Its shape, which looks like a praying hand (hence its name) is caused by a genetic mutation. Because this fruit is seen as a lucky charm, it was an offering to Buddha. It is picked in winter, like most citrus fruits.

Nutrients > This citrus fruit is low in calories and contains very little sugar. It is rich in micronutrients and contains vitamins such as B, C and E.

Use > This unusual fruit has no juice. It is eaten only for the aromatic notes of its skin. In preserves or zest, its sweet notes recall those of lemon and orange.

CHERRIES

Source > Cherries are the (summer) fruit of the cherry tree. The first signs of cherry pits go back to the Neolithic era (6000 to 2200 BCE), but it wasn't until Roman times that cherries were cultivated. There are more than 600 varieties of cherries: the best known are Bigarreau, Burlat and Bing. Cherries are picked starting at the beginning of May (the blooming of the cherry tree heralds the start of spring) until mid-August.

MORE INFO

The cherry blossom tree is called sakura in Japan. Every year, when it flowers, the Japanese celebrate this majestic tree and its pale pink blossoms.

Nutrients > Cherries contain antioxidant pigments. They are a source of vitamins, especially A, B9 and C. They are also rich in carbohydrates.

Use > The red flesh is very sweet, juicy and delicate. Cherries are used raw, cooked, in a compote or in preserves, in pies, cakes, clafoutis or Black Forest cake. They pair very well with chocolate, pistachio, coconut and almond.

> **GOOD TO KNOW**
> Cherry stems are used by herbalists for their diuretic properties; the pits can be used to fill a cushion and then heated or frozen to soothe pain or reduce bruising. Every part of the cherry is good!

CRANBERRIES

Source > Cranberries are a red summer fruit from a bush that grows in North America and Europe, especially France. They are harvested at the end of summer.

Nutrients > This fruit is low in calories and rich in antioxidants. It contains pigments (flavonoids) and in particular is a source of vitamin C. Cranberries contain minerals such as potassium. Their flavonoid and mineral salt levels are high.

Use > Cranberries have a very acidic flavor and are often sold frozen, as sauce (with whole berries or jellied) or dried. They pair well with dried fruit. They are used in cakes or dried in energy bars.

DRAGON FRUIT

Source > Dragon fruit, or pitaya, is the (exotic) fruit of a cactus native to South America. Its name (given to it in Vietnam, where it was imported in the 19th century) comes from vines that the cactus forms around trees, like a dragon wrapping itself around its prey. Dragon fruit is picked once it is fully ripe and the skin is nicely colored. It can have white or pink flesh, depending on the variety.

Nutrients > Because dragon fruit is rich in water, it is good for hydration. Also, it has antioxidant properties because it is high in vitamin C. It is a source of fiber and magnesium.

Use > Eaten fresh or puréed, dragon fruit is perfect raw in pastry or in a fruit salad. Its juicy, sweet flesh brings pear notes.

FIGS

Source > Figs are from the fig tree, native to Asia. They are summer fruits that can be picked until fall. Fig trees have been grown in the Mediterranean region for thousands of years (archeological digs mention figs as of 9400 BCE), making figs the oldest domesticated fruit. There are more than 800 varieties of figs with a range of appearances and colors.

Nutrients > Figs are low in calories and have a low GI (35). They are rich in fiber. Figs are dense in minerals such as potassium and copper and in B vitamins. They contain precious antioxidants: 100 g of figs contain the recommended daily serving of antioxidants.

Use > Its flesh is tender, and its sweet flavor has berry notes. Figs are used raw or as preserves: as fillings for cakes, in pies or in small pieces in a cake. They are also delicious with baked almond cream, fresh raspberries or roasted with vanilla.

GRAPEFRUIT

Source > Grapefruit is the (citrus) fruit of the grapefruit tree, native to Asia.

Nutrients > Like its cousin the orange, grapefruit is rich in vitamin C, which boosts the immune system. It is low in calories and has a low glycemic load. It is a source of fiber and antioxidants, which are found in its pigments.

Use > Grapefruit has a sweet/sour, slightly bitter taste. It is used for its juice, zest and peel. Because the peel is very bitter, it needs to be blanched up to five times before being used for preserves. It pairs with pineapple, cinnamon and juniper berry. Grapefruit can be found freshly cut into segments on the top of pies, in sorbet or stewed in a cake.

> **GOOD TO KNOW**
> Grapefruit is sometimes confused with pomelo. The latter is a cross between an orange and a grapefruit; its skin is thinner and it is smaller than a grapefruit.

GRAPES

Source > Grapes are the fruit of the vine. Since Roman times (and possibly earlier), this fruit has been used to make wine.

Nutrients > Grapes are one of the fruits with the most sugar. They are a source of fiber and B vitamins, vitamin C and antioxidants (polyphenols and tannins in red wine). Grapes are also a source of minerals and trace elements, especially potassium.

Use > Grapes are not often used fresh in pastries but are found with their fruity and sweet notes in the form of raisins in Viennese pastries and cakes. They pair very well with almond, peanut and peach.

KIWIS

Source > Kiwis are the (exotic) fruit of a vine native to China. The name comes from New Zealand, where they were imported: people saw a resemblance to the kiwi bird (which is brown, small and hairy). There are many varieties of different sizes, shapes and colors. They are picked in winter.

Nutrients > Kiwis are rich in vitamins such as C, A and K1. They have powerful antioxidant properties, contain many minerals and are a good source of fiber. Kiwis are also a source of vitamins B6 and B9.

Use > Kiwi flesh is juicy, sweet and tender. Kiwis are rarely used in pastry making but are found raw, as a jelly or fruit spread, mainly on the top of a cake or pie.

KUMQUATS

Source > Kumquats are a citrus fruit that grows on the kumquat tree, native to China. Today, they are grown all over the world in temperate regions. People like to cross the kumquat with other citrus fruits to make hybrids, such as limequat, lemonquat or calamansi.

Nutrients > Kumquats are a low-calorie fruit. They are an excellent source of fiber and have antioxidant properties. They are a source of essential nutrients including vitamins A, C and B9.

Use > Raw, stewed, as preserves... Kumquats are found in many recipes in both pastry making and chocolate making. Their flavor is tart and sweet. As decoration on a dessert plate, they can be in the form of a compote, preserves, raw or in sorbet. They are also used as preserves or marmalade in a cake or as jelly in a chocolate. Kumquat pairs well with almond, chestnut and vanilla.

LEMONS

Source > Lemons are the (citrus) fruit of the lemon tree, a tree native to Asia that was exported around the world over the centuries. In Roman times, lemons were used for their healing properties. Lemon trees have several flowering periods, which is why their fruit is available all year long. They are especially generous in winter.

Nutrients > Lemons have one of the highest concentrations of vitamin C. Their citric acid levels and mineral content are also significant, especially calcium and iron.

Use > The flavor is sour, and all parts can be consumed. The zest flavors cakes, doughs, cookies and creams. The skin is used for making preserves. The juice is found in creams and syrups. Any remaining bits of lemon are chopped, dried and ground to make powder and flavor recipes in the same way as the zest. Lemon goes with many ingredients, especially basil, chocolate, thyme and rosemary.

LIMES

Source > Limes are a citrus fruit from the lime tree, native to the Arabian Peninsula. They are picked in winter.

Nutrients > Limes are high in fiber and low in fat. They are rich in vitamin C and contain calcium, magnesium, phosphorus, iron and fiber. They also have pigments with antioxidant effects.

Use > The juicy flesh is slightly bitter and is more acidic than lemon. Limes are used for their juice, for their zests or in preserves. Lime flavors mixtures. It can also be used with baking soda to replace baking powder.

LYCHEES

Source > Lychees, fruit of the lychee tree, native to China, are also called "Chinese cherries" and are considered a great delicacy. They were introduced in the 18th century on the islands of Réunion and Madagascar. They are picked in winter.

Nutrients > Lychees have high water content and are also an excellent source of vitamin C. They have antioxidant properties and are source of soft fiber; they are high in potassium.

Use > Lychee flesh is very juicy, delicate and sweet. It can be used raw or puréed. It goes well with rose, raspberry (such as the great pastry chef Pierre Hermé's famous raspberry-lychee macaron) or grapefruit.

MANDARINS

Source > Mandarins come from the mandarin tree, a tree native to Asia that was imported into Europe and America in the 19th century. Its name is inspired by the silk robes worn by mandarins (public officials). They are eaten mainly in fall and winter (when they are picked). They are similar to clementines, a 19th-century hybrid that was even more popular thanks to its milder, sweeter notes.

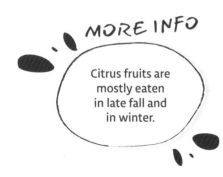

MORE INFO

Citrus fruits are mostly eaten in late fall and in winter.

Nutrients > Mandarins are a citrus fruit that is rich in carbohydrates without being high in calories. They are high in calcium, potassium and vitamin C and have strong antioxidant properties.

Use > Mandarins have a tangy, sweet flavor. All the parts can be eaten, from the peel to the juice, as with lemons. They pair perfectly with vanilla, chestnut, almond and hazelnut. The zest and juice are used in cakes, stewed or used as preserves for decoration.

MANGOES

Source > Mangoes are native to forests in India. It has been said that Buddha prayed in the shade of a mango tree. In many countries, mangoes have been considered a luxury until recently and were mainly kept for special celebrations. Today they are eaten more regularly, and they are more and more popular in pastry making.

Nutrients > Mangoes have antioxidant properties thanks to their pigments and are a good source of vitamin C. They also have a good amount of soluble fiber.

Use > Their fruity flesh, very flavorful and tender, is used raw and diced for pies, in a coulis, in a compote, or thinly sliced and marinated for decoration. They pair with apricot, pineapple, passion fruit, coconut and cardamom.

MELONS

Source > Melons grow on vines. They are grown in the Mediterranean region and around the world in temperate zones. There are many varieties of melons, with one of the most popular being the very sweet Charentais melon (a kind of cantaloupe), with orange flesh. It is picked in summer.

Nutrients > Melons contain a lot of water and few calories; they are good diuretics and thirst-quenchers. They are a source of provitamin A and vitamin C, giving them beneficial qualities when it comes to oxidation and inflammation. This fruit is rich in minerals and antioxidants through its pigments and vitamins. It is also a source of fiber.

Use > Thanks to its sweet, tasty, juicy flesh, this fruit can be eaten raw, pickled or juiced. Melon is used as decoration: in balls or slices or on a tart. In the form of sorbet or in a summer granita, it can also be blended to make juice in a cup or a dessert. It goes perfectly with mint, strawberry, orange and watermelon.

ORANGES

Source > Oranges are the (citrus) fruit of the orange tree, native to Asia. Oranges, the queens of citrus, are eaten mainly in fall and winter. There are sweet oranges (which we present here) and bitter ones. Long considered a luxury (they were a big treat at Christmas), oranges became more widely available and popular; they are now in the top 10 of the most commonly eaten fruits.

Nutrients > Oranges, like other citrus fruits, are rich in vitamin C. They contain a lot of antioxidants, which combat oxidative stress, and soluble fiber. They are low in calories but a source of carbohydrates and offer good micronutrients, such as calcium and magnesium.

Use > Like lemons, oranges can be used in many different ways. Their zest, peel and juice are used in countless pastry recipes: preserves, compotes, sorbets, fruit spreads and more. They pair well with apricot, chocolate, fig, juniper berry and strawberry.

PASSION FRUIT

Source > Passion fruit is an exotic fruit discovered in the 17th century in Brazil. It grows on a tropical vine called passionflower and was initially used for medicinal and therapeutic purposes. It got its name from Catholic missionaries who, upon seeing the flower, saw Christ's crown of thorns, with the petals representing the apostles. The fruit is ready for picking when it turns from green to purple, red or orange and its skin starts to wrinkle slightly.

Nutrients > Passion fruit is an excellent source of fiber. It contains vitamin C, which gives it an antioxidant effect. It is also a source of iron.

Use > The flesh of passion fruit is juicy, sweet and sour, with crunchy black seeds covered in orange pulp. Raw or puréed, it is used often in pastry making and is found as fillings for cakes, in sorbets or as juice. It goes perfectly with exotic fruits, coriander seeds and milk chocolate.

PEACHES

Source > Peaches are the fruit of the peach tree, native to China. They are picked in summer. Of the 300 varieties of peaches, we find above all yellow peaches, vine peaches, flat peaches and white peaches.

Nutrients > Peaches are a source of soft fiber, which gently activates the bowels. They are rich in vitamin C and contain provitamin A and pigments that protect the cardio-vascular system.

Use > They are often used in pastry making as people love their juicy, sweet and tender flesh. Peaches are used raw, cooked, marinated, stewed, poached, in pies, in cake fillings, as decoration, in sorbets… They pair with blackberries, thyme, vanilla and cherry. Peach melba goes well with vanilla ice cream.

PEARS

Source > Pears are the fruit of the pear tree, native to Central Asia. There are two distinct types: soft pears (originally from Europe) and firmer, rounder pears (originally from China). They are picked from summer until winter. There are many varieties: popular ones include Bartlett, Williams, Beurré Giffard, Comice and Conference.

Nutrients > Pears are high in dietary fiber. They have antioxidant levels that are higher or lower depending on the color of the skin, with varieties having reddish-orange skin being highest in antioxidants. They contain a variety of minerals, trace elements and vitamins, especially vitamin C.

Use > With their sweet, fruity flavor, pears pair perfectly with almond, chocolate, cinnamon, chestnut and walnut. They are used raw, poached, cooked in a pie, in mousse or simmered as part of a cake, like the legendary pear Charlotte. They oxidize once the skin is removed; drizzling them with lemon juice keeps them from turning brown.

PERSIMMONS

Source > Persimmons are the fruit of the persimmon tree, native to Asia (especially eastern China), which arrived in Europe only about a thousand years ago and acclimatized to the Mediterranean region. They are picked in the fall.

Nutrients > Persimmons are rich in vitamin C and antioxidants, with extremely high levels of provitamin A. They thus contribute to healthy skin. They are a source of fiber, minerals and trace elements such as potassium, calcium and manganese.

Use > Sweet, with juicy flesh, persimmons can be bitter. They are used fresh, cooked in a crumble, marinated with spices or roasted. They pair with berries, 4-spice mix (cloves, nutmeg, ginger and pepper) and almond.

PINEAPPLES

Source > Pineapples are an exotic fruit that is picked in winter. The plant originated in South America. There are around six varieties of pineapple, including the Victoria, which is known for its sweet flesh.

Nutrients > Pineapple is rich in fiber. It also has antioxidant properties, especially through its pigments, mainly carotenoids, and vitamin C content. It is also a good source of minerals and trace elements. Bromelain is an enzyme found in the pineapple's central stem and is important because of its ability to predigest protein.

Use > Its yellow flesh is very sweet, juicy and at times slightly acidic. It goes well with other exotic fruits, vanilla and coriander (seeds and leaves). It can be enjoyed fresh, puréed, in preserves, roasted, flambéed, in a cake or as diced fresh fruit to decorate the top of a cake.

PLUMS

Source > Plums come from plum trees. Mirabelle, damson and greengage plums are in the same family.

Nutrients > Plums are nutritionally dense. They are rich in antioxidants, fiber, B vitamins, vitamins C and K, as well as minerals and trace elements, especially potassium, iron and magnesium.

Use > They have traditionally been used in pies (cooked or raw). Jam is made from plums; they can also be roasted, fried or made into a compote to serve as a dessert or as a filling for cakes. They work well with almond, vanilla or another of their family members, such as mirabelle plums.

MORE INFO

A prune is a dried plum.

POMEGRANATES

Source > Pomegranates come from the pomegranate tree, native to Persia (Iran). They have been grown in the Mediterranean region for centuries but also in Central Asia. In various religions, the pomegranate is a symbol of life and fertility, no doubt because of its many seeds. The fruit is picked between the end of summer and the end of fall.

Nutrients > Pomegranates are one of the fruits with the strongest antioxidant and anti-inflammatory properties owing to their extremely high vitamin C content but also their tannins. They are full of minerals and trace elements.

Use > As fresh fruit or in juice form, pomegranate has been popping up more and more lately, popular especially for its antioxidant superpower. Its seeds are juicy, slightly bitter and acidic. They are used mainly to decorate cakes, as juice or jellied as decoration on a dessert plate.

QUINCE

Source > Eaten as early as Greek Antiquity, quince is the fruit of the quince tree, a small tree native to Iran. The biblical name translates as the "Golden Apple." Today, the best known and most popular variety comes from Crete, Greece. Quince is grown in a Mediterranean climate and is eaten in fall.

Nutrients > Quince is rich in insoluble fiber, especially pectin. Quince is therefore a satisfying fruit. It helps to reduce cholesterol and blood sugar levels. Rich in tannins, it is also a source of potassium and copper.

Use > This pear-shaped fruit has a firm, sweet flesh. It is only eaten cooked. It is used mainly in jellies, jams, pies or fruit spreads. It pairs with all citrus fruits, almond and spices such as cinnamon or nutmeg.

RASPBERRIES

Source > These are the fruit of the raspberry bush, native to mountainous areas of Western Europe and North America. They are eaten mainly in spring and summer. It wasn't until the 19th century that they began to be grown for their flavor attributes. They can be deep pink but also white, yellow or black.

Nutrients > Raspberries are very high in antioxidants. They are one of the fruits with the highest mineral densities, with significant quantities of iron, magnesium and calcium. They are also very high in vitamin C and fiber – especially insoluble fiber, found in their small seeds that are rich in cellulose, and soluble fiber in the form of pectin in their flesh.

Use > Their flesh is soft and has a sweet and sour flavor. They go well with all red fruits, almond, apricot and peach. Raspberry pie is a perennial winner! Among traditional pastries, there is also the famous Framboisier cake. Whether fresh, as preserves or baked in dough, raspberries are a delight.

REDCURRANTS

Source > Redcurrants are the fruit of the currant bush. Wild redcurrants grow in the Nordic countries of Europe and in cold mountain regions. There are multiple varieties, and they are picked in summer. They can be red, pink or black, depending on the variety.

Nutrients > Redcurrants are rich in vitamin C and antioxidants. They are also high in minerals, with a significant amount of potassium. Also, redcurrants contain a lot of pectin.

Use > Known for their sweet and sour flavor, redcurrants are popular in pastry making, in cakes, as a coulis or jelly on a cake, or in sorbet. They go with almond, red fruits and peach.

STRAWBERRIES

Source > Humans have been eating strawberries since Antiquity. This berry was discovered on wild strawberry plants in the Americas, but it wasn't until the Middle Ages that strawberries were grown in private gardens. There are many varieties. They have different shapes and a more or less sweet flavor, depending on the variety. They are picked at the end of spring and throughout the summer.

Nutrients > Strawberries are rich in minerals and in vitamins A, E, C and B9 (the latter is crucial for pregnant women) and are not too high in sugar. They are rich in pigments (which have antioxidant properties), promoting cardiovascular and eye health. Strawberries are also a source of fiber.

Use > Strawberries are used raw or puréed, in pies, cake fillings or mousses. Strawberries are one of the most popular fruits in pastry making due to their sweetness and tender flesh. Many classic recipes use them, such as charlottes and strawberry pie. They pair well with almond, chocolate, raspberry and coconut.

WATERMELON

Source > Watermelon is the fruit of the creeping vine of the same name. It is picked in summer. It is known for its thirst-quenching properties, being 90% water. It is said that in Antiquity, the Egyptians offered pieces of this fruit to visitors to welcome them.

Nutrients > This fruit is saturated with water but also fiber, with very few calories. It contains different vitamins, such as provitamin A, B vitamins (including B6) and vitamin C. Watermelon has antioxidants due to its pigments.

Use > Although juicy and sweet, watermelon is rarely used in pastry making. It is mainly eaten fresh, shaped into balls on a summer pie or in a fruit salad. It pairs well with cinnamon, lime, chili pepper and melon.

WILD STRAWBERRIES

Source > Wild strawberries are the fruit of the wild strawberry plant, a perennial native to Europe and North America. Its cultivation goes back to the 14th century. Crossbreeding made this fragile fruit more resistant and just as flavorful. They are picked in spring and summer.

Nutrients > Like most fruits, wild strawberries contain some good nutrients. They contain a lot of water and vitamins A and C, which stimulate the immune system and help to fight against fatigue. Also, they are rich in vitamin B9 and contain antioxidants.

Use > The delicateness and taste of this fruit mean that we use it as is to decorate a pie or choux pastry. Tiny and elegant, they pair with the same ingredients as strawberries.

Vegetables

✧

Long live the combination of vanilla and sweet potato in a sweet compote, cucumber and Granny Smith apple in a delicious crumble, carrot and spices in a scrumptious cake, or red pepper and raspberry in a sophisticated sorbet! Vegetables have recently crept into pastry making by way of some bold recipes.

Of course, not everyone loves using them in this way, so in this chapter I chose ingredients that suit pastry best – those that blend into a sweet dessert most easily, for pastries that are more tempting, tasty and healthy. Rich in fiber and minerals, and low in sugar, they deserve a place in healthy pastries, to which they can add zest and whimsy!

THE SIX VEGETABLE FAMILIES

Vegetables can be classified into the following six families:

> **FLORET VEGETABLES:** They are often picked before their florets open, otherwise they lose their flavor. These vegetables can be eaten raw or cooked.

Examples: artichokes, cauliflower, broccoli...

> **LEAFY VEGETABLES:** As their name indicates, only the leaves are eaten: raw, in a salad, with seasoning to bring out the flavor, or in some cases cooked.

Examples: cabbage, spinach, lettuce, endive, celery...

> **FRUIT VEGETABLES:** These are the fruits of a plant that are treated as vegetables because of their unsweetened or mildly sweet flavor. They are generally grown in sunny regions.

Examples: cucumbers, peppers, zucchini, tomatoes...

> **SEED VEGETABLES:** These are commonly called legumes. Only the seeds from the pods are eaten.

Examples: beans, chickpeas, lupins, lentils...

> **BULB VEGETABLES:** Some of these grow underground and others aboveground. In each case, only the bulb is eaten, not the leaves or the flowers. That is where most of the plant's nutrients are.

Examples: onions, shallots, garlic...

> **ROOT VEGETABLES/TUBERS:** The root of these vegetables, the part found under-ground, is the part that is eaten.

Examples: beets, carrots, parsnips...

BEETS

Source > Beets are a root vegetable that is harvested from October to March and eaten in winter. There are three kinds: sugar beets (for making sugar), fodder beets (for animal feed) and garden beets (more than 130 varieties: yellow, white, purple... including the familiar red beet). Here, we are talking about garden beets.

Nutrients > Beets are an excellent source of antioxidants, which give them their color. They are very rich in essential micronutrients. We often think beets contain too much sugar; and yet, their carbohydrate levels are reasonable and their nutrient profile very good. Studies even show that one of their antioxidants, but also their high fiber content, helps lower blood sugar. They also contain vitamins A, K and B9. And, like most vegetables, they contain vitamin C. Beets also offer a wide range of minerals: magnesium, iron, sodium and potassium.

Use > Beets have a sweet flavor. With their reddish-purple color, they are a natural red dye used to color cookies, macarons or cakes. They pair well with chocolate, apple and red fruits. They are mainly used cooked, as a purée, as this makes them easier to blend into mixtures. They can also be cold pressed for juice.

CARROTS

Source > Carrots are a root vegetable, native to Asia (specifically, Iran and Afghanistan). They were originally used as an aromatic herb for their tops. Many varieties exist, in a range of colors: orange, white, yellow and purple. Carrots were domesticated in the 10th century in Asia Minor, before spreading to Europe. Early carrots are available from April to July, new carrots until October, and winter carrots for the entire fall and winter.

Nutrients > Carrots are an excellent source of beta-carotene, with strong antioxidant properties. They also contain vitamin A and a good amount of B vitamins and vitamin C. As well, they have significant levels of phosphorus and potassium and are a good source of fiber.

Use > Carrots color cakes with their orange hue and are sweet and mild flavored. They can be used grated in carrot cake, whole in an apple-carrot tarte Tatin, as juice in a sauce, or as jelly or sorbet. They go well with spices and dried fruit.

CELERY

Source > Celery is a leafy vegetable that originated in the Mediterranean region. Many years ago, it was used more for medicinal purposes and decoration than for cooking. It arrived in North America in the early 1800s. Following selection and domestication, it was grown so its stalks could be eaten (we distinguish celery, whose root is not used, from celery root). It is available all year long.

Nutrients > Celery has high water content. It contains less glucose than the average vegetable and is low in calories. It is made up of fiber but has less of it than other vegetables. However, it contains significant amounts of potassium and vitamins C, B (especially B9), A and K. It also contains calcium, copper and manganese.

Use > Its flavor is slightly sweet and has dominant aniseed notes. Mainly, the stalks are cold extracted to get the juice, which can be used in a sorbet or jelly. Celery is very fibrous; it can also be used finely diced. It goes well with Granny Smith apple, citrus fruit and verbena.

CELERY ROOT

Source > Celery root has the same origins as celery but is a root vegetable. It is eaten from October to March.

Nutrients > Celery root is an excellent source of dietary fiber and minerals, especially potassium and phosphorus. Also, it is rich in vitamins, such as vitamins K, B5, B6 and B9, and is a source of vitamin C when eaten raw. Celery root has antioxidant properties.

Use > Celery root has a slight aniseed sweet flavor. It is peeled and steamed to make a purée. It brings smoothness to a cream and softness to baked goods. It pairs very well with the same flavors that work with celery.

CUCUMBER

Source > Cucumbers are a fruit vegetable that appeared in India at least 3,000 years ago, before quickly spreading around Asia and the Middle East, arriving much later in Europe. There are different varieties of cucumbers, in different sizes. The English cucumber, for example, is the best known; the spiny cucumber looks like a pickle. Cucumbers can be eaten from early spring until fall.

Nutrients > Cucumbers have high water content and are one of the lowest-calorie vegetables. This summer vegetable is a source of fiber and essential micronutrients, vitamins and minerals: vitamin C, potassium, sodium and phosphorus.

Use > With its watery flavor, neutral but slightly bitter, cucumber is ideal for processing with or without the peel to make sorbet. It can be cold extracted for its juice to make a jelly or grated into a cake. It pairs with all flavors, especially citrus fruit, mint and rhubarb.

FENNEL

Source > Fennel is a leafy vegetable native to the Mediterranean. For a long time, it was grown for its seeds and its fruits, as a condiment. It has been used in cooking since Antiquity. It is eaten from May to December.

Nutrients > Fennel is a low-calorie vegetable that is high in fiber, potassium, sodium, phosphorus, calcium, vitamin B9 and vitamin C. It also has strong antioxidant properties.

Use > With its strong aniseed notes, fennel is very fragrant. It pairs very well with ginger, citrus fruits such as bergamot, and pine nuts. It can be cooked and puréed to be added to a cake or other baked goods. It can also be diced or poached in a tea infusion.

PARSNIPS

Source > Parsnips are a root vegetable native to Europe. They are mainly grown in northern countries. Parsnips were out of fashion for some time but found their way back into dishes in the early 2000s. They are harvested in the fall.

Nutrients > They have several benefits, especially their high amount of insoluble fiber, which is higher than that of other vegetables. They contain many vitamins and minerals, such as vitamin B9, vitamin C, potassium and manganese. They are also a source of antioxidants.

Use > The flesh of parsnips has a mild, slightly sweet flavor. In pastry making, they are puréed, which involves peeling and steaming them. They provide a creamy texture to cream. Grated raw, they bring moistness to a cake. They go very well with citrus fruit, such as orange, 4-spice mixture, dried fruit and hazelnut.

RED KURI (POTIMARRON) SQUASH

Source > Red kuri squash is a member of the squash family. Like pumpkin, it is a fruit vegetable. It is native to South America. Traces of it that have been found show that it existed before 2000 BCE in Peru. There are several varieties, found in different countries, such as Hokkaido squash in Japan. Red kuri squash is eaten in fall.

Nutrients > This squash is particularly high in beta-carotene, which gives it strong antioxidant properties. It is also a source of trace elements and vitamins C and E. It contains a lot of water and dietary fiber.

Use > It has a sweet, round, delicate flavor. Peeled and steamed, it becomes a purée that can be added to cakes or put in a pie. It is also used in drinks as a replacement for milk, due to its creamy texture. It pairs with dried fruit, spices such as cardamom, cinnamon and chocolate.

RED PEPPERS

Source > Also called sweet peppers, red peppers are a fruit vegetable from South America. They were cultivated for the first time in Mexico, then imported to the Mediterranean region. Unlike many vegetables, there is no wild version. There are different varieties of peppers with different shapes and colors, depending on their ripeness. The high season for this vegetable is summer.

Nutrients > Made of more than 90% water, peppers are summer vegetables. They are rich in antioxidants, vitamin C, minerals, trace elements (iron, calcium, potassium, phosphorus, manganese, copper) and fiber. Red peppers are the ripest and are the richest in vitamins C, B6 and E and beta-carotene. Yellow peppers, the intermediate stage of ripening, are the mildest and sweetest. They are rich in beta-carotene and vitamin B9. Green peppers are picked before they are ripe: they are an excellent source of vitamin K and are the richest in flavonoids, which are powerful antioxidants.

Use > They have sweet, slightly bitter notes, and their flesh is juicy. When puréed, they can be made into a sorbet or a coulis. When diced, they can be preserved or cooked to make marmalade. They pair perfectly with raspberry, chocolate and citrus fruit.

SWEET POTATOES

Source > Sweet potatoes are a tuber native to tropical regions of the Americas that were brought to Europe by Christopher Columbus. Today, this vegetable is available year-round.

Nutrients > Sweet potatoes have a low glycemic index and antioxidant properties thanks to the presence of beta-carotene. They are rich in fiber and vitamins A, B6 and C. Also, they contain potassium and manganese.

Use > Their sweet orange flesh works well in pastry making. Steamed and puréed, they are used as decoration, in cake recipes for their moistness, or in a flan for their tender texture. They are also enjoyed in drinks, such as in sweet potato lattes. They go perfectly with vanilla, chocolate and coconut.

MORE INFO

Pumpkin and squash have the same nutrients and are used in similar ways.

ZUCCHINI

Source > Zucchini is a fruit vegetable native to Mexico. It then spread throughout the American continent and was imported into Europe in the 16th century. In the 20th century, it became popular in Italy, where it is called "Italian squash." It is available in different sizes and colors. It grows from June to September.

Nutrients > Zucchini has few calories but a lot of water (promoting a feeling of fullness), fiber, vitamin C and B vitamins. Zucchini is rich in antioxidants and is a source of phosphorus, magnesium and potassium.

Use > With its neutral and watery flavor, zucchini pairs easily with other flavors. This is the vegetable that is most used in pastry making. Peeled or not, it is used grated in chocolate, pistachio or citrus fruit cakes.

CALENDAR OF SEASONAL FRUITS & VEGETABLES

Winter

Spring

January

Fruits

- Apple
- Banana
- Buddha's hand
- Dragon fruit
- Grapefruit
- Kiwi
- Lemon
- Lychee
- Mandarin
- Orange
- Passion fruit
- Pear
- Pineapple

Vegetables

- Beet
- Carrot
- Celery
- Celery root
- Parsnip
- Sweet potato

April

Fruits

- Apple
- Banana
- Dragon fruit
- Kiwi
- Kumquat
- Mango
- Orange
- Pear
- Pineapple
- Strawberry

Vegetables

- Early carrot
- Cucumber

February

Fruits

- Apple
- Banana
- Buddha's hand
- Dragon fruit
- Grapefruit
- Kiwi
- Kumquat
- Lemon
- Lychee
- Mandarin
- Orange
- Passion fruit
- Pear
- Pineapple

Vegetables

- Beet
- Carrot
- Celery root
- Parsnip
- Sweet potato

May

Fruits

- Banana
- Cherry
- Dragon fruit
- Kumquat
- Mango
- Raspberry
- Strawberry

Vegetables

- Early carrot
- Cucumber
- Fennel

March

Fruits

- Apple
- Banana
- Buddha's hand
- Dragon fruit
- Grapefruit
- Kiwi
- Kumquat
- Lemon
- Lychee
- Orange
- Passion fruit
- Pear
- Pineapple

Vegetables

- Beet
- Carrot
- Celery root
- Sweet potato

June

Fruits

- Apricot
- Banana
- Cherry
- Dragon fruit
- Mango
- Peach
- Raspberry
- Redcurrant
- Strawberry
- Watermelon

Vegetables

- Early carrot
- Cucumber
- Fennel
- Zucchini

Summer

July

Fruits
- Apricot
- Bilberry
- Blackberry
- Cherry
- Cranberry
- Dragon fruit
- Fig
- Grape

- Mango
- Melon
- Raspberry
- Red currant
- Peach
- Plum
- Strawberry
- Watermelon

Vegetables
- Early carrot
- Celery
- Cucumber
- Fennel
- Red pepper
- Zucchini

August

Fruits
- Apricot
- Bilberry
- Blackberry
- Cherry
- Cranberry
- Blackcurrant
- Fig
- Grape

- Melon
- Raspberry
- Red currant
- Peach
- Pear
- Plum
- Strawberry
- Raspberry

Vegetables
- New carrot
- Celery
- Cucumber
- Fennel
- Red pepper
- Zucchini

September

Fruits
- Apple
- Apricot
- Blackberry
- Bilberry
- Blackcurrant
- Cherry
- Dragon fruit
- Fig

- Grape
- Melon
- Pear
- Plum
- Pomegranate
- Raspberry
- Red currant

Vegetables
- New carrot
- Celery
- Cucumber
- Fennel
- Red pepper
- Zucchini

Fall

October

Fruits
- Apple
- Blackberry
- Dragon fruit
- Fig
- Grape
- Persimmon

- Pear
- Pineapple
- Plum
- Pomegranate
- Quince

Vegetables
- Beet
- New carrot
- Celery
- Celery root
- Fennel
- Parsnip
- Red kuri squash
- Sweet potato

November

Fruits
- Apple
- Dragon fruit
- Kiwi
- Lemon
- Mandarin

- Pear
- Persimmon
- Pineapple
- Pomegranate
- Quince

Vegetables
- Beet
- Carrot
- Celery
- Celery root
- Fennel
- Parsnip
- Red kuri squash
- Sweet potato

December

Fruits
- Apple
- Dragon fruit
- Grapefruit
- Kiwi
- Lemon
- Mandarin
- Mango

- Orange
- Pear
- Persimmon
- Pineapple
- Pomegranate
- Quince

Vegetables
- Beet
- Carrot
- Celery
- Celery root
- Fennel
- Parsnip
- Red kuri squash
- Sweet potato

CHAPTER 7

Oleaginous fruits
and oil seeds

INTRODUCTION

Mmmm... Can you smell that delicious aroma?

That sweet scent of almonds, hazelnuts, coconut or toasted sesame seeds?

As a spread, a crispy topping or ingredients in baking, oleaginous fruits and oil seeds delight our taste buds.

Thanks to their unsaturated fat content, they are also excellent for our health.

Last but not least, they are packed with protein, vitamins and minerals (calcium, zinc, iron, magnesium)!

Oleaginous fruits

AVOCADOS

Source > Avocados likely originate from the south-central area of Mexico and Guatemala. There are a dozen major varieties, including Hass, the most common, with a coarse purplish-black skin. The fruit doesn't ripen until after it is picked.

Nutrients > Avocado is the healthy fat star. It lets you fill up on omega-9 and take in a significant quantity of vitamins B9 and K1.

Use > Once the flesh is puréed, it often replaces butter as it can act as a texturing agent in a fruitcake, cream or mousse. It pairs very well with chocolate, mango, strawberry and lemon, thanks to its round notes.

FRESH COCONUTS

Source > Coconut is the fruit of the coconut palm tree. This tree, native to Southeast Asia, is now found in most countries in the tropical belt.

Nutrients > Coconut is rich in fiber, which is a real advantage. And that's not all: it contains a significant amount of iron and potassium as well. It is also very high in saturated fatty acids, which explains why the oil crystallizes at room temperature.

Use > Coconut is a multipurpose fruit. It can be made into oil, purée, milk, water, powder, flour or cream. It is therefore often used in pastry making and can be added to all recipes. It pairs perfectly with all exotic fruits, chocolate and citrus fruit, owing to its fruity and milky notes.

GREEN OLIVES

Source > Grown in the Mediterranean region for more than 5,000 years, green olives are one of the oldest fruits. They are only used in pastry making in oil form.

Nutrients > Olives contain sodium chloride, whose main ingredient is salt. Also, this small fruit is high in fiber.

Use > Olive oil can be delicate, sometimes a little spicy, even peppery, when it is young. It can be used in fruitcake or paired with chocolate, citrus fruit and aromatic herbs such as thyme or rosemary.

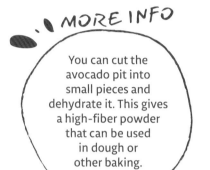

MORE INFO

You can cut the avocado pit into small pieces and dehydrate it. This gives a high-fiber powder that can be used in dough or other baking.

Oleaginous dried fruits (nuts)

ALMONDS

Source > Almonds grow on an almond tree, native to East Asia. They are found both in pastry making and in the medicine of our ancestors, because of their many therapeutic properties. There are two types: bitter and sweet. Bitter almonds, which are toxic because of the presence of hydrocyanic acid, are found, after being treated, in the form of bitter almond extract. Sweet almonds are the ones we snack on. They are picked during two periods: fresh almonds for a very short season (beginning of summer) and dried almonds from the end of summer to fall.

Nutrients > Almonds are especially high in fiber, vitamin E and calcium.

Use > Almonds are found in various forms in many pastry recipes: with or without skin, toasted, powdered, as paste, flour, toffee or oil. The best-known use may be in macarons or frangipane cake. They can also be eaten fresh. Due to their round, sweet notes, they pair with all fruits and spices in pastry making.

BRAZIL NUTS

Source > Brazil nuts are the seed in the shell of the fruit of the Brazil nut tree, native to the Amazon rainforest. The nut is eaten by the Indigenous peoples of Amazonia as a superfood. It is harvested from December to March.

Nutrients > Brazil nuts have a higher concentration of micronutrients than walnuts. This multiplies the benefits. To top it off, they come second for magnesium levels, after flaxseeds.

Use > Although they are not often used in pastry making, they can be used in various ways, like almonds or hazelnut. Their mild flavor and roundness in the mouth allow them to pair with all fruits and spices.

CASHEWS

Source > This nut (seed) comes from the cashew tree. It is dried and shelled.

Nutrients > When it comes to vegetable protein, it shares the crown with the almond. But when it comes to vitamin K1, the cashew beats the almond.

Use > Cashews are often used to make vegan cheeses, creams and yogurts.

CHESTNUTS

Source > Chestnuts are wrapped in a reddish skin and contained in a shell (burr), which opens on its own when the fruit is ripe. They weigh 5 to 30 g, depending on the species. The smallest chestnuts are often preferred, as they have a better flavor. They are harvested in fall.

Nutrients > This fruit has a surprising feature: it is low in fat but high in carbohydrates – almost like a starch, which gives it a mild flavor. It is also high in fiber, trace elements and minerals.

Use > Chestnuts are very popular in France. They are eaten in multiple ways: puréed, flour, cream, glazed... and they have many different applications in pastry making. They pair very well with chocolate, pear and vanilla.

CHESTNUT OR HORSE CHESTNUT?
Here are six ways to tell the difference...

	Horse chestnut	Chestnut
1	Toxic	Edible
2	Thick green burr before falling from the tree, with small, short spikes	Brown burr with many fine, long spikes
3	One burr contains 1 fruit; occasionally 2 fruits	2 or 3 fruits per burr
4	Round shape	Flat, triangular shape with a pointy end
5	Palm-shaped leaves	Long single leaves
6	Tree found in cities	Tree found in forests and orchards

IS CHESTNUT PURÉE MADE FROM HORSE CHESTNUTS?
No – it's made from edible chestnuts. After the skin is removed, it can be made into a cream or paste.

HAZELNUTS

Source > Hazelnuts come from the hazel tree, native to Asia. They are picked from the end of summer to the end of fall. Hazelnuts are protected by their shell and their involucre (fused petals below the shell).

Nutrients > Hazelnuts are number one among oil seeds when it comes to protein and fat. But they are also rich in vitamins and minerals, especially calcium, magnesium, potassium and vitamin E!

Use > Hazelnut is the star of spreads. It is a popular ingredient in pastry making thanks to its round notes. Hazelnuts are often used after being lightly toasted, with or without the skin (peeled), crushed, powdered, as paste, as praline or sometimes as oil. They pair easily with chocolate, coffee, red fruits and citrus fruits.

MACADAMIA NUTS

Source > Macadamia nuts, native to Australia, are round. For 5,000 years, they have been eaten by Indigenous peoples there, but they only became known in Europe in the 19th century. They are named for John Macadam, a Scottish chemist and physician.

Nutrients > Get out your best nutcracker so you can fill up on iron and manganese! This nut will also cover some of your fiber needs.

Use > Macadamias are used crushed or as praline. They have a mild, round flavor thanks to their high fat content. They go easily with chocolate, vanilla and nuts with stronger flavors, such as hazelnuts and walnuts.

PECANS

Source > Pecans are native to the Americas and were imported into Europe in the 16th century. They grow on pecan trees. Like pistachios and almonds, pecans are encapsuled in a hard shell. When the fruit is ripe, the shell opens.

Nutrients > A natural way to enhance your intake of omega-9 is to eat pecans. This nut is also rich in magnesium and phosphorus.

Use > Pecans are found in pastry in various forms: whole, crushed, as paste or as praline. They have a strong flavor and pair well with other nuts, such as almond, but also with vanilla, chocolate and pear.

PINE NUTS

Source > Pine nuts are the seeds found behind the scales of pinecones on pinyon pine trees. They are used in cooking or as a natural remedy. In Greek and Roman times, they were seen as aphrodisiacs.

Nutrients > This nut is one of the richest in iron.

Use > Whole, crushed, toasted, as praline... pine nuts are mainly used in Asian pastries. They go with citrus fruits, orange blossom and stone fruits.

PISTACHIOS

Source > Pistachio trees are originally from Asia Minor. They were introduced to the Mediterranean region more than 2,000 years ago. The pistachio fruit of the tree sits in a shell that opens when the fruit is ripe.

Nutrients > Pistachios are different from their oleaginous cousins due to their vitamin C content (which is rare for nuts). They also have high levels of potassium and beta-carotene.

Use > In their raw form, pistachios are eaten like almonds. They are commonly used in Asian pastries as well as French pastries. Pistachios pair with cherry, raspberry, citrus fruit and stone fruit (peaches, apricots...).

WALNUTS

Source > Walnuts come from the walnut tree, which is popular for both its fruits and its precious wood. There are several nut-producing varieties; they are harvested in fall. This fruit has existed for millions of years.

Nutrients > Walnuts have qualities similar to other nuts, especially a significant amount of fiber, calcium and magnesium but also vitamin B, omega-3 and other minerals.

Use > They are used whole, powdered, as praline or as oil. Their woody notes pair perfectly with caramel, pear and honey.

MORE INFO

Pure pistachio paste is naturally dark green and has a slightly bitter pistachio flavor. However, because of its high cost, it is often mixed with almond paste and green dye.

Oil seeds

BLACK SESAME SEEDS

Source > Cousins of golden sesame seeds, black sesame seeds come from a different variety, grown in Asia. They are found in Asian cooking and, more and more, in French pastries.

Nutrients > The nutritional benefits in the sesame seed family are genetic. The nutrients of black sesame seeds are more concentrated than golden ones. They are also rich in fiber, iron and magnesium.

Use > With their bitter, toasted notes, they go perfectly with coconut, exotic fruits and raspberry. They are used in the same forms as golden sesame seeds. Their dark hue colors creams, crusts and baked goods, in which they are especially used as a paste.

CHIA SEEDS

Source > Chia seeds come from the plant Salvia hispanica, a member of the mint family that is native to Mexico and Central America. The Mayans and the Aztecs grew this plant for thousands of years for its exceptional nutritional properties. Today, chia seeds are considered one of the superfoods. Chia comes in a black variety and a white one. It's known as a mucilaginous seed: it contains a mucilage that is rich in pectin, giving it the ability to make a gel when wet.

Nutrients > If you are looking for a concentration of fiber, omega-3 and magnesium, chia seeds are the right choice. You'll also get some iron and several B vitamins.

Use > They are popular with vegans for their binding and gelling properties. After being soaked in water, they swell and make a gel. They can thus replace eggs in creams, for example. They pair well with dairy products, exotic fruits and red fruits.

FLAXSEEDS

Source > Flaxseeds come from the flax plant. Flax is made into linen textiles, but its seeds are used in pastry making for their nutritional qualities. Their color can range from brown to yellow.

Nutrients > Like flaxseed oil, flaxseeds are omega-3 superstars. Also, they come first for magnesium content. They also contain vitamin B, minerals and trace elements.

Use > Flaxseeds are used whole, toasted or as flour. However, for their nutrients to offer benefits, they must be eaten ground. Their neutral flavor has a mild hazelnut taste.

GOLDEN SESAME SEEDS

Source > Sesame seeds come from an aromatic oleaginous plant and are mainly produced in Africa and India. The seeds are a golden color when ripe; white once the hull is removed.

Nutrients > Sesame seeds are a mineral powerhouse: they contain in particular calcium, iron, magnesium and zinc. For vitamins, B9 is the most present.

Use > In many cultures, sesame seeds are used in various dishes and desserts, such as Chinese nougat or Asian baked goods. We find them whole, ground, toasted, as praline or as oil. With their subtle and delicate flavor, they pair easily with chocolate, honey and coffee.

POPPY SEEDS

Source > Black (or blue) poppy seeds come from a plant belonging to the poppy and opium poppy family. Opium, morphine and codeine extracts from the opium poppy do not come from the seeds but from a milky substance in the immature pods.

Nutrients > Poppy seeds are high in calcium and have significant amounts of iron, magnesium and zinc. You can eat as many as you like!

Use > Poppy seeds have a mild hazelnut flavor. Despite their small size, they add some originality to recipes, giving crunch to a cake or decorating bread. They are paired with citrus fruit, raspberry and nuts.

PUMPKIN SEEDS

Source > The first traces of pumpkin seeds were found in fossilized mammoth dung. The mammoths disseminated the seeds, which helped the plants reproduce. Originally, pumpkin was very bitter, and was not eaten by humans. Since then, many hybridizations have been developed. Although there are more than 800 varieties of squash, only pumpkin, butternut squash and gourd are grown for their flesh and their seeds.

Nutrients > Pumpkin seeds are a great source of vegetable protein and fiber. Also, you will fill up on omega-3 and -9. A good combo!

Use > Whole, crushed, toasted, as purée or as praline... Pumpkin seeds work with cherry, pistachio and chocolate in desserts.

SUNFLOWER SEEDS

Source > The seeds are found in the center of the sunflower. They have been used by Indigenous peoples in the Americas for more than 8,000 years in food as well as medicine as they have many benefits. They are harvested in early autumn.

Nutrients > Sunflower seeds are rich in fiber: that is a great reason to eat them. They also contain magnesium, vitamin E and phosphorus.

Use > Sunflower seeds are found in baking and pastry making. They are used whole, toasted, as praline or in the form of oil. They have a neutral taste, which allows them to pair easily with other flavors.

MORE INFO

In some Asian countries, poppy seeds are prohibited from being sold.

Which nuts and oil seeds can be used for which pastries?

As an oil, powder or paste... oleaginous fruits and oil seeds are available in many forms. This allows us to make all kinds of recipes. The table below will guide you to the right ones for your needs!

Use	Which oleaginous fruit or oil seed?	In what form?
To decorate a cake	All except olive and avocado	Whole, crushed, powder
In a mixture or as decoration	All except olive and avocado	Whole, crushed, powder
To replace or complement butter	All except olive	Purée
To complement or replace flour	Dried fruits and deoiled seeds	Flour
To add softness to baked goods/cakes or to make an emulsion in cream	All	Oil
As a pastry filling or to flavor cream	All except olive and avocado	Praline
To replace water and/or milk	All except olive and avocado	Milk
To replace cream	Dried fruit and coconut	Cream

CHAPTER 8

Spices

INTRODUCTION

Spices are a treasure when it comes to cooking. They have added flavor to dishes and desserts in all times and places.

Coveted as much for their therapeutic benefits as for their flavoring properties, spices have played an active role in the daily lives of the people who use them. At times used for honoring the dead, or as incense in religious ceremonies, they were added to the medicinal books of the greatest healers for their powerful benefits. What's more, thanks to their aromatic power, they have enhanced festive meals and added their unique flavors to traditional dishes and beverages throughout the ages.

From caves in Israel to the Egyptian pyramids, from India to South America, from the Mayans to the Greeks, spices have traveled through time and around the world. The major explorers always brought back spices from their travels to import and grow them in new lands.

The countless available spices are a playground for creativity. We have chosen those that are suited to pastry making. They are added in small amounts, are low in calories and are rich in antioxidants. Who could ask for more?

What is a spice?

The spice comes from the most aromatic parts of the plant. A plant produces odors from its roots to its fruits, which helps it to ward off predators or attract insects that will help it reproduce. Depending on the plant, we can find these aromatic compounds in different places:

> **In the stem**

The stem allows water and nutrients to circulate in the plant. Very few spices come from this part, but cinnamon (dried bark) and lemongrass do.

> **In the roots and underground stems**

The roots draw water and nutrients from the soil and bring them into the plant. Licorice is one example. Underground stems (rhizomes or bulbs) allow sugars and nutrients to be stored. These are the plant's energy reserves. This category includes galangal, ginger and turmeric.

> **In the fruit**

The fruit follows the flowering of the plant. It contains one or more seeds, allowing the plant to reproduce.

Note: not all fruits are spices. Only a few, through their concentration of aromatic substances, are considered as such, like vanilla, pepper or chili pepper.

> **In the seeds**

Seeds contain the plant's precious DNA. It is therefore essential for the plant to protect them by having them produce powerful aromatic substances. Many seeds give spices in this way: tonka bean, star anise and cardamom, for example.

> **In the flower and leaves**

Flowers are very elegant, and for good reason: their mission is to attract pollinators (insects, birds…) to be fertilized. The male part of the flower (stamen) offers them its nectar and pollen so these can be carried to the pistil, the reproductive part of female flowers. For this union to happen, the flower gives off a seductive perfume. In the spice family, we find those that have an especially concentrated scent, such as saffron or clove.

You can pair and blend these aromatic treasures in many ways. You will find some suggestions for combinations and uses in the following pages. Give your creativity free rein!

Star anise

Nutmeg

Saffron

Rose

Turmeric

Sumac

Cinnamon

Pepper

Chili
pepper

Cardamom

Ginger

Pink
peppercorn

Salt

Tonka bean

Vanilla

Star
anise

Licorice

Spices from the bark and stem

CEYLON CINNAMON

Source > Cinnamon is the inner bark of the cinnamon tree, native to Sri Lanka, India, and Myanmar. This spice was used in the Greco-Roman era. As of 1600 BCE, it was used for incense for funeral rites. Today it is grown in hot and humid climates, especially in Asia. Some of the best cinnamon in the world is from Vietnam. The bark is dried and then rolled up.

Nutrients > Cinnamon is very low in calories and contains a significant amount of manganese and a smaller amount of iron. It also contains antioxidants (beta-carotene and vitamin C), like many spices. Also, it is rich in fiber: more than half its weight is dietary fiber.

Aromatic notes > Woody, floral, hot.

Pairings > Apple, pear, peach, plum, cherry, cardamom, star anise.

CASSIA, OR CHINESE CINNAMON

Cassia, the most consumed variety that is sold in most supermarkets, is part of the same family as Ceylon cinnamon, but its bark is thicker and darker. Its aromatic notes are stronger and spicier. Also, because cassia cinnamon contains coumarin (see below), it should be eaten in small quantities (Ceylon cinnamon doesn't contain coumarin).

CAUTION: COUMARIN

Coumarin is an aromatic substance that is naturally present particularly in cassia cinnamon (significantly less in Ceylon cinnamon) and tonka beans. Since July 2008, the recommended daily limit is 0.1 mg coumarin/kg (0.05 mg/lb) body weight. Beyond this amount, it would be toxic to the liver, so it is important to limit consumption of products containing coumarin. **In the US, selling tonka beans to eat has been illegal since 1954.**

LEMONGRASS

Source > Lemongrass, also called Indian verbena, is a plant native to Asia. It grows in tropical and subtropical regions. During the harvest, from May to October, the stems are firm. The leaves can also be used to flavor recipes.

Nutrients > Lemongrass is rich in minerals and B vitamins.

Aromatic notes > Citrus fruit, herbaceous, tangy.

Pairings > Citrus fruit, coconut, mango, apple, pineapple, cardamom, Sichuan pepper, ginger.

Spices from the roots/rhizomes

CHICORY

Source > Chicory is the root of the chicory plant. It is dried, roasted and ground into powder.

Nutrients > Chicory is very high in fiber – useful for reducing the glycemic index of recipes. Another strong point: its calcium and iron levels are significant. Like tea and coffee, it contains tannins, which tend to block the absorption of iron (from plant sources).

Aromatic note > Coffee.

Pairings > Pear, chocolate, vanilla.

GALANGAL

Source > Galangal is a tropical plant in the ginger family and is native to Asia. It is also ginger's closest cousin, with more lemony and peppery notes. There are three kinds of galangal; lesser galangal is used most.

Nutrients > Galangal contains flavonoid polyphenols that give it strong antioxidant powers.

Aromatic notes > Hot, tangy, peppery.

Pairings > Chocolate, citrus fruit, exotic fruits, nuts.

GINGER

Source > Ginger is a rhizome that is grown mainly in Asia. Used for more than 3,000 years, especially by Indian and Chinese people, it was one of the first Asian spices to arrive in Europe, around the fourth century BCE. It is harvested nine months after planting, when its leaves start to dry out.

Nutrients > It contains a significant quantity of antioxidants as well as various minerals, such as manganese, magnesium and copper. Ginger is also a source of vitamin B9.

Aromatic notes > Woody, tangy, spicy.

Pairings > Chocolate, citrus fruit, exotic fruits, rhubarb, pear.

POLYPHENOLS

Polyphenols are substances found in flowers and spices. They are powerful antioxidants. Hundreds of different polyphenols can be found in edible flowers, plants and spices.

LICORICE

Source > Licorice is the rhizome of the licorice plant, native to Southern Europe and Asia. The Egyptians, the Greeks and the Romans chewed it to freshen their breath and quench their thirst. Consumed in the 12th century for its medicinal properties, it was later used in the first candies. The rhizome is harvested by digging up the entire plant once it has reached the age of 4 to 5 years. The rhizomes are washed and left to dry for several months.

Nutrients > Licorice contains glycyrrhizic acid. This small molecule is known for its sweet taste, which means licorice can be used as a sweetener. Licorice has antioxidant properties.

However, in too-large amounts, this molecule can be harmful to human health (water retention, increased blood pressure, loss of potassium in the body).

Another precaution to take: those who are pregnant, have high blood pressure or have kidney failure should avoid eating black licorice in any form.

Aromatic notes > Aniseed, woody.

Pairings > Cinnamon, citrus fruit, exotic fruits, coffee.

> **NOTE**
> A compound called anethol gives the aniseed flavor to licorice, fennel seeds and anise.

TURMERIC

Source > Turmeric, also called Indian saffron, is the rhizome of a tropical plant from the ginger family. Since Antiquity, Indian people have used it in many different ways – in cooking, textiles, medicines and cosmetics.

Nutrients > This spice is made of a pigment called curcumin, which gives it its orangey-yellow color. This substance contains turmeric's antioxidant properties and some other benefits. It is also a good source of vitamin C. Turmeric contains precious micronutrients, such as iron and manganese.

Aromatic notes > Bitter, woody, earthy.

Pairings > Star anise, ginger, cardamom.

Spices from fruits

CAROB

Source > This fruit comes from the carob tree, a member of the legume family native to the eastern Mediterranean. It comes in a long pod, changing in color from green to brown, when it becomes ripe. The pods are picked by hand, then the seeds and pulp are removed, dried and ground to make carob bean gum. With its fruity notes, it can also be used to make molasses.

Aromatic notes > Milk chocolate, vanilla, sweet.

Pairings > Coffee, vanilla, nuts.

CHILI PEPPER

Source > Chili peppers are native to Central and South America. The Aztecs grew them for their rituals or to flavor their drinks. There are more than 20 different chili peppers, from paprika to Espelette pepper to cayenne pepper, classified according to their aromatic strength, which is related to how much capsaicin is present. Whatever the variety, once the pepper is ground, the aromatic notes disappear, leaving only spicy notes.

Aromatic notes > Spicy, fruity.

Pairings > Chocolate, exotic fruits, raspberry, cherry.

COCOA BEANS

Source > Cocoa beans are found in cocoa pods, the fruit of the cacao tree. Once the pod opens, the beans are removed, then the white pulp (called "mucilage") around the beans is removed. It is used to make a paste or syrup. Next, the beans are fermented, then naturally sun dried. At this stage, they are called "raw" (they have not been heated above 45 °C). In most cases, they are then roasted at up to 140 °C to develop the flavors. There are two differences between roasted and raw cocoa beans:

> Roasted beans have more complex and developed aromatic notes than raw beans.

> Raw beans offer significant nutrients compared to roasted beans (including minerals, especially magnesium, trace elements and antioxidants, which are partly altered during heating).

Aromatic notes > Fermented, sour.

Pairings > Vanilla, coffee, pear, banana, orange.

GREEN CARDAMOM

Source > Cardamom is a fruit native to India, where it has been used in cooking but also for its medicinal properties for more than 2,000 years. The green pod-shaped fruits are dried to be eaten as a spice. Each pod contains 15 to 20 seeds.

Aromatic notes > Citrus fruit, herbaceous, minty.

Pairings > Milk chocolate, clementine, apricot, apple, pear, raspberry, cherry, vanilla.

JUNIPER BERRY

Source > Known since Antiquity, juniper berries were used by the Egyptians to relieve digestive problems and urinary infections. Mistakenly called "berries," they are spherical female seed cones (galbuli). The fruit is picked when ripe and then dried to provide the spice.

Aromatic notes > Citrus fruit, floral, woody.

Pairings > Chocolate, citrus fruit.

MASTIC

Source > Mastic is an aromatic resin obtained by making incisions in the stem and major branches of the mastic tree. In Greek and Roman times, people chewed mastic, as they did with licorice, to freshen the breath. Mastic is the root of the Greek word *mastichon* (in English, "masticate"), meaning "to chew." This spice is mainly used in Asian pastries. It is a translucent pale-yellow color.

Aromatic notes > Pine, peppery, floral.

Pairings > Apple, fig, orange blossom, rose water, pistachio, orange.

NUTMEG

Source > Nutmeg comes from the fruit of the nutmeg tree. This spice was greatly valued for its rarity and its aphrodisiac qualities. In the 16th century, demand was so high that it became more precious than gold. The nutmeg trade was a monopoly for a long time; it was only at the end of the 19th century that the French managed to cultivate it. Most nutmeg now comes from Indonesia and Grenada. The seed is found inside a fruit; it is surrounded by a lacy covering (aril or mace), also called flower of nutmeg. The mace is dried and used as a spice as well. The seed is red when it is fresh and orangey when it is dry.

Aromatic notes > Woody, (light) clove, sweet.

Pairings > Apple, pear, ginger, cinnamon.

PEPPER

Source > Pepper is a berry native to Southwest India that grows on the black pepper (Piper nigrum) vine. The berries are in clusters, like grapes. The different colors of pepper are related to how they are harvested (see below). Other berries use the name "pepper" but do not belong to the Piper nigrum species, such as Sichuan pepper, cayenne pepper and Timut pepper. We call these false peppers.

Pepper variety	Source (most common)	Aromatic notes	Production
Green	India, Madagascar	Fruity, not very spicy	The fruit is picked as it begins to ripen, then is either preserved in brine, dehydrated or freeze dried.
Black	Cambodia (Kampot), Malaysia (Sarawak), China (Sichuan), Madagascar (Voatsiperifery)	The spiciest and most full bodied	The seeds, which are green, are harvested before ripening. They are fermented and sun dried, giving them their color and aromatic power.
Red	Cambodia (Kampot), India (Puducherry)	Fruity, sweet, not very spicy	The berries are red until fully ripe. They are picked and dried, away from direct light to preserve their color. They are rarer and more expensive than other peppers.
White	Madagascar, Cambodia (Kampot)	The mildest of all the peppers, with vegetable notes	The berries are harvested when ripe, when they are red. They are soaked in salted water to remove their red outer layer, the pericarp. What is left is the white seed, which is then dried.

PINK PEPPERCORNS

Source > Pink peppercorns are native to South America. The berry, which is actually a drupe (a stone fruit, like the apricot) and not a peppercorn, is picked and dried. The pink shell contains the stone.

Aromatic notes > Sweet, fruity, spicy.

Pairings > Exotic fruits, red fruits, citrus fruit.

STAR ANISE

Source > Star anise is the fruit of the badian tree. This star-shaped fruit is divided into carpels (seed-bearing structures). It is picked before it is ripe, then dried in the sun until the seeds are visible and it turns a brownish-red color.

Aromatic notes > Aniseed, peppery.

Pairings > Apricot, apple, exotic fruits, pear.

SUMAC

Source > Sumac resembles a berry but is actually a drupe (stone fruit) from the sumac, a small wild tree. After being picked, it is crushed and dried.

Aromatic notes > Fruity, tangy, woody, salty.

Pairings > Mango, pineapple, bergamot, lemon, red fruits.

VANILLA

Source > Vanilla is a bean that grows on an orchid, *Vanilla planifolia*, which is native to Mexico. People in many countries tried to cultivate it, without success. It wasn't until 1841, on the island of Réunion (formerly Île Bourbon), that an enslaved 12-year-old boy, Edmond Albius, used the process for hand pollination with the vanilla flower. This discovery earned him his freedom. The island became the first vanilla producer in the world, and Edmond's process is still the standard technique for pollinating vanilla flowers. The fresh beans, which are green, are harvested, then submerged in water at 140 °F (60 °C) for up to 3 minutes. They then go through a sweating phase for up to 2 weeks, during which they turn black. They are dried for 3 to 4 weeks, then aged to enhance the vanillin flavor. Depending on the geographic location and ecosystem where the vanilla grows, it develops very different flavors.

Aromatic notes > Vary according to where it is grown.

Pairings > Pairs with all ingredients in pastry making.

MORE INFO

Vanilla beans must be stored in an airtight container away from the light, in the fridge or freezer.

NOTE
Vanilla extract is commonly available. To choose the best quality, check on the label that it is made from natural extracts, with 35% alcohol.

Spices
from seeds

ANISE SEEDS

Source > Green anise comes from a plant whose flowers and seeds resemble those of fennel. Much used since Antiquity for its therapeutic properties, it is commonly found in pastries, liqueurs and wine for its licorice flavor and sweet taste. Although it is close enough to fennel that the two can be confused, anise has spicier notes.

Aromatic notes > Licorice, spicy.

Pairings > Lemon, quince, apple, pear.

CORIANDER

Source > We talk about coriander seeds, but they are really the fruits of a hardy plant. The flowers produce these small, round fruits containing two very aromatic seeds. Coriander has been used for more than 8,000 years in the Mediterranean region. This spice is found in some alcohols, such as Chartreuse and gin.

Aromatic notes > Citrus fruit, floral.

Pairings > Orange, apple, pear, chocolate, red fruits.

FENNEL SEEDS

Source > Fennel fruits look like long, tiny green seeds that are found inside little yellow flowers. This spice, highly prized in the Mediterranean region, has been used since Greek Antiquity for its medicinal properties.

Aromatic notes > Anise seeds, lemony.

Pairings > Plum, fig, almond, citrus fruit, green apple.

TONKA BEANS

Source > Tonka beans come from teak, a very large tree native to South America.

Nutrients > Tonka beans must be eaten only occasionally, as they contain coumarin (an aromatic substance that is toxic for the body if too much is consumed; see page 128). The beans are banned in the US.

Aromatic notes > Almond, amber.

Pairings > Chocolate, pear, hazelnut, citrus fruit.

Spices from flowers and leaves

LEMON MYRTLE

Source > Myrtle is a tree native to Australia. The spice is made with the leaves, which are dried and then ground. Indigenous peoples have used them for millennia to heal wounds (antiseptic) or in cooking for its aromatic perfume.

Aromatic notes > Citrus fruit, peppery, herbaceous.

Pairings > Quince, pear, plum, apple, banana.

ROSE

Source > This spice, in the form of rose water, is from the Damask rose. The perfume is in the buds and on the petals, which are dried or distilled. This spice is used in pastry making (especially Asian pastries, where it is commonly found), cosmetics and perfumes.

Aromatic notes > Floral.

Pairings > Strawberry, raspberry, cherry, almond, pistachio, vanilla, lychee.

SAFFRON

Source > The spice is made from the pistils of the saffron crocus flower (crocus sativus). The moment for picking them is short, as it must be done before the flower's petals open. The harvested pistils must be red. Throughout history, this spice has always been coveted, especially by royalty, because it is so rare.

Aromatic notes > Honey, musky, floral.

Pairings > Citrus fruit, chocolate, mango, honey, pear, strawberry.

Salt

How can we talk about spices, which help to elevate dishes, without mentioning salt, a wonderful flavor enhancer? Salt is an essential ingredient in pastry making. During cooking, it helps give color to dough. Its salty flavor pairs well with many ingredients and enhances the flavor of pastries. It also helps to preserve foods.

WHAT IS THE DIFFERENCE BETWEEN FLEUR DE SEL, COARSE SALT AND FINE SALT?

Fleur de sel is salt that has finely crystallized on the surface of shallow pools of seawater. It is the first salt that salt workers collect, and they do so with great care. The white salt crystals are very rich in minerals, as magnesium and calcium are concentrated on the water's surface once evaporation has taken place.

Coarse salt is found below the surface of the water. It is used as is or processed to make fine salt.

THERE ARE MANY TYPES OF SALT, DEPENDING ON THEIR SOURCE AND HOW THEY ARE PRODUCED. HERE ARE A FEW:

REFINED (TABLE) SALT: INDUSTRIAL

This salt is treated so it is composed only of NaCl (sodium chloride, the chemical formula for salt). It no longer contains the trace elements that are naturally present. It is mined, bleached and then crushed to the desired granule size. Due to this treatment, it keeps longer than it would in its natural state. It is, however, enriched with iodine and fluoride and contains an anti-caking agent. Refined or table salt is usually a form of fine salt.

FRENCH GRAY SEA SALT: THE BEST FOR OUR HEALTH

This salt is obtained naturally, after evaporating water from salt marshes. Its gray color comes from the clay from which the "eyelets" (basins) of salt marshes are made; this gives it magnesium, potassium and calcium.

Gray salt can be in the form of fine or coarse salt and has a higher moisture content than many other salts. Since it has not undergone any processing, it retains its nutrients.

BLACK HIMALAYAN SALT: POLLUTION FREE

Black salt, also called kala namak, is a rock salt from South Asia. Given how long ago it was formed, it has the benefit of being free of pollution. Traditionally, it is extracted in blocks from the rock, then heated at a high temperature with carbon and a mix of different seeds. This gives it its black color. Its eggy flavor is due to its sulfur content.

Like its cousin pink salt, it contains potassium. Also, it has alkalizing properties for the body (allowing it to fight acidity).

PINK HIMALAYAN SALT: A DISTINCTIVE COLOR

This rock salt is mined from the foothills of the Himalayas; it is raw and unrefined. Its pink tints are due to the presence of iron oxide.

Iron in the form of iron oxide is not well absorbed by the body; we must rely on other animal and plant sources (beef, offal, seafood, green vegetables, legumes or oleaginous fruits and oil seeds) to meet our iron needs. Also, this salt is not iodized: iodine requirements that are usually met by salt are not met with this one. Again, it is important to eat a variety of foods (yes, even salt!).

BLACK HAWAIIAN SEA SALT: FROM THE LAND OF VOLCANOES

This is a blend of black sea salt and black lava salt with activated carbon. It has smoky aromatic notes.

It is lower in sodium than classic salt: it is therefore ideal for reducing sodium consumption. The activated carbon in this salt is a real advantage as it offers many benefits, including detoxifying the body.

Tips for choosing, storing and using spices

CHOOSING

> Choose spices that you will actually use.

> Buy whole spices, not ground, in small quantities.

STORING

Whether spices are dried or fresh, in all cases, they are fragile foods, to be stored away from light and heat.

> Keep them in sealed glass jars.

> Store in a cupboard away from the light yet easily accessible for cooking.

USING

> Use a spice grinder, a zester or a mortar and pestle, depending on the spices you want to use, and grind them just before using.

CHAPTER 9

Flowers

INTRODUCTION

In Antiquity, the Greeks and the Romans grew edible flowers for medicinal purposes.

In the 19th century, flowers appeared in food in various forms: in infusions, syrups and salads. However, toward the end of the 20th century, edible flowers were set aside. Recently, they became trendy and are finding themselves on our plates once again, after having given acclaimed performances in palaces and starred restaurants.

It is thanks to the new generation of chefs that flowers are in vogue again: these chefs know how to showcase their delicate aspects – from orange blossom's sweet and tangy perfume to nasturtium's peppery notes – and pair flavors to persuade the public. Today, flowers have their rightful place in home pastry making, where, as you will see, they add color, whimsy and surprising tastes.

The nutritional value of edible flowers

˙ʅ

Flowers, which contain a lot of water, have relatively few calories and are beautiful and delicious. They are also nutritionally dense, owing to their richness in trace elements, vitamins and minerals. Their petals even contain essential fatty acids: omega-3 and -6. And they have high concentrations of pigments with antioxidant powers! Eating flowers is therefore an opportunity to fill up on antioxidants and prebiotics, which are indispensable for the health of our microbiota.

Depending on the flower, you will also find vitamins C, F, B1 and B2, beta-carotene, calcium, phosphorus and iron.

Like spices, even though they are eaten in small quantities, flowers teem with wonderful benefits and antioxidant superpowers.

IMPORTANT

Warning: not all flowers are edible, and some are lethal. Choose flowers that are known to be edible and avoid being adventurous.

It is essential to eat flowers that have not been treated with pesticides and are produced in ways that respect the environment.

Flowers in pastry making

˙ʅ

ACACIA FLOWERS

Source > Acacia flowers are white. The acacia tree is a member of the pea (Fabaceae) family. It is native to North America but also grows in the Southern Hemisphere. The name "acacia" comes from the Greek word *akis* ("spine"). There are more than 1,500 species of acacia in the world. The flowering season for the acacia is very short: May and June.

Aromatic notes > Floral

Pairings > Apple, pear, apricot

ANISE HYSSOP FLOWERS

Source > Anise hyssop is a hardy herbaceous plant native to North America. It was used by Native Americans for its medicinal properties. Its tubular purple-blue flowers release a strong aniseed scent with licorice notes that attracts insect pollinators.

Aromatic notes > Licorice, minty

Pairings > Chocolate

BASIL FLOWER

Source > Basil is a plant native to Southeast Asia. It was long considered a magic herb by the Greeks, the Romans and the Egyptians. It was imported at least 4,000 years ago into Egypt and then spread to other countries over time. Basil needs a tropical or Mediterranean climate; today, this aromatic plant is grown in many places, including France, Italy, Central Europe and the western and southern US. Like all flowers, basil flowers are rich in antioxidants. The flowers typically grow in summer.

Nasturtium

Thyme   Calendula   Rose   Lave

Borage

Marigold

Hypericum

ler

Gaillardia
(Blanket Flower)

Chamomile

Aromatic notes > Basil

Pairings > Strawberry, peach, lemon, mango

BLACK ELDERFLOWER BLOSSOM

Source > Black elderflower is a shrub native to Central Europe. It is found in Europe, Western Asia, North Africa and North America. There are different species of elderflower. The blossom is especially rich in flavonoids and minerals. It flowers from May to June.

Aromatic notes > Sweet

Pairings > Rhubarb, strawberry, pear, almond, blackberry

BORAGE FLOWERS

Source > Borage is native to Syria; from there, it spread rapidly in the Mediterranean region and North Africa. It has been known since the Middle Ages for its many medicinal properties but also in cooking. It is especially rich in the essential fatty acids omega-3 and -6. The flowers can be picked from May to August.

CHAMOMILE FLOWER

Source > Roman chamomile (*Chamaemelum nobile*) is a plant native to Europe and North Africa. It was a symbol of the sun, and its essential oil was used to embalm the dead, including Pharaoh Ramses II. Its petals are popular in cooking, medicines and cosmetics, especially because of their flavonoids. The flowers bloom from June to September.

Aromatic notes > Apple, floral, bitter

Pairings > Apple, pear, peach, mango

CHERRY BLOSSOM

Source > Cherry trees are native to Greece, from where they were then propagated in many countries. In Japan, people gather for Hanami, a celebration of the cherry blossoms. Cherries flower in March or April, depending on the variety, for only about 10 days. The blossoms are rich in plant sugars and antioxidants, especially owing to their flavonoid polyphenols (see page 129) and tannins (see page 144). Be sure to choose an edible, rather than a decorative, blossom.

Aromatic notes > Fruity, floral

Pairings > Matcha, kidney bean, strawberry, cherry

DANDELION FLOWER

Source > The cultivation of dandelions began in France in the 19th century. The plant is native to Europe; it was then propagated in North America and Africa. Its yellow flowers are picked in spring. The leaves, which can be consumed as a tea, are rich in vitamin C and beta-carotene, two powerful antioxidants. Good to know: the stems and roots are also edible.

Aromatic notes > Slightly bitter, slightly sweet

Pairings > Chocolate, honey

USES

> Flavor butter or oil
> Infuse in a cream or syrup
> Add to sweet dough, jelly or sorbet
> Decorate a cake

GERANIUM FLOWER

Source > The scented geranium (*Pelargonium*) is native to Southern Africa. It is known by its flowers that are shaped like a crane's bill. Its magnificent flowers, rich in antioxidants, are delicious and fruity; they bring rose, hazelnut, lemon or apple flavors, depending on the species. Scented geranium leaves, which are also edible, are even more flavorful than the flowers! Note that geraniums are toxic to horses, cats and dogs.

Aromatic notes > Rose, lemon

Pairings > Melon, raspberry, rhubarb

LAVENDER FLOWER

Source > Lavender is native to the Mediterranean region. The Romans used it for its antioxidant properties and its distinctive calming scent.

Aromatic notes > Lavender, bitter

Pairings > Almond, apricot, peach

LINDEN FLOWER

Source > The linden flower is from the large leaf linden tree. The tree is native to Southern and Central Europe. During the French Revolution, the linden became a symbol for freedom. Its flowers are rich in vitamin C. Note: frequent use of linden has been linked with heart damage. DO NOT USE if you have heart disease.

Aromatic notes > Honey

Pairings > Pistachio, apricot, pear, raspberry

MARIGOLD (CALENDULA)

Source > The *Calendula* genus of marigold, or pot marigold, is a flower native to the Mediterranean region. It flowers from June to September. It contains many antioxidants and flavonoids. Note: Though all *Calendula* genus marigolds are edible, not all marigolds of the *Tagetes* genus are edible. Ensure that the type of marigold you use is safe to eat.

Aromatic notes > Peppery

Pairings > Citrus fruit, pear, apple

MEADOWSWEET FLOWER

Source > Meadowsweet is a flowering herb that grows in damp soils. It is native to Central Europe. It can be found in Western Asia and in North America. It is picked in summer.

Aromatic notes > Bitter almond, vanilla

Pairings > Chocolate, strawberry, raspberry

NASTURTIUM FLOWER

Source > Nasturtium is a plant native to South America. Its nickname is Indian cress. Nasturtiums arrived in North America in the 18th century. They are especially rich in polyphenols and antioxidants. The plant flowers from June until the first frost.

Aromatic notes > Peppery

Pairings > All flavors

ORANGE BLOSSOM

Source > Orange blossoms are white. They are the flowers of the Seville (bitter) orange tree, native to China. They were used first in China, then spread to Arab countries, the Mediterranean region, Europe and later Florida. They are rich in antioxidants. Orange blossoms are harvested from March to July.

Aromatic notes > Sweet, floral, tangy

Pairings > Almond, pistachio, citrus fruit, raspberry, strawberry

PINEAPPLE SAGE FLOWER

Source > Pineapple sage is a plant belonging to the mint (Lamiaceae) family, native to Mexico. Its name comes from its fruity scent, which is reminiscent of pineapple. Its flowers are rich in vitamins and minerals. This plant flowers in fall and is sensitive to cold.

Aromatic notes > Pineapple

Pairings > Apricot, peach, mango, pineapple, lemon

POPPY FLOWER

Source > The poppy is native to the eastern Mediterranean, North Africa and Asia. The flower is very rich in vitamin C and in polyphenols. Poppies grow mainly in spring. Oriental and Breadseed varieties may cause a skin reaction in children.

Aromatic notes > Neutral, bitter, slightly sweet

Pairings > Berries, peach, nectarine, chocolate

PURPLE BEE BALM FLOWER

Source > Purple bee balm is a hardy rhizomic plant native to eastern North America, where it grows in forests, underbrush and prairies. Its flowers, which attract honeybees and birds, release mint and bergamot scents.

Aromatic notes > Orange

Pairings > Red fruits, citrus fruit

ROSE BLOSSOM

Source > Roses, which grow on rose bushes, have been celebrated since Antiquity for their beauty, scent and colors. The cultivation of this flower – the most cultivated flower in the world – began around 5,000 years ago in China. Some rose bushes are called repeat-flowering because they flower several times within a growing season. The petals contain minerals, vitamin A, vitamin C, vitamin E and essential fatty acids. They are also a source of protein. This pretty flower is an antioxidant powerhouse!

Aromatic notes > Sweet

ROSEMARY FLOWERS

Source > Rosemary is native to Southern Europe. It has long been used in cooking but also for its medicinal properties. Depending on the climate zone where it grows, it can flower in spring, summer and fall. Its flowers are very rich in antioxidants.

Aromatic notes > Rosemary

Pairings > Apricot, peach, raspberry, nectarine

ST. JOHN'S WORT FLOWER

Source > This herbaceous plant is native to Europe, North Africa and Central Asia. It has since spread around the world. Its name refers to St. John the Baptist, whose feast is in late June, around the time the flowers start to bloom (June to September).

Aromatic notes > Black tea

Pairings > Lemon, apricot, peach, lemon balm

SWEET CLOVER BLOSSOM

Source > Clover is an herbaceous plant in the Fabaceae (pea) family. Its generic name is *Melilotus*, from the Greek *meli* ("honey") and *lotos* ("lotus"). It is very rich in coumarins (important: see information on page 128) and flavonoids. The plant flowers from June to October. There are different clovers of different colors.

Aromatic notes > Vanilla

Pairings > Goes with all flavors

Pairings > Strawberry, raspberry

THYME FLOWER

Source > Thyme is a small shrub with wonderful aromatic and medicinal properties that has been known since thousands of years before the common era. It is often found in sunny zones, such as the Mediterranean region. Its flowers are rich in antioxidants. Thyme flowers can be picked from May to July.

Aromatic notes > Thyme

Pairings > Apricot, lemon, strawberry, grapefruit

VIOLET BLOSSOM

Source > Violets are native to the Mediterranean region, where they have been known since 400 BCE for their many benefits. For example, they were used to make a crown to reduce migraines. Their flowers are very rich in vitamins A and C as well as minerals. Violets flower in spring, but some also flower in fall.

Aromatic notes > Floral

Pairings > Redcurrant, raspberry, passion fruit

CHAPTER 10

Aromatic herbs

INTRODUCTION

✦

Aromatic herbs and microgreens are valuable additions to a recipe, as they allow you to give pastries a unique aromatic signature.

Here you will discover the ones that, dried or fresh, pair best with sweet notes.

They have many benefits: to make the most of these, there's nothing better than using fresh herbs. The ideal is to add them at the end of cooking or to make a cold infusion.

Aromatic herbs

Herb	Pairings	Use
Basil	strawberry, lemon	
Dill	apple, lemon	
Lemon balm	apple, pear, lemon, berries	
Mint	chocolate, lemon, strawberry, pineapple	
Pineapple sage	strawberry, lemon, pomegranate, pineapple	Dried or fresh, they are used as infusions in creams or syrups, finely chopped or mixed with fruit
Rosemary	apricot, peach, rhubarb, fig	Blended to make a sweet pesto or a sauce
Sorrel	peach, apricot	
Tarragon	cherry, raspberry, blackberry, apricot	
Thyme	apricot, peach, lemon, honey	
Verbena	strawberry, bergamot, peach, raspberry, pear	

BASIL

Nutrients > Basil is rich in antioxidants and vitamin K. This aromatic plant also contains good amounts of water, iron, copper and manganese, magnesium, potassium, phosphorus and calcium. Fresh basil is also rich in vitamins B9, C and A.

DILL

Nutrients > Dill offers a lemony taste with subtle aniseed notes and is very rich in antioxidants, vitamins C and B9, iron, manganese, potassium and calcium. It also contains other B vitamins, vitamin E, zinc and copper.

LEMON BALM

Nutrients > Lemon balm is particularly rich in flavonoids, which are powerful antioxidants. It contains vitamins A and E as well as magnesium and calcium.

MINT

Nutrients > Mint is a source of iron, manganese, magnesium, calcium and phosphorus. It has antioxidant properties. Mint also contains several vitamins: A, B, C and E.

PINEAPPLE SAGE

Nutrients > Its name comes from its pronounced pineapple notes. It has strong anti-oxidant properties and contains vitamins K, A and B6 as well as iron. Its red flowers, with subtle notes, can also be eaten.

ROSEMARY

Nutrients > Rosemary is an excellent source of iron and vitamin B9 as well as manganese, calcium and potassium. It also contains vitamin C and other B vitamins, and its richness in flavonoids offers significant antioxidants.

SORREL

Nutrients > Given that many people today are low in magnesium, you have to wonder why everyone doesn't eat sorrel! It is rich in fiber, vitamins, minerals and trace elements. It especially meets our needs in provitamin A (100% of the recommended intake for 100 g) and vitamin C (three quarters of the recommended intake for 100 g), with antioxidant properties strengthened by the presence of carotenoids. It also contains potassium, a precious mineral for the body's acid-base balance.

TARRAGON

Nutrients > Tarragon is one of the aromatic herbs that are powerful antioxidants. This plant is a source of vitamin K and iron. Tarragon can also be a source of manganese if it is dried.

THYME

Nutrients > Thyme is an incredible source of iron, vitamin C and beta-carotene, with good antioxidant properties. This aromatic plant is also a source of calcium, manganese, potassium, copper, B vitamins and vitamin K (only in dried thyme).

VERBENA

Nutrients > We should always have verbena at hand – for its delicious scent but also for its many benefits related to its high levels of polyphenols, especially flavonoids, and its aromatic compounds.

Microgreens

Many microgreens can nicely enhance sweet desserts, for esthetic reasons and/or their flavor. Here you will discover the ones most used in pastry making.

It is possible, as with aromatic herbs, to grow the ones that suit you at home.

WHAT IS A MICROGREEN?

A microgreen is a vegetable or herb seed that is germinated and then exposed to the light. In one week, microgreens appear: small stems with leaves.

They are aromatic but above all contain a concentration of benefits up to 40 times higher than in aromatic herbs.

Microgreen	Aromatic note	Pairings
Anise	aniseed – tarragon	coconut, apple
Apple blossom	tangy – green apple	green apple, lemon, banana, mango, peach
Atsina	sweet aniseed	apricot, peach, lemon, apple
Basil	clove	citrus fruit, apricot, peach, pineapple
Green shiso	aniseed – mint	lime, pineapple, raspberry, chocolate
Jasmine	jasmine	cherry, raspberry, chocolate
Lime	aniseed – lemon	dark chocolate, citrus fruit
Red shiso	cumin	peach, mulberry, orange, apple, pear
Syrha	mildly sour	apricot, peach, fig, raspberry, passion fruit

PRODUCTION METHOD

1 > Choose the seeds you want to grow.

2 > Soak the seeds in a water bath for 6 to 8 hours.

3 > Choose 2 identical shallow trays (about 4 cm high) and make drainage holes in one of them.

4 > Pour some water into the tray without holes. Add organic compost to the tray with the holes.

5 > Place the seeds on the compost until they cover it completely. Place this tray on top of the tray that has water in it.

6 > Spray the seeds and compost with water.

7 > Cover for 3 days with a third tray.

8 > Remove the top tray and let the microgreens grow for 1 week in the light. Ensure the bottom tray contains water.

That's it! They are ready to be picked and eaten right away.

CHAPTER 11

Natural thickeners and dyes

INTRODUCTION

Pastry making is an art where the ingredients use chemistry and certain agents to enhance the texture, color, appearance and flavor of the final product.

It is a skill in which technique is at the service of what is both delicious and beautiful. Whatever you are making, the thickener always plays a major role, in terms of both the texture and the shelf life. Dyes help to enhance the appearance so your creation is also a delight for the eyes.

What is a thickener?

A thickener is an additive that does not bring any nutrients but plays a purely technical role in the recipe. It binds with liquids to thicken, create a gel or emulsify a mixture. These additives can be classified based on their function, as follows:

> **Thickener:** increases the viscosity of a mixture

> **Gel:** gives the consistency of a gel to a cream- or fruit-based mixture

> **Stabilizer:** keeps sponge cakes soft, keeps ice cream from melting for longer and increases a product's shelf life

> **Emulsifier:** helps to combine two ingredients that don't mix naturally

> **Binder:** brings together solid particles

> **Aerator:** makes it possible to incorporate air through whipping to give an airy and fluffy texture

Thickeners are either proteins:	Or polysaccharides from:
plant: pea, wheat or soy protein **animal:** gelatin or eggs	**plants:** pectin, guar, carob, tara...
	algae: alginate, agar agar, carrageenan
	fermentation of micro-organisms: xanthan, gellan...
	a synthesis process: cellulose derivatives

ACACIA FIBER

Also called acacia gum, it comes from the sap of the acacia tree that oozes out of the trunk and looks like hard resin. The gum is harvested, dissolved, then filtered and dried. It is colorless, odorless and flavorless. It is high in fiber and is marketed as a dietary supplement or thickener.

Acacia gum dissolves perfectly in cold water. Use an amount equaling 0.2% to 0.5% of the total mass of the recipe to incorporate it. It mainly replaces starch. It has both thickening and emulsifying properties. It can be used to bind or thicken creams, such as pastry cream. It is also used in yeast doughs, such as brioches, or in other baked goods, for a softer texture.

AGAR AGAR

Agar agar comes from a red alga from which the mucilage is extracted, which is then dehydrated.

It is used in very small quantities to gel mousses, jellies or whipped ganaches. Agar agar must be diluted with water and brought to a boil to activate it. Gelling happens during the cooling phase and is thermo-reversible (becomes viscous when heated). Agar agar has no flavor and is often used to replace gelatin or pectin.

AQUAFABA

Aquafaba is made at home with the cooking water from chickpeas. Chickpea protein is released into the cooking water and then concentrated after partial evaporation.

Once cooled, the aquafaba is whipped to create a fluffy texture, like whipped egg whites.

It is used to make plant-based mousses or meringues.

CAROB BEAN GUM

This gum comes from the kernels of the carob tree. After the kernels are washed, the seeds are removed and turned into powder. This is not the same as carob powder (flour), which is made from carob pulp and pods.

To thicken a sauce or give texture to ice cream, use 2 to 10 g/kg. It is mixed with some dry ingredients from the recipe, then added to the whole mixture. Used cold, it is mixed in a blender; used hot, it is brought to a boil in a liquid.

GELATIN

Gelatin comes from the collagen of animal and fish bones and skins. It is not considered an additive but an ingredient.

It is pale yellow and is used in powdered or leaf form. The powder is added to cold water (7 times its weight) for 1 hour, then the mixture is heated to at least 131 °F (55 °C). It can be used right away or kept in the fridge.

The leaves are soaked one by one in a bowl of cold water for 1 hour. After the water is squeezed out, they are ready to be used in the recipe.

GUAR GUM

Guar gum is extracted from the seed of the guar bean plant. It can be used in two ways:

Used cold, add 0.5% to 2% guar gum based on total weight and combine the gum with the mixture.

To make gluten-free bread, add 4 g for 400 g flour (1% guar gum).

It is found in many recipes for ice cream and sorbet to stabilize their creamy texture.

INULIN

This fiber comes from chicory or agave. Inulin is known for its high fiber. It is water soluble and, once mixed, has a gelatinous texture. It is considered a prebiotic and is also marketed as a dietary supplement.

It is often used in ice cream and sorbet in a ratio of 50 to 100 g/kg (5 to 10%). It is mixed with the recipe's dry ingredients and brought to a boil.

KONJAC GUM

Konjac gum or flour comes from a tuber native to Asia. It has been known for thousands of years for its natural thickening properties. It has a greasy, sticky texture and, in some recipes, can replace butter. Like alginate, it gives texture to both cold and hot mixtures.

Its flavor is neutral, and it is added to a mixture containing water. The gelling is irreversible once activated.

PEA PROTEIN

It comes from yellow split peas, which are very rich in protein and are made up of essential amino acids. It has aerating properties like egg whites and can therefore be used to make a vegan version of whipped egg whites, like aquafaba, using a ratio of 0.5% to 2% pea protein for the total liquid in the recipe. Important: people with a peanut allergy might have an anaphylactic reaction to pea protein.

PSYLLIUM

It comes from the husks of psyllium seeds, which are very high in fiber. It is recommended as a dietary supplement, as it is a probiotic that promotes intestinal health. It is also found under the name "blond psyllium," but black and brown versions are available too.

Some of the sugar in baking or a meringue recipe can be replaced with psyllium. This is an easy way to lower the glycemic index.

Use 20 g psyllium per 400 g (5%) flour in a bread recipe.

SODIUM ALGINATE

Sodium alginate comes from a brown alga from which the algine, an element in the alga's cell wall, is extracted. It offers the alga great flexibility. In pastry making, it is mixed with water; it has no flavor or odor. It is activated with calcium, even in very small quantities.

To use it, mix with a small amount of sugar from the recipe (to avoid lumps) and add to the mixture while stirring. The obtained gel is irreversible. It is the ideal thickener for gelling fruit preserves and preserving their micro-nutrients, such as vitamins.

Natural dyes

Here are some ingredients to add color to your pastries and baked goods naturally:

> **Red dye:** beets or dried strawberries

> **Reddish-orange dye:** paprika

> **Yellow dye:** turmeric

> **Light green dye:** matcha

> **Blue dye:** spirulina

> **Brown dye:** cocoa powder or coffee grounds

> **Black dye:** activated carbon

Vitamins & minerals
Nutrients at a glance

Name ●······○

Where to find them ●······○

Benefits ●······○

Vitamin A
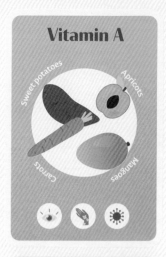
Sweet potatoes, Apricots, Mangoes, Carrots

Vitamin B6

Nuts and seeds, Avocados, Whole grains, Bananas, Legumes

Vitamin B8

Green leafy vegetables, Eggs, Nuts and seeds

Vitamin B9

Green leafy vegetables, Whole grains, Legumes, Citrus fruits

Vitamin B12

Dairy products, Enriched plant-based beverages, Eggs

Calcium

Dairy products, Green vegetables, Nuts and seeds

Copper

Green vegetables, Dark chocolate, Legumes, Nuts and seeds

Iron

Green vegetables, Legumes, Nuts and seeds

Iodine

Dairy products, Eggs, Seaweed

Sodium

Salt, Seaweed

Zinc

Whole grains, Legumes

Omega-3

Flaxseeds, Canola oil, Flaxseed oil, Soy, Nuts

Omega-6

Grape seed oil, Olive oil, Sunflower oil, Nuts and seeds

Vitamin B1

Whole grains · Nuts and seeds · Legumes

Vitamin B2

Green leafy vegetables · Almonds · Eggs

Vitamin B3

Sunflower seeds · Whole grains · Legumes

Vitamin B5

Eggs · Dairy products · Avocados · Legumes

Vitamin C

Berries · Kiwi · Citrus fruits · Peppers · Papayas

Vitamin D

Margarine · Fromage blanc · Eggs

Vitamin E

Avocado · Vegetable oils · Nuts and seeds

Vitamin K1

Green leafy vegetables · Vegetable oils

Magnesium

Nuts and seeds · Bananas · Cocoa · Avocados

Phosphorus

Whole grains · Dairy products · Nuts and seeds

Potassium
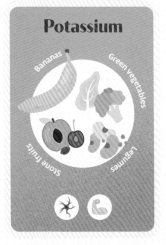
Bananas · Green vegetables · Stone fruits · Legumes

Selenium

Brazil nuts · Eggs

Omega-9

Olive oil · Walnut oil · Olives · Avocado oil

Fiber

Whole grains · Fruits and vegetables · Whole-grain flour · Legumes · Nuts and seeds

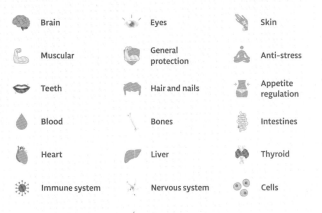
Brain · Eyes · Skin
Muscular · General protection · Anti-stress
Teeth · Hair and nails · Appetite regulation
Blood · Bones · Intestines
Heart · Liver · Thyroid
Immune system · Nervous system · Cells
Fatigue reduction · Energy

155

The benefits of nutrients

Strengthening the body from within

Blood

Carbohydrates > Are the first source of energy used by the body when it needs to move

Fiber > Helps to limit blood sugar spikes

Vitamin K > Helps blood to clot

Immune system

Protein > Helps the body heal more quickly

Iron > Fights against winter viruses

Vitamins C and D > Strengthen the immune system

Muscles

Protein > Maintains muscle mass to keep the body strong

Calcium and potassium > Activate muscle contraction, which makes movement possible

Head

Omega-3 and -9 > Allow good brain development and brain function

Beta-carotene > Helps the body make vitamin A; it is also an antioxidant that helps fight free radicals

Potassium > Helps the nervous system perform

Vitamin A and omega-3 > Contribute to good vision

Calcium and vitamin D > Promote strong teeth

Thyroid

Iodine > Is essential for a healthy thyroid! The thyroid is a small gland that produces hormones to regulate vital functions such as sleep, growth, energy use and hunger.

Heart

Vitamin E and omegas-3 and -9 > Help keep the heart healthy

HDL cholesterol > Eliminates excess cholesterol and prevents cardiovascular disease

Digestive system

Fats > Are indispensable for building up energy reserves

Omega-9 > Regulates cholesterol levels

HDL cholesterol > This is the good cholesterol; it absorbs excess cholesterol in the blood

Fiber > Optimizes bowel function and limits diarrhea and constipation

Lactic acid bacteria > Promote balanced intestinal flora

Bones

Vitamin D > Maintains calcium levels

Calcium and vitamin K > Strengthen bones

Omega-3 > Is especially helpful for avoiding joint stiffness

Cells

B vitamins > Support cell multiplication

Vitamins C and E > Are antioxidants that are especially effective in fighting free radicals (unstable atoms made by the body) and slowing down cell death

Omega-9 > Help make cells strong (incorporated into cell membrane)

Zinc > Is an antioxidant that helps keep skin and hair soft

Recipes

DEAR BAKERS,
WELCOME TO THE TASTIEST PART OF THIS BOOK!

I am delighted to share my secrets with you for creating desserts that are both delicious and balanced, taking advantage of the many choices of ingredients that Mother Nature offers us.

In this section you will find a variety of recipes, from sweet pastry that will enhance your favorite pies to a flavorful marble cake, not to mention my own original creations. Because I want to meet the needs of a range of diets and consider common food allergies, I have included gluten-free, low-GI and vegan alternatives.

You will also find ideas to tailor recipes to your taste. I encourage you to experiment, make these recipes your own and adapt them to your lifestyle. Baking should be enjoyable! I hope these recipes will inspire you to explore new flavors while taking care of yourself and all those who will eat these desserts.

Many of the specialty ingredients can be purchased at well-stocked health food or natural food stores and various online sources. Specialty bakeware can also be purchased through various online sources.

Here are a few tips and tricks before you begin:

SAY GOODBYE TO COMMERCIAL BAKING POWDER

For 2 tsp (10 g) homemade baking powder replacement:

- Mix 1 tsp (5 g) baking soda (base) + 1 tsp (5 g) lemon juice (acid)
- Add it to the mixture just before baking.
- If you have to let the mixture rest, add this leavening agent to the batter just before baking.

WE LOVE ORGANICS!

We prefer organic products for ingredients that are unrefined and free of added chemicals, especially citrus fruits, whose zest we love to add to our baking. The cherry on top is that we are also helping to promote sustainable agriculture by preserving biodiversity.

BLEND DIFFERENT FLOURS

Does your pantry contain only one type of flour? Do you want to try mixing several flours together? See page 33 to choose the one(s) that meet your expectations. But be careful: some flours have a strong taste, while others can tint the batter with their dark color or give a very crumbly result. It's up to you to choose the right combination!

COOKING METHOD

Baking or dehydrating: time and temperature can vary depending on the equipment you use and how much of something you're cooking. Stay alert. When the cooking time or temperature is off, you may need to start over...

MARGARINE OR BUTTER?

Both will work. You can replace one with the other. All recipes in this book that call for butter use unsalted butter.

Here is an easy recipe for homemade margarine:

- 7 tbsp (100 g) coconut oil
- 6 tbsp + 2 tsp (100 g) cashew butter
- 2 tsp (10 g) olive oil
- 3 tbsp + 1 tsp (50 g) water

Blend all ingredients and store in a container.

COW'S MILK OR PLANT-BASED BEVERAGE?

You can interchange these liquids in equal quantities.

And if you want to make your own plant-based beverages, here is a brief guide:

OILSEED- AND FRUIT-BASED BEVERAGE (EXAMPLE USING ALMONDS)

Oil seeds and fruits	Ingredients	Directions
almond, hazelnut, coconut, chestnut, cashew, sesame seed...	with whole almonds	Soak 1 oz (30 g) almonds for 24 hours. Strain and add 1¼ cups (300 g) water. Purée in a blender for 1 minute. Sieve. Refrigerate the liquid, and dry the almond sediment at 200 °F (100 °C) in the oven to make a powder.
	with pure almond paste	Combine 10% of pure oilseed or fruit paste with 90% water. Purée in a blender and use right away, or refrigerate and mix before using.

GRAIN- AND LEGUME-BASED BEVERAGE (EXAMPLE USING OATS)

Grains and legumes	Ingredients	Directions
spelt, rice, oat, quinoa, buckwheat, soy...	with flakes	Purée 1⅔ oz (50 g) oats with 2 cups (500 g) water in a blender for 30 seconds to 1 minute to avoid having any residue. For a perfectly smooth beverage, strain the liquid.
	with flour	Purée 10% flour with 90% water in a blender for 1 minute.

LET'S UPCYCLE!

Citrus fruit > After you use the zest and juice of a citrus fruit, cut the remainder of the fruit into small pieces and dry them in the oven at 200 °F (100 °C), in a dehydrator or under a warm sun for several days. Then grind well in a high-powered blender or food processor until you get a powder.

Sprinkle the powder in cake batter, madeleine batter or sweet dough.

Vanilla > After you use the seeds from the pod, dry the pod in the air for several days. Once it is very dry, you can grind it to a powder. Store it in an airtight container.

Add it to butter or homemade margarine, shortcrust dough, sponge or cake.

Eggshells > Eggshells are very rich in calcium, magnesium and iron. Consuming them is easy. Boil the shells, dry them and grind in a high-powered blender or food processor. Now you have a food supplement with a neutral flavor that you can sprinkle on your meals.

Tea > After you use tea leaves to make an infusion, dry them and grind them to make a powder. Perfect for flavoring batter, dough and sponge cakes.

Fruit > Fruit peels can be dehydrated, then ground to a powder in a high-powered blender or food processor. Store this powder in an airtight container and add to cake batter or cookies for extra fiber.

Bread > Stale bread can be made into croutons. To do this, cut the bread into cubes. Add a little olive oil and crushed garlic. Mix well and bake at 200 °F (100 °C) or toast them in a skillet until golden. You can also use stale bread to make bread pudding.

Leftover cake and sponge > You can crumble leftovers and use them for a cheesecake base or pudding or to make cake pops (shape them into balls, then coat them in chocolate glaze).

Basic
recipes

Sweet dough

gluten   nuts

Makes four 3-inch (8 cm) diameter tarts • Preparation: 20 minutes • Baking time: 12 minutes

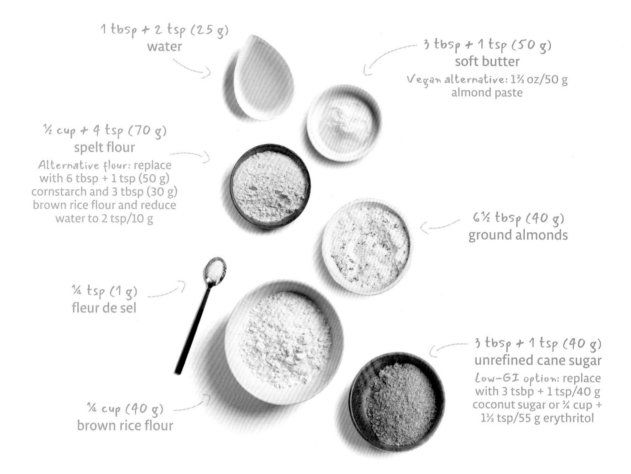

1 tbsp + 2 tsp (25 g)
water

3 tbsp + 1 tsp (50 g)
soft butter
Vegan alternative: 1⅔ oz/50 g
almond paste

½ cup + 4 tsp (70 g)
spelt flour
Alternative flour: replace
with 6 tbsp + 1 tsp (50 g)
cornstarch and 3 tbsp (30 g)
brown rice flour and reduce
water to 2 tsp/10 g

6½ tbsp (40 g)
ground almonds

¼ tsp (1 g)
fleur de sel

3 tbsp + 1 tsp (40 g)
unrefined cane sugar
Low-GI option: replace
with 3 tsbp + 1 tsp/40 g
coconut sugar or ¼ cup +
1½ tsp/55 g erythritol

¼ cup (40 g)
brown rice flour

DIRECTIONS

- In a bowl, combine sugar, flours and ground almonds.
- Add water and fleur de sel, then add butter; stir using a spatula until dough forms.
- Roll out to ⅛ inch (3 mm) thick between two sheets of parchment paper.
- Bake at 325 °F (160 °C) for 12 to 15 minutes.

Jazz it up

Jazz up your raw dough with chia seeds, black sesame seeds, lemon thyme powder, lemon powder or processed fennel seeds.

Shortcrust pastry

 egg   nuts

Makes 40 sticks • Preparation: 20 minutes • Baking time: 12 minutes

2 tbsp (30 g)
water

6½ tbsp (40 g)
ground almonds

3 tbsp (35 g)
date sugar

½ tsp (2 g)
fleur de sel

½ cup (60 g)
oat flour
Alternative flour: replace
with brown rice flour

COCONUT LEMON GLAZE

⅓ cup (40 g)
coconut flour

3 tbsp + 1 tsp (50 g)
almond butter

3 tbsp + 2 tbsp (50 g)
cocoa butter

3 tbsp + 1 tsp (50 g)
butter
Vegan alternative: replace
with 2 tbsp/30 g water and
4 tsp/20 g applesauce

2 tbsp + 2 tsp (20 g)
unsweetened
desiccated coconut

Lemon zest

SHORTCRUST PASTRY

- In a stand mixer fitted with the paddle attachment, beat butter and date sugar.
- Gradually add salt, flours, ground almonds and water; beat until the dough forms.
- Roll out the dough between two pieces of parchment paper to ¼ inch (0.5 cm) thick.
- Cut out sticks that are ½ inch (1 cm) wide by 4 inches (10 cm) long.
- Place in the freezer for 15 minutes.
- Place the sticks on a non-stick baking sheet and bake at 325 °F (160 °C) for 12 minutes.

COCONUT LEMON GLAZE

- In the microwave, melt cocoa butter, then add almond butter.
- Mix well.
- Place the sticks in the freezer for a few minutes and then dip them in warm 95 °F (35 °C) glaze and decorate them with coconut mixed with lemon zest.

Jazz it up

Jazz up the sticks after glazing them by adding dried rose petals, sesame seeds or tea powder.

Choux pastry

egg

nuts*

Makes 15 1-inch (2.5 cm) choux • Preparation: 40 minutes • Baking time: 20 minutes

6 tbsp + 2 tsp (100 g)
water

¼ cup (30 g)
corn flour

3 tbsp + 1 tsp (50 g)
neutral oil or grape
seed oil

6 tbsp + 2 tsp (100 g)
milk or plant-based beverage

Recipe for homemade
plant-based beverage
(page 161)

½ tsp (2 g)
fine gray salt

½ tsp (2 g)
unrefined cane
sugar

7 tbsp (70 g)
brown rice flour

3
eggs

DIRECTIONS

- In a saucepan, heat milk or plant-based beverage, water, oil, sugar and salt, without bringing to a boil, for 30 seconds.
- Off the heat, add sifted flours all at once.
- Still off the heat, use a wooden spoon to stir the dough for 30 seconds to help release the steam.
- Once the dough pulls away from the sides of the saucepan, transfer it to the bowl of a stand mixer fitted with the paddle attachment and beat to cool it down.
- When it has cooled to just warm, while beating, gradually pour in beaten eggs until you get the desired texture. You should get a smooth, glossy dough that makes a V when it comes off the beater paddle.
- Pipe onto a non-stick baking sheet, then bake at 350F (180 °C) for 20 to 30 minutes, until golden.

GOOD TO KNOW
To avoid lumps in the dough, heat liquids just to 170 °F (80 °C) before adding the flours. Here, the corn flour can form lumps when it is mixed into a liquid hotter than 170 °F (80 °C).

* depending on the plant-based beverage used

Jazz it up

Turn your choux
into savory versions (called
gougères in French) by replacing
the sugar with pepper and by
adding ⅓ cup (40 g) grated cheese
(Emmental, hard sheep's
milk cheese, Comté…).

Sponge cake roll

egg

gluten

Makes one 12 x 16-inch (30 x 40 cm) sponge • Preparation: 20 minutes • Baking time: 8 minutes

2
egg whites

2
egg yolks

2
eggs

3 tbsp + 1 tsp (40 g)
unrefined cane sugar
Low-GI option:
replace with ¼ cup/50 g erythritol

⅓ cup (40 g)
spelt flour
*Alternative flour: replace
with 6 tbsp + 2 tsp/50 g
tigernut flour*

2½ tbsp (20 g)
arrowroot starch

DIRECTIONS

- Sift flour and arrowroot starch.
- In a bowl, using an electric mixer, beat eggs, egg yolks and sugar to a fluffy texture.
- In a separate bowl, using clean beaters, beat egg whites.
- Gently fold egg whites into the egg and sugar mixture.
- Sprinkle in the flour and starch and stir gently.
- Spread on a 12 x 16-inch (30 x 40 cm) rimmed baking sheet lined with a silicone mat.
- Bake at 350 °F (180 °C) for 8 minutes.

Vegan alternative

¾ cup + 2 tbsp (200 g) plain unsweetened vegan yogurt
3 tbsp + 1 tsp (50 g) plant-based beverage
¾ tsp (4 g) cider vinegar
½ cup + 1½ tbsp (80 g) all-purpose flour
3 tbsp (40 g) granulated raw sugar
1 tsp (4 g) psyllium husk powder
¼ tsp (1 g) baking soda
¼ tsp (1 g) fine gray salt

¼ to ½ tsp (1 to 2 g) turmeric powder
2 tbsp (30 g) neutral oil

- Whisk together yogurt, plant-based beverage and cider vinegar and let sit for 10 minutes.
- Meanwhile, in a bowl, combine flour, sugar, psyllium, baking soda, salt and turmeric.

- Once the 10 minutes are up, add oil to the yogurt mixture and mix well. Then add everything to the bowl containing the flour. Whisk.
- Spread on a 12 x 16-inch (30 x 40 cm) rimmed baking sheet lined with a silicone mat.
- Bake at 350 °F (180 °C) for 12 minutes.

Jazz it up

Jazz up your rolled sponge using natural dyes such as phycocyanin (blue), turmeric (yellow), paprika (red) or matcha or spirulina (green).

To add some decoration and/or flavor, sprinkle dried flowers before spreading the batter on the baking sheet, then bake.

Soft almond sponge cake

gluten egg

Makes one 7-inch (18 cm) cake • Preparation: 20 minutes • Baking time: 16 minutes

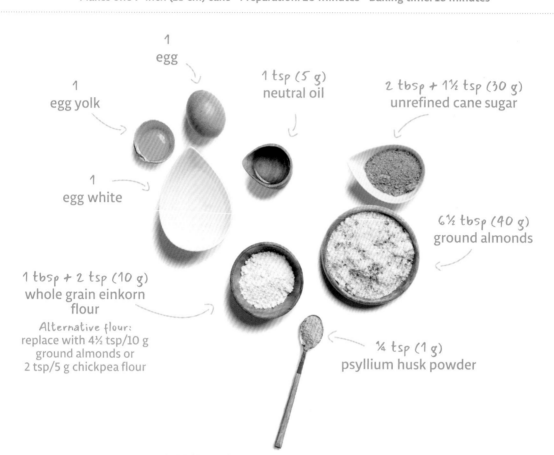

1
egg

1
egg yolk

1 tsp (5 g)
neutral oil

2 tbsp + 1½ tsp (30 g)
unrefined cane sugar

1
egg white

6½ tbsp (40 g)
ground almonds

1 tbsp + 2 tsp (10 g)
whole grain einkorn
flour

Alternative flour:
replace with 4½ tsp/10 g
ground almonds or
2 tsp/5 g chickpea flour

¼ tsp (1 g)
psyllium husk powder

DIRECTIONS

- Preheat the convection oven to 325 °F (160 °C).
- Grease a 7-inch (18 cm) springform or round pan with neutral oil.
- In a bowl, use a whisk to combine egg and egg yolk with sugar.
- Stir in ground almonds, then einkorn flour and psyllium.
- Using an electric mixer, whip egg white until firm. The texture should be supple and somewhat fluffy (like shaving cream). Using a spatula, fold into the mixture.
- Pour the mixture into the pan.
- Bake at 340 °F (170 °C) for 16 minutes.
- Let cool before removing from pan.

For an extra-soft result, using an electric mixer, beat egg, yolk and sugar to a fluffy texture, pour the mixture into the pan and bake at 325 °F (160 °C) for 20 minutes.

For thin cakes, pour the mixture into two 7-inch (18 cm) pans and bake at 325 °F (160 °C) for 16 minutes.

Vegan alternative ⸜

Replace the egg white with 2 tbsp + 1 tsp (30g) aquafaba (chickpea cooking/ can water) and replace the eggs with 1 tbsp (15 g) grape seed oil and 4 tsp (10 g) cornstarch mixed with the flour.

Jazz up your almond cake by adding slivered almonds, slivered hazelnuts, lemon zest or your choice of spice.

Baba dough

egg

Makes 30 small babas or one large baba that serves 8 • Preparation: 30 minutes • Rising time: 1 hour
Baking time: 10 minutes for individual babas – 20 minutes for 1 large baba

4
eggs

3 tbsp (25 g)
cornstarch

¼ oz (8 g)
fresh compressed
or 1 tsp/3 g
instant yeast

3 tbsp + 1 tsp (25 g)
tigernut flour

¾ cup + 1½ tsp (125 g)
brown rice flour

2 tsp (10 g)
water

¼ tsp (1 g)
salt

1 tsp (6 g)
honey

3 tbsp + 1 tsp (50 g)
butter

DIRECTIONS

- In a stand mixer fitted with the paddle attachment, mix yeast, water and honey. Add flours, cornstarch, salt, diced butter and two-thirds of the eggs. Switch to the dough hook and knead on low speed until the dough is smooth, glossy and pulls away from the sides of the bowl.

- Add the remaining eggs and knead until the dough is elastic and pulls away from the sides of the bowl.

- Lightly grease a 7-inch (18 cm) pan or the molds, ensuring to only fill half of the pan or molds with dough.

- Let rise, uncovered, for 40 minutes to 1 hour at 82 to 86 °F (28 to 30 °C).

- Bake for 10 minutes at 350 °F (180 °C) for individual babas or 20 minutes for a large baba.

- Remove from pan or molds, let cool and store in airtight containers at room temperature or in the freezer.

Vegan alternative 🌱

¼ oz (8 g) fresh compressed or 1 tsp
instant yeast
4 tsp (20 g) plant-based beverage
1½ tsp (6 g) unrefined cane sugar
1 cup + 6½ tbsp (190 g)
all-purpose flour
½ tsp (2 g) sea salt
4 tbsp + 2 tsp (70 g) soy cream
3 tbsp + 2 tsp (55 g) margarine

- In a stand mixer fitted with the paddle attachment, mix yeast, plant-based beverage and sugar. Add flour, salt and soy cream. Switch to the dough hook, knead on low speed for 1 minute and add margarine. Knead again for 5 minutes until the dough is elastic and pulls away from the sides of the bowl.
- Lightly grease the molds and divide the mixture, ensuring to only fill half of the pan or molds with dough.
- Let rise, uncovered, for 40 minutes to 1 hour at 82 to 86 °F (28 to 30 °C), then bake 10 minutes at 350 °F (180 °C).
- Remove from pan or molds.

Meringues

Makes 20 small meringues • Preparation: 20 minutes • Baking time: 2 hours

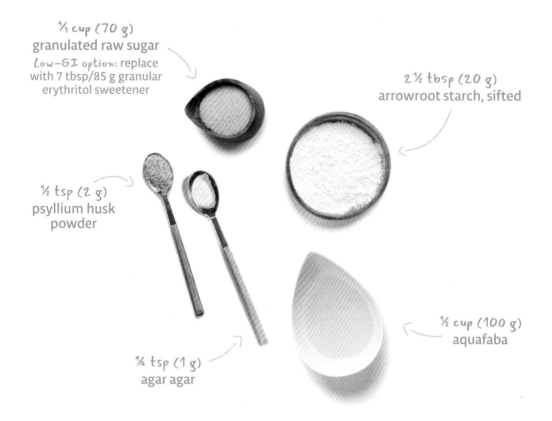

⅓ cup (70 g) granulated raw sugar

Low-GI option: replace with 7 tbsp/85 g granular erythritol sweetener

2½ tbsp (20 g) arrowroot starch, sifted

½ tsp (2 g) psyllium husk powder

¼ tsp (1 g) agar agar

½ cup (100 g) aquafaba

DIRECTIONS

- In a saucepan, stir together sugar, agar agar and aquafaba. Heat the mixture, then bring to a boil.
- Transfer the mixture to a bowl. Using an electric mixer, whip the mixture into a meringue until thick and glossy.
- Using a spatula, fold in sifted arrowroot starch and psyllium.
- Pipe onto a baking sheet lined with a silicone mat and let dry in the oven at 195 °F (90 °C) for at least 2 hours.

Jazz it up

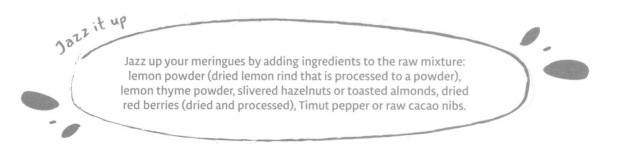

Jazz up your meringues by adding ingredients to the raw mixture: lemon powder (dried lemon rind that is processed to a powder), lemon thyme powder, slivered hazelnuts or toasted almonds, dried red berries (dried and processed), Timut pepper or raw cacao nibs.

Crème anglaise

egg

nuts*

Serves 2 • Preparation: 10 minutes • Cooking time: 2 minutes

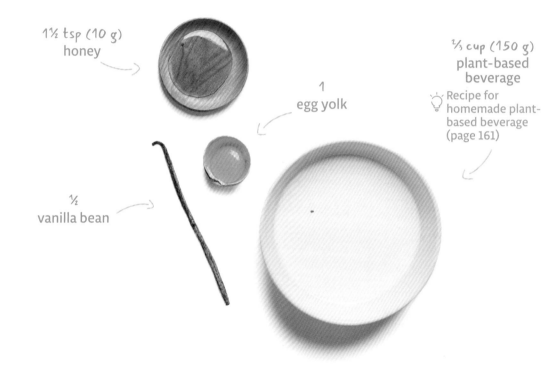

1½ tsp (10 g)
honey

1
egg yolk

⅔ cup (150 g)
plant-based
beverage

Recipe for
homemade plant-
based beverage
(page 161)

½
vanilla bean

DIRECTIONS

- Split vanilla bean pod and scrape out the seeds; add seeds to a saucepan with plant-based beverage and stir. Heat. In a bowl, whisk honey with egg yolk. Pour warm plant-based beverage over the egg yolk mixture while whisking, then return to saucepan and cook, stirring with a spatula until it coats the spatula. The cream should be smooth.

- Pour into a bowl, cover with wrap to touch, refrigerate and enjoy when it's cool.

Vegan alternative

½ vanilla bean
⅔ cup (150 g) plant-based beverage
(Recipe for homemade plant-based
beverage page 161)
2½ tsp (10 g) unrefined cane sugar
4 tsp (10 g) cornstarch
Pinch turmeric powder
Pinch sea salt

- Split vanilla bean pod and scrape out the seeds, add seeds to a saucepan with the plant-based beverage and stir. Heat. In a small bowl, whisk the cane sugar with cornstarch, turmeric and salt. Pour the hot beverage over the dry ingredients while whisking, then return to the saucepan and cook, stirring with a spatula until it coats the spatula. The cream should be smooth.
- Pour into a bowl, cover with wrap to touch, refrigerate and enjoy when it's cool.

* depending on the plant-based beverage used

Pastry cream

nuts*

Makes 1 cup (250 mL) • Preparation: 20 minutes • Cooking time: 3 minutes

Pinch (0.2 g)
turmeric powder

2 tbsp (30 g)
coconut oil

½
vanilla bean

1 tbsp + ¾ tsp (10 g)
arrowroot starch

1 tbsp (15 g)
brown sugar

1 cup (250 g)
plant-based beverage
Recipe for homemade
plant-based beverage
(page 161)

DIRECTIONS

- In a saucepan, heat plant-based beverage with sugar. Pour a small amount over the arrowroot starch and stir.

- Pour the arrowroot mixture back into the saucepan. Split vanilla bean pod and scrape out the seeds; stir seeds into the mixture.

- Bring to a boil for about 30 seconds, then turn off the heat. Stir in coconut oil and turmeric.

- Cover with wrap to touch and refrigerate right away.

Jazz it up

Jazz up your pastry cream by adding grated tonka bean, grated fresh ginger or ground cardamom. Please note: tonka bean is banned from consumption in the US (see details on its toxic ingredient coumarin on page 128).

* depending on the plant-based beverage used

Lemon curd

Makes 1 cup (250 mL) • Preparation: 20 minutes • Cooking time: 3 minutes

Zest of ½ lemon

3 tbsp (40 g) cocoa butter or homemade margarine (see recipe on page 160)

2 tbsp (40 g) honey
Low-GI option: replace with 2⅓ tbsp (30 g) erythritol

6 tbsp + 2 tsp (100 g) water

2 tbsp (15 g) arrowroot starch

4 oz (120 g) unsweetened lemon purée

DIRECTIONS

- In a saucepan, whisk together lemon purée, lemon zest and water with honey and arrowroot starch, then bring the mixture to a boil.
- Pour into a measuring jug. Add cocoa butter or margarine, then stir until smooth.
- Cover with wrap to touch and refrigerate.

Peanut butter ice cream

Serves 2 to 4 • Preparation: 10 minutes • Cooking time: 2 minutes • Freezing time: 2 hours

1¼ cups (300 g) water
6½ tbsp (100 g) peanut butter, unsweetened
1 tbsp + ¾ tsp (10 g) arrowroot starch
¼ cup (40 g) chopped dates
1 tbsp (20 g) honey

- In a saucepan, bring water, peanut butter and arrowroot starch to a boil.
- Pour the mixture over the dates and honey and stir.
- Pour into small silicone molds. Freeze.
- To make the ice cream, remove from molds and purée in a blender. Sprinkle with chopped peanuts, if desired. Eat right away.

Tip

My tip for all the ice cream recipes: pour the mixture into an ice cube tray or silicone molds to remove and purée more easily.

Chocolate ice cream

Serves 2 to 4 • Preparation: 15 minutes • Cooking time: 2 minutes • Freezing time: 2 hours

3⅓ oz (100 g) 64% dark chocolate, chopped or pieces
¾ cup + 3 tbsp (260 g) coconut cream
4 tbsp + 2 tsp (70 g) almond beverage
1¼ tsp (3 g) arrowroot starch
1½ tsp (10 g) honey
1 tsp (4 g) fleur de sel

- Melt the chocolate.
- In a saucepan, heat coconut cream with almond beverage, arrowroot starch and honey and while whisking, bring to a boil.
- Pour liquid over the chocolate and whisk.
- Pour into small silicone molds. Freeze.
- To make the ice cream, remove from molds and purée in a blender. Add fleur de sel and eat right away.

Coffee ice cream

soy

nuts

∗

Serves 2 to 4 • Preparation: 10 minutes • Cooking time: 2 minutes • Freezing time: 2 hours

⅔ cup (150 g) vegan cream
⅔ cup (150 g) almond beverage
¼ cup (20 g) coffee beans
¾ cup + 4 tsp (200 g) cashew butter
2 tbsp (40 g) honey

- In a blender, purée cream, almond beverage, coffee beans, cashew butter and honey, then freeze. It's okay if little bits of coffee beans remain, these will give the ice cream some crunch.
- Pour into small silicone molds. Freeze.
- To make the ice cream, remove from molds and purée in a blender. Eat right away.

  If you don't have coffee beans, you can use ⅓ cup (40 g) ground coffee.

Vanilla – orange blossom ice cream

nuts*

∗

Serves 2 to 4 • Preparation: 15 minutes • Cooking time: 2 minutes • Freezing time: 2 hours

1 vanilla bean
1 cup + 2 tsp (250 g) plant-based beverage
3 tbsp + 1 tsp (45 g) granulated raw sugar
1⅓ tbsp (12 g) arrowroot starch
2 tsp (10 g) orange blossom water
¼ cup (50 g) aquafaba

- Split vanilla bean pod and scrape the seeds. Add seeds to a saucepan with plant-based beverage and heat. In a small bowl, whisk sugar with arrowroot starch. Add ¼ of the hot plant-based beverage, whisk, then pour the mixture into the saucepan.
- Keep whisking and bring to a boil.
- Refrigerate.
- When cooled, using an electric mixer, whip aquafaba until thick and glossy. Add orange blossom water and whipped aquafaba to the cream mixture.
- Pour into small silicone molds. Freeze.
- To make the ice cream, remove from molds, purée in a blender and eat right away.

* depending on the plant-based beverage used

Apricot thyme sorbet

Serves 2 to 4 • Preparation: 5 minutes • Freezing time: 2 hours

1⅓ cup (300 g) washed and stones removed apricots
6 tbsp + 2 tsp (100 g) apple juice
2 pinches dried lemon thyme
2 tbsp (40 g) honey

- In a blender, purée apricots, apple juice, thyme and honey.
- Pour into small silicone molds. Freeze.
- To make the sorbet, remove from molds and purée in a blender. Eat right away.

Pineapple coconut sorbet

Serves 2 to 4 • Preparation: 5 minutes • Freezing time: 2 hours

1⅓ cup (300 g) peeled, trimmed and chopped pineapple
6 tbsp + 2 tsp (100 g) coconut milk
Zest and juice of 1 lime
1 tbsp + 2 tsp (30 g) coconut cream

- In a blender, purée pineapple, coconut milk, lime juice and coconut cream.
- Stir in lime zest.
- Pour into small silicone molds. Freeze.
- To make the sorbet, remove from molds and purée in a blender. Eat right away.

Exotic mango, banana and passion fruit sorbet

Serves 2 to 4 • Preparation: 15 minutes • Freezing time: 2 hours

1¼ cup (200 g) peeled and stone removed mango
½ cup (100 g) peeled passion fruit
1 cup (90 g) peeled banana
2 tsp (8 g) grated gingerroot

- Purée mango, passion fruit, banana and ginger in a blender.
- Pour into small silicone molds. Freeze.
- To make the sorbet, remove from molds and purée in a blender. Eat right away.

Raspberry, lychee and galangal sorbet

Serves 2 to 4 • Preparation: 15 minutes • Freezing time: 2 hours

1 cup (200 g) peeled and stones removed lychees
1⅔ cup (200 g) raspberries
2½ tsp (10 g) grated galangal
2 tbsp (40 g) honey

- Peel the lychees and remove the stones.
- In a blender, purée lychees, raspberries, galangal and honey.
- Pour into small silicone molds. Freeze.
- To make the sorbet, remove from molds and purée in a blender. Eat right away.

Classic
recipes

Crepes

egg

nuts*

Makes 6 crepes • Preparation: 10 minutes • Resting time: 2 hours • Cooking time: 10 minutes

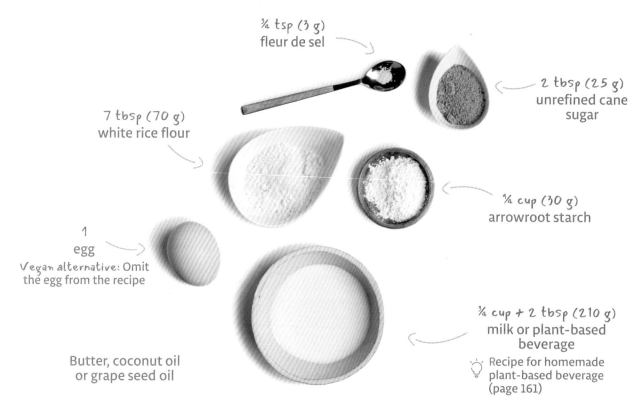

¾ tsp (3 g)
fleur de sel

2 tbsp (25 g)
unrefined cane
sugar

7 tbsp (70 g)
white rice flour

¼ cup (30 g)
arrowroot starch

1
egg
Vegan alternative: Omit
the egg from the recipe

¾ cup + 2 tbsp (210 g)
milk or plant-based
beverage
💡 Recipe for homemade
plant-based beverage
(page 161)

Butter, coconut oil
or grape seed oil

DIRECTIONS

- In a bowl, whisk together egg, milk, cane sugar and fleur de sel.
- In a large bowl, combine rice flour and arrowroot starch. Gradually pour in liquid and stir until the mixture is smooth.
- Let rest for 2 hours. Stir again.
- Heat a skillet with a little butter, coconut oil or grape seed oil. Using a ladle, pour batter into the skillet and rotate the pan to spread the batter over the whole surface. Cook until bottom is golden and, using a spatula, turn over the crepe and cook until the other side is golden.

Jazz it up

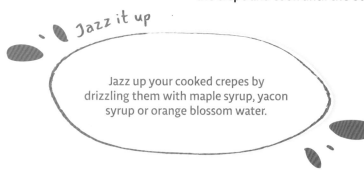

Jazz up your cooked crepes by drizzling them with maple syrup, yacon syrup or orange blossom water.

* depending on the plant-based beverage used

Waffles

gluten   egg   nuts*

Serves 4 • Preparation: 15 minutes • Cooking time: 20 minutes

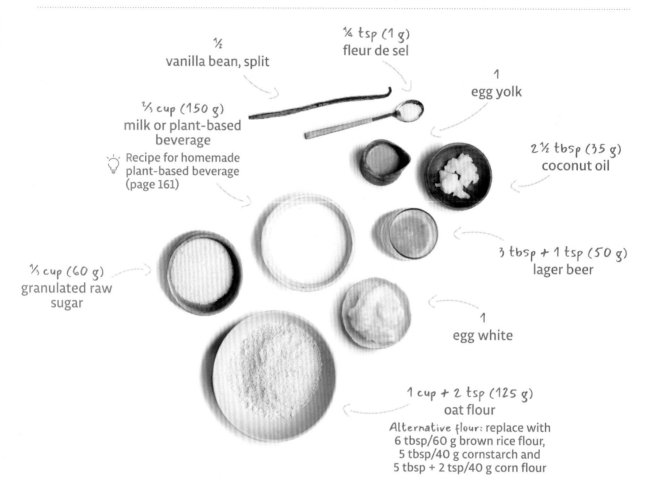

½
vanilla bean, split

¼ tsp (1 g)
fleur de sel

1
egg yolk

⅔ cup (150 g)
milk or plant-based
beverage

💡 Recipe for homemade
plant-based beverage
(page 161)

2½ tbsp (35 g)
coconut oil

3 tbsp + 1 tsp (50 g)
lager beer

⅓ cup (60 g)
granulated raw
sugar

1
egg white

1 cup + 2 tsp (125 g)
oat flour
Alternative flour: replace with
6 tbsp/60 g brown rice flour,
5 tbsp/40 g cornstarch and
5 tbsp + 2 tsp/40 g corn flour

DIRECTIONS

- In a small saucepan, heat milk over medium-low heat just until bubbles form around the edge; add coconut oil and let melt. Remove from heat and let cool.
- In a bowl, whisk together egg yolk with milk and beer.
- Sift the oat flour into a separate bowl. Add sugar, fleur de sel and seeds scraped from the vanilla bean.
- Gradually whisk the liquids into the dry ingredients.
- Let the batter rest in the fridge for 1 hour.
- In a bowl, using an electric mixer, whip the egg white until you get the texture of shaving cream and gently fold it into the mixture.
- Cook right away on a lightly greased waffle iron according to manufacturer's directions. Sprinkle with nut butter and poppy seeds, if desired.

TIP

Put a layer of batter onto the surface of the waffle iron, add hazelnut butter (or another nut butter) in the middle and add more batter on top. Cook.

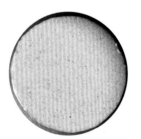

Vegan alternative 🌱

Omit the egg yolk; replace the egg white with 2 tbsp (30 g) aquafaba and add a pinch of turmeric.

* depending on the plant-based beverage used

Jazz it up

Jazz up your waffles
by adding lemon zest,
fennel seeds or ground
flax seeds.

Pancakes

egg   gluten

Makes 8 pancakes • Preparation: 15 minutes • Skillet cooking time: 15 minutes

½ tsp (2 g)
baking soda

2 tsp (3 g)
psyllium husk powder

2 tbsp + 1 tsp (30 g)
unrefined cane sugar

½ cup (125 g)
coconut milk

½ tsp (2 g)
lemon juice

½ cup (60 g)
whole spelt flour
Alternative flour:
replace with 6 tbsp/60 g
brown rice flour)

½
vanilla bean, split

1
egg
Vegan alternative: replace
with 4 tsp/20 g mashed
banana and additional
4 tsp/20 g coconut milk

¼ cup (40 g)
brown rice flour

DIRECTIONS

• In a bowl, whisk together egg and sugar.

• Whisk in coconut milk, flours and psyllium; add seeds scraped from the vanilla bean.

• In a small bowl, mix lemon juice and baking soda and add it to the batter.

• Heat a skillet, oil it lightly and, using a ladle, add about ¼ cup (60 mL) of batter per pancake.

• Cook for 1 minute until bottom is golden and, using a spatula, turn over the pancakes and cook until golden and firm.

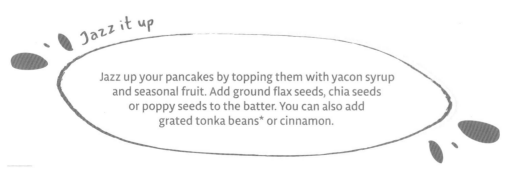

Jazz it up

Jazz up your pancakes by topping them with yacon syrup and seasonal fruit. Add ground flax seeds, chia seeds or poppy seeds to the batter. You can also add grated tonka beans* or cinnamon.

* Caution: tonka beans are banned in the US as they contain coumarin (an aromatic substance that is toxic for the body if too much is consumed; see page 128).

Chocolate babka

 gluten   nuts*

Makes 1 babka • Preparation the day before: 5 minutes • Preparation: 40 minutes
Resting time: 2 x 1 hour • Baking time: 20 minutes

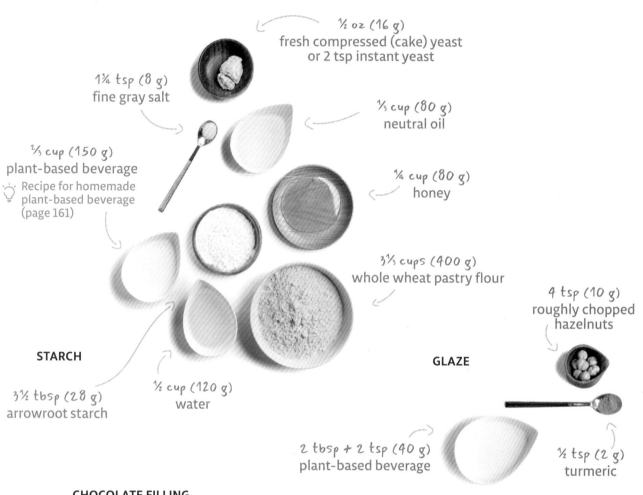

½ oz (16 g)
fresh compressed (cake) yeast
or 2 tsp instant yeast

1¼ tsp (8 g)
fine gray salt

⅓ cup (80 g)
neutral oil

⅔ cup (150 g)
plant-based beverage

¼ cup (80 g)
honey

Recipe for homemade
plant-based beverage
(page 161)

3⅓ cups (400 g)
whole wheat pastry flour

4 tsp (10 g)
roughly chopped
hazelnuts

STARCH

GLAZE

3½ tbsp (28 g)
arrowroot starch

½ cup (120 g)
water

2 tbsp + 2 tsp (40 g)
plant-based beverage

½ tsp (2 g)
turmeric

CHOCOLATE FILLING

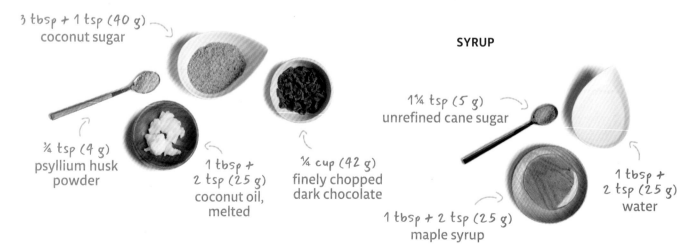

3 tbsp + 1 tsp (40 g)
coconut sugar

SYRUP

1¼ tsp (5 g)
unrefined cane sugar

¾ tsp (4 g)
psyllium husk
powder

1 tbsp +
2 tsp (25 g)
coconut oil,
melted

¼ cup (42 g)
finely chopped
dark chocolate

1 tbsp +
2 tsp (25 g)
water

1 tbsp + 2 tsp (25 g)
maple syrup

* depending on the plant-based beverage used

STARCH

- Make the starch the day before: in a saucepan, combine arrowroot with water. Cook over high heat and, using a whisk, stir until thickened. Let rest in the fridge for at least 2 hours.

BABKA

- In the bowl of a stand mixer using the dough hook, mix honey and yeast. Add flour, salt, oil and plant-based beverage. Knead the dough for 2 minutes.
- Add the starch mixture to the dough. Knead on medium speed for 10 minutes, until the dough pulls away from the sides of the bowl. Let rest for at least 1 hour at room temperature.

CHOCOLATE FILLING

- In a double boiler, melt dark chocolate with coconut oil.
- Stir in coconut sugar, then psyllium. Set aside.

ASSEMBLY

- Shape the dough into a rectangle.
- Using a spatula, spread the chocolate filling on the dough.
- Roll the dough lengthwise. Cut into two pieces and twist them around each other.
- Place the dough in a greased round 7-inch (18 cm) cake pan.
- Let rise for 1 hour at 86 °F (30 °C).
- Make the glaze by combining the plant-based beverage and turmeric.
- Using a brush, glaze the top of the babka and garnish with hazelnuts.
- Bake at 350 °F (180 °C) for about 20 minutes.

SYRUP

- Combine cane sugar, water and maple syrup. Boil. Let cool. Soak the cooked babka in the syrup.

Lemon cake

Makes 1 cake • Preparation: 20 minutes • Resting time: 1 hour • Baking time: 45 minutes

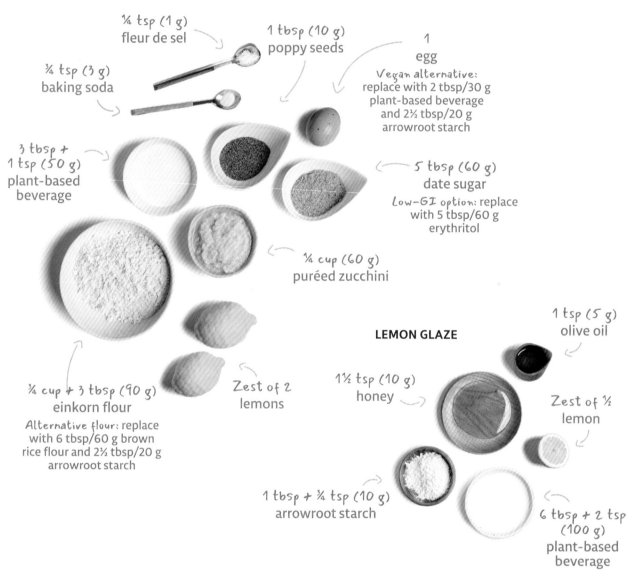

¼ tsp (1 g)
fleur de sel

1 tbsp (10 g)
poppy seeds

1
egg
Vegan alternative:
replace with 2 tbsp/30 g
plant-based beverage
and 2⅓ tbsp/20 g
arrowroot starch

¾ tsp (3 g)
baking soda

3 tbsp +
1 tsp (50 g)
plant-based
beverage

5 tbsp (60 g)
date sugar
Low-GI option: replace
with 5 tbsp/60 g
erythritol

¼ cup (60 g)
puréed zucchini

LEMON GLAZE

1 tsp (5 g)
olive oil

¾ cup + 3 tbsp (90 g)
einkorn flour
Alternative flour: replace
with 6 tbsp/60 g brown
rice flour and 2⅓ tbsp/20 g
arrowroot starch

Zest of 2
lemons

1½ tsp (10 g)
honey

Zest of ½
lemon

1 tbsp + ¾ tsp (10 g)
arrowroot starch

6 tbsp + 2 tsp
(100 g)
plant-based
beverage

CAKE

- Combine flour with zucchini and date sugar.
- Add plant-based beverage, egg, baking soda, lemon zest, poppy seeds and fleur de sel.
- Pour batter into a greased 5- by 1.5-inch (12 by 4 cm) deep round cake pan. Bake in 325 °F (160 °C) oven for 20 minutes.

LEMON GLAZE

- Heat plant-based beverage with arrowroot starch and honey. Whisk until thickened. Off the heat, add olive oil and lemon zest.
- Glaze the cake once it has been removed from the pan and has cooled.

Jazz it up

Jazz up your lemon cake by adding grated gingerroot, ground cardamom or tea powder (see page 161) to the cake batter.

Banana bread

gluten

Makes 1 loaf • Preparation: 20 minutes • Resting time: 1 hour • Baking time: 45 minutes

1
egg
Vegan alternative: replace with 4 tsp/10 g cornstarch, 4 tsp/20 g oil and 4 tsp/20 g mashed banana

¼ cup (60 g) grape seed oil

1½ tbsp (20 g) granulated raw sugar

4 g baking soda

1½ tbsp/20 g unrefined cane sugar

⅓ cup (40 g) green banana flour

¾ tsp (4 g) lemon juice

1 whole banana + 1 for decoration

4 tsp (20 g) yacon syrup or maple syrup (1) + 4 tsp (20 g) for decoration (2)

6 tbsp (60 g) brown rice flour

⅔ cup (160 g) mashed banana

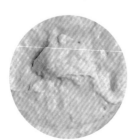

DIRECTIONS

- Peel one banana and cut it lengthwise and then in half crosswise.
- Arrange the banana pieces on the bottom of a greased 5- by 1.5-inch (12 by 4 cm) deep round cake pan and drizzle with syrup (1).
- In a bowl, whisk together mashed banana with oil and egg. Stir in sugars and sifted flours. Combine baking soda with lemon juice and stir it into the cake mixture.
- Pour the cake mixture over bananas in the pan.
- Bake at 300 °F (150 °C) for 45 minutes.
- After removing the cake from the pan, decorate with a diagonally sliced banana and drizzle with syrup (2).

Jazz it up

Jazz up your banana bread by adding to the batter some four-spice mixture (equal amounts of nutmeg, clove, cinnamon and ginger), citrus zest or chopped nuts or by replacing the grape seed oil with peanut oil.

Carrot cake

gluten   egg   nuts

Makes 1 cake • Preparation: 20 minutes • Resting time: 1 hour • Baking time: 45 minutes

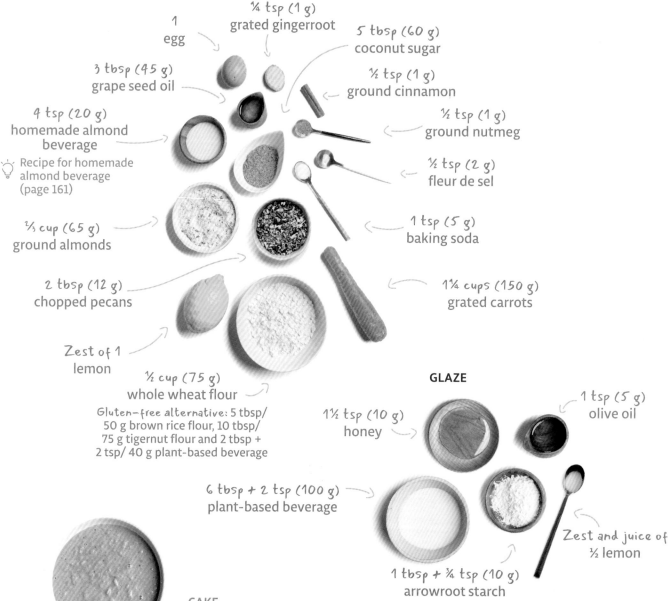

1
egg

¼ tsp (1 g)
grated gingerroot

5 tbsp (60 g)
coconut sugar

3 tbsp (45 g)
grape seed oil

½ tsp (1 g)
ground cinnamon

4 tsp (20 g)
homemade almond
beverage

Recipe for homemade
almond beverage
(page 161)

½ tsp (1 g)
ground nutmeg

½ tsp (2 g)
fleur de sel

⅔ cup (65 g)
ground almonds

1 tsp (5 g)
baking soda

2 tbsp (12 g)
chopped pecans

1¼ cups (150 g)
grated carrots

Zest of 1
lemon

½ cup (75 g)
whole wheat flour

Gluten-free alternative: 5 tbsp/
50 g brown rice flour, 10 tbsp/
75 g tigernut flour and 2 tbsp +
2 tsp/ 40 g plant-based beverage

GLAZE

1½ tsp (10 g)
honey

1 tsp (5 g)
olive oil

6 tbsp + 2 tsp (100 g)
plant-based beverage

1 tbsp + ¾ tsp (10 g)
arrowroot starch

Zest and juice of
½ lemon

Vegan alternative

Replace egg with ¼ cup
(30 g) grated carrot, 2½ tbsp
(20 g) arrowroot starch
and 2 tbsp + 2 tsp (40 g)
plant-based beverage.

CAKE

• In a standard mixer fitted with a paddle attachment, combine all ingredients.
• Pour the mixture into a greased 5- by 1.5-inch (12 by 4 cm) deep round cake pan.
• Bake at 325 °F (160 °C) for 45 minutes.
• Let the cake cool.

GLAZE

• Heat the plant-based beverage with arrowroot starch and honey. Whisk until thickened. Off the heat, add the oil, lemon juice and zest.
• Cover the cake with the glaze.

Marble cake

egg   nuts

Makes 1 cake • Preparation: 20 minutes • Resting time: 30 minutes • Baking time: 25 minutes

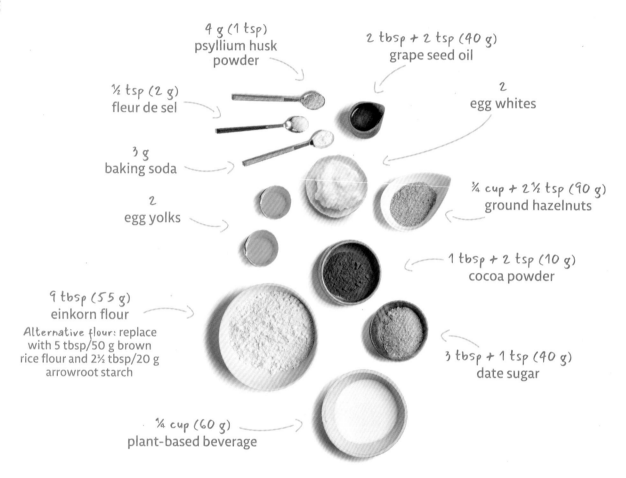

4 g (1 tsp)
psyllium husk
powder

2 tbsp + 2 tsp (40 g)
grape seed oil

½ tsp (2 g)
fleur de sel

2
egg whites

3 g
baking soda

¾ cup + 2½ tsp (90 g)
ground hazelnuts

2
egg yolks

1 tbsp + 2 tsp (10 g)
cocoa powder

9 tbsp (55 g)
einkorn flour

Alternative flour: replace
with 5 tbsp/50 g brown
rice flour and 2½ tbsp/20 g
arrowroot starch

3 tbsp + 1 tsp (40 g)
date sugar

¼ cup (60 g)
plant-based beverage

Vegan alternative

Replace the egg whites with
¼ cup (60 g) aquafaba and
the yolks with 2 tbsp (30 g)
plant-based beverage.

DIRECTIONS

- In a bowl, using an electric mixer, beat egg whites until stiff peaks form.
- In a large bowl, using an electric mixer, beat sugar with the ground hazelnuts, psyllium, egg yolks and fleur de sel. Sift einkorn flour with the baking soda and beat into the hazelnut mixture.
- Mix in plant-based beverage and oil. Gently fold in the beaten egg whites.
- Divide the mixture into two equal portions and fold cocoa powder into one.
- Into a greased 5- by 1.5-inch (12 by 4 cm) deep round cake pan, pour ⅓ of the plain batter and ⅓ of the chocolate batter. Repeat the process two more times and, using a spatula, swirl the batter to give it a marbled look.
- Place the pan in the fridge for 30 minutes.
- Bake at 325 °F (160 °C) for 20 minutes.

Jazz it up

Jazz up your marble cake, once it has cooled, by brushing the top of the cake with argan oil or grape seed oil. You can also sprinkle raw cocoa nibs on top.

nuts

Brownie
❦

Makes 1 brownie cake • Preparation: 20 minutes • Baking time: 20 minutes

**6 tbsp (90 g)
plant-based beverage**
💡 Recipe for homemade
plant-based beverage
(page 161)

**3 tbsp (40 g)
unrefined cane sugar**
Alternative sugar:
replace with 2⅓ tbsp/30 g
coconut sugar or 2 tbsp/30 g
yacon or maple syrup)

**4 tsp (10 g)
cornstarch or
2 tsp/5 g
arrowroot starch**

**10 tbsp (60 g)
ground
almonds**

**1 tsp (5 g)
baking soda**

**¼ tsp (1 g)
fleur de sel**

**1 tsp (5 g)
cocoa powder**

**1 tsp (5 g)
lemon juice**

**6½ tbsp (70 g)
chopped 66% dark
chocolate**

**1½ tbsp (15 g)
brown rice flour**

**3 tbsp (50 g)
applesauce**

**6 tbsp + 2 tsp (50 g)
chopped pecans
or hazelnuts**

DIRECTIONS

- Using a double boiler, melt the chocolate.
- In a small saucepan, bring plant-based beverage to a simmer and pour it over the chocolate in three pours. Whisk. Add applesauce, then sugar. Sift flour, cornstarch and cocoa powder. Add to the mixture with the ground almonds, fleur de sel and chopped nuts.
- Combine baking soda and lemon juice and add to the batter.
- Grease a 5- by 1.5-inch (12 by 4 cm) deep round cake pan and fill it no more than three-quarters full with batter.
- Bake at 160 °C for about 20 minutes.

Jazz it up

Jazz up your brownie by adding chicory or instant coffee to the batter.

You can also add sesame seeds or ground flaxseed.

Madeleines with lemon zest

egg

Makes 6 madeleines • Preparation: 20 minutes • Resting time: 30 minutes • Baking time: 10 minutes

4 tsp (20 g)
butter, melted

2 tsp (15 g)
honey

2 tbsp + 1 tsp (30 g)
granulated raw sugar

1
egg

2 tbsp + 1 tsp (30 g)
unrefined cane sugar

Low-GI option: Add ¾ tsp/3 g psyllium powder and replace the sugars with 6 tbsp + 2 tsp/80 g erythritol

2 tsp (10 g)
plant-based
beverage

½
vanilla bean, split

¾ tsp (3 g)
baking soda

¾ tsp (3 g)
lemon juice

6 tbsp + 2 tsp (50 g)
whole wheat pastry
flour

Alternative flour: replace
with ¼ cup + 1½ tsp/45 g
brown rice flour and 1 tbsp
+ ¾ tsp/10 g arrowroot
starch)

Zest of 1
lemon

¼ tsp (1 g)
fleur de sel

DIRECTIONS

- In a bowl, using a whisk, mix egg, sugars, lemon zest and seeds scraped from the vanilla bean.
- Add flour, then plant-based beverage, fleur de sel and butter.
- In a small bowl, mix baking soda and lemon juice. Add to the batter.
- Let rest in the fridge 30 minutes.
- Using a brush, grease the madeleine molds with oil.
- Spoon the madeleine mixture into the molds to fill each mold about three-quarters full.
- Preheat the oven to 375 °F (190 °C) and bake for 10 minutes.
- Remove the pan from the oven and, using a spatula, remove the madeleines right away. Brush the madeleines with honey.

Jazz it up

Jazz up your madeleines by
adding chia seeds, poppy seeds,
tea powder, orange blossom
water or dried chamomile
flowers to the batter.

Vegan alternative

6 tbsp + 2 tsp (50 g) whole wheat pastry flour (T80)
1 tbsp + ½ tsp (15 g) granulated raw sugar
Zest of 1 lemon
½ vanilla bean, split
2 tbsp + 2 tsp (40 g) plant-based beverage
¼ tsp (1 g) fleur de sel
4 tsp (20 g) grape seed oil
¼ tsp (1 g) baking soda
¼ tsp (1 g) lemon juice

- Mix flour with sugar, lemon zest and seeds scraped from the vanilla bean. Add plant-based beverage, fleur de sel and oil.
- In a small bowl, mix baking soda and lemon juice. Add to the batter.
- Let rest in the fridge for 30 minutes.

- Spoon the madeleine mixture into the molds to fill each mold about three-quarters full.
- Preheat the oven to 375 °F (190 °C) and bake for 10 minutes.
- Remove the pan from the oven and, using a spatula, remove the madeleines right away. Brush the madeleines with honey.

Financiers

egg

nuts

Makes 15 financiers • Preparation: 20 minutes • Baking time: 12 minutes

¾ tsp (3 g)
fleur de sel

3 tbsp + 1½ tsp (45 g)
unrefined cane sugar

6 tbsp + 1½ tsp (60 g)
poppy seeds

3
egg whites
Vegan alternative:
replace with 6 tbsp/90 g
plant-based beverage)

1½ cup (20 g)
slivered almonds

2 tbsp (45 g)
honey
Low-GI option: replace
with 2 tbsp/30 g yacon
syrup

3½ tbsp (45 g)
brown rice flour

1 cup (105 g)
ground almonds

2 tbsp (30 g)
butter, melted

DIRECTIONS

- Using a spatula, mix egg white with honey and cane sugar. Add fleur de sel, rice flour and ground almonds.
- Mix and add butter.
- Grease individual financier molds of 1.5-inch (4 cm) diameter and spoon batter into each mold about two-thirds full.
- Sprinkle poppy seeds and slivered almonds on top.
- Bake at 325F (160 °C) for 12 minutes.

Jazz it up

Jazz up your financiers by flavoring the batter with orange blossom water, elderflower (infused in warm oil) or tea powder. Once they are baked, brush them with a thin layer of cocoa butter and arrange dried flower petals, such as lavender, rose or cornflower, on top.

Cookies

eggs nuts

Makes 8 to 10 cookies • Preparation: 20 minutes • Resting time: 1 hour • Baking time: 12 minutes

1
egg

3 tbsp + 1 tsp (50 g)
grape seed oil

2 tsp + 2 tsp (40 g)
hazelnut butter

¾ tsp (3 g)
psyllium husk
powder

2 tbsp + 1 tsp (30 g)
unrefined cane sugar

¼ tsp (1 g)
fleur de sel

1½ tbsp (30 g)
honey

¼ cup (40 g)
chopped
chocolate or chips

1⅓ cups (125 g)
einkorn flour
Alternative flour: replace
with 3 tbsp + 2¾ tsp/30 g
cornstarch and 7 tbsp/70 g
brown rice flour

PREPARATION

- In the bowl of a stand mixer fitted with the paddle attachment, mix all ingredients until the dough is well blended.
- Let rest in the fridge for 1 hour.
- Roll the dough into 8 to 10 balls, space apart on a parchment paper-lined baking sheet and press down lightly.
- Bake at 350 °F (180 °C) for 12 minutes. Let cool and drizzle with honey, if desired.

Vegan alternative

Omit the egg and add 1 tbsp + 2 tsp (25 g) plant-based beverage. Press down the balls of dough before baking.

Crème caramel
ᆞᆞ

Serves 1 • Preparation: 20 minutes • Saucepan cooking time: 10 minutes • Refrigeration time: 2 hours

nuts*

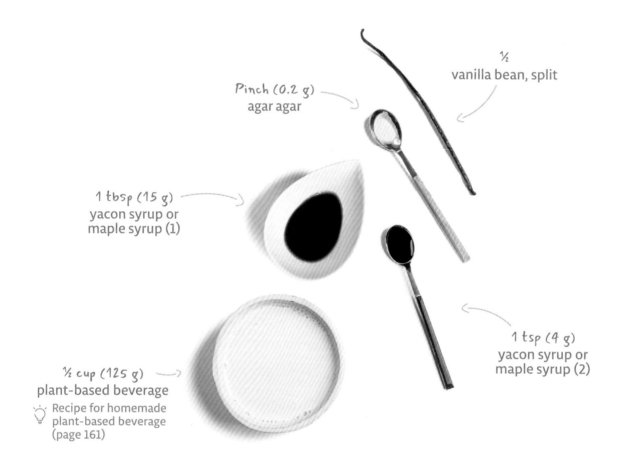

Pinch (0.2 g)
agar agar

½
vanilla bean, split

1 tbsp (15 g)
yacon syrup or
maple syrup (1)

1 tsp (4 g)
yacon syrup or
maple syrup (2)

½ cup (125 g)
plant-based beverage
Recipe for homemade
plant-based beverage
(page 161)

PREPARATION

- Pour the syrup (1) into the bottom of a ramekin and freeze.
- In a saucepan, combine plant-based beverage and syrup (2) with agar agar and the seeds scraped from the vanilla bean and heat gently.
- Bring to a boil.
- Pour into the ramekin containing the frozen syrup.
- Refrigerate for 2 hours, then gently unmold.

* depending on the plant-based beverage used

Chocolate mousse with fleur de sel

nuts*

Serves 4 • Preparation: 20 minutes • Saucepan cooking time: 2 minutes • Refrigeration time: 1 hour

¼ tsp (1 g)
grated gingerroot

¼ cup (60 g)
almond beverage

💡 Recipe for homemade plant-based beverage (page 161)

3
egg whites

Vegan alternative: replace with 7 tbsp/90 g aquafaba

¼ tsp (1 g)
fleur de sel

3⅓ oz (100 g)
64% dark chocolate, chopped
(use raw chocolate to enjoy all its nutritional benefits)
Low GI alternative: use sugar-free chocolate)

PREPARATION

- In a double boiler, melt chocolate.
- In a saucepan, heat plant-based beverage for 30 seconds and pour it over the chocolate.
- Using an immersion blender, emulsify until you get a smooth and glossy ganache. Let cool 15 minutes in the fridge.
- Using an electric mixer, beat the egg whites into firm peaks and using a spatula, gradually add the chocolate ganache.
- Fold in fleur de sel and ginger.
- Pour into glass bowls or small dishes.
- Refrigerate for 1 hour.

Jazz it up

Jazz up your chocolate mousse by adding raw cacao nibs or replacing the ginger with grated tonka bean,* ground cardamom or chicory powder.

* Caution: tonka beans are banned in the US as they contain coumarin (an aromatic substance that is toxic for the body if too much is consumed; see page 128).

Energy balls

nuts

Preparation: 20 minutes

3 tbsp (20 g)
dried banana slices

½ tsp (5 g)
flax seeds

7 tbsp (70 g)
pitted dates

⅔ cup (60 g)
chestnut flour

6 tbsp (45 g)
whole almonds

3½ tbsp (35 g)
dried cranberries

1 cup + 3 tbsp (140 g)
dried apricots

¾ cup + 4 tsp (100 g)
unsweetened
desiccated coconut

PREPARATION

- In a food processor, combine banana slices, flax seeds, dates, chestnut flour, almonds, apricots, cranberries and coconut; pulse to blend.
- Roll batter into bite-size balls.
- Store in a sealed container at room temperature for one week or freeze for up to one month.

Jazz it up

Jazz up these energy balls by adding sesame seeds, sunflower seeds or bee pollen. You can replace the chestnut flour with ½ cup (60 g) green banana flour.

Healthy Bounty bars

Makes 5 bars • Preparation: 45 minutes • Freezing time: 1 hour

1½ tsp (10 g)
honey

2 tsp (10 g)
coconut oil

⅔ cup (150 g)
coconut milk

CHOCOLATE COATING

5 oz (150 g)
66% dark chocolate,
chopped

¾ cup + 4 tsp (100 g)
unsweetened desiccated
coconut

4 tsp (20 g)
grape seed oil

COCONUT BAR

- In a bowl, mix all ingredients, then divide to fill 5 sections of 5 x 1-inch (12 x 2.5 cm) silicone finger molds. Place in the freezer for 1 hour, remove from mold and dip in the chocolate coating.

CHOCOLATE COATING

- In a double boiler, melt chocolate with oil at 45 °C.
- Using a fork, dip the coconut bars. Tap to remove excess chocolate and let set on parchment paper or a silicon mat.

Jazz it up

Jazz up your homemade coconut bars by adding chia seeds or raw cacao nibs to the coconut mixture. Dress up your bars by dipping them in desiccated coconut before the chocolate sets or drizzle them with some of the melted chocolate.

Healthy Snickers bars

peanuts

Makes 10 bars • Preparation: 45 minutes • Freezing time: 1 hour

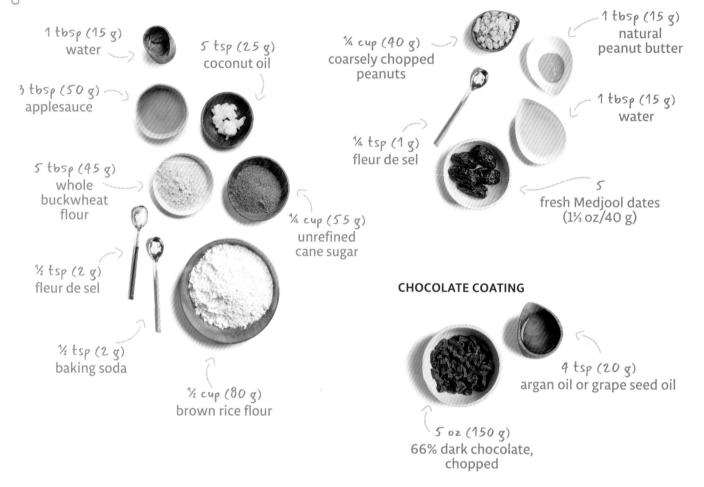

SHORTBREAD BASE

1 tbsp (15 g) water

5 tsp (25 g) coconut oil

3 tbsp (50 g) applesauce

5 tbsp (45 g) whole buckwheat flour

½ tsp (2 g) fleur de sel

½ tsp (2 g) baking soda

¼ cup (55 g) unrefined cane sugar

½ cup (80 g) brown rice flour

HEALTHY CARAMEL

¼ cup (40 g) coarsely chopped peanuts

1 tbsp (15 g) natural peanut butter

1 tbsp (15 g) water

¼ tsp (1 g) fleur de sel

5 fresh Medjool dates (1⅓ oz/40 g)

CHOCOLATE COATING

4 tsp (20 g) argan oil or grape seed oil

5 oz (150 g) 66% dark chocolate, chopped

SHORTBREAD BASE

- In a stand mixer fitted with the paddle attachment, beat cane sugar and coconut oil.
- Add applesauce and water. Beat until blended.
- Gradually add fleur de sel, flours and baking soda.
- Roll until ⅓ inch (1 cm) thick between two pieces of parchment paper.
- Cut strips of dough the size of 5 x 1-inch (12 x 2.5 cm) silicone finger cookie molds and place them in the molds.
- Bake at 340F (170 °C) for 20 minutes. Let cookies cool in molds.

HEALTHY CARAMEL

- In food processor, purée dates with peanut butter and water until smooth.
- Stir in fleur de sel. Pipe about 1 tbsp (15 g) of caramel into the silicone molds, on top of the baked shortbread, then sprinkle with peanuts and press them in well.
- Place in the freezer for 1 hour.

CHOCOLATE COATING

- In a double boiler, melt dark chocolate with the oil at 45 °C, then, using a fork, dip the bars in it.
- Let set on a silicone mat or a baking mat.

Original
creations

Buckwheat vanilla
mille feuille

᠆ᢆ᠆

MAKES 10 PASTRIES

QUICK PUFF PASTRY • ½ cup + 4 tsp (190 g) **spelt flour** • 7 tbsp (60 g) **buckwheat flour** • ½ cup (125 g) **water**, cold • ⅔ cup (150 g) **butter**, cold, diced in ½-inch (1 cm) cubes • 1¼ tsp (5 g) **fleur de sel** • **unrefined cane sugar**, for sprinkling

VANILLA PASTRY CREAM • 2 cups (500 g) **plant-based beverage** • 1½ tbsp (30 g) **honey** • 1 **vanilla bean** • 2 **egg yolks** • 6 tbsp (50 g) **cornstarch or potato starch** • ¼ cup (60 g) **coconut oil** • pinch **turmeric powder**

BUCKWHEAT PRALINE • 1 cup (200 g) **whole grain buckwheat** • 1¾ cup (200 g) **almonds**, chopped • ½ cup + 5 tsp (200 g) **yacon syrup or maple syrup** • 1¼ tsp (5 g) **fleur de sel**

QUICK PUFF PASTRY

In a food processor, combine flours with cold water and fleur de sel.

Add butter and mix until combined with small pieces of butter still visible in the dough.

Place the dough on the worktop and turn it into a ball.

Roll it out into a rectangle that is three times longer than it is wide.

Fold the first third to the middle of the dough and the last third up and over the first fold.

Turn the dough a quarter turn so the fold is on your right.

You have just given your dough one turn. Repeat these three steps to give it another turn.

Refrigerate, covered, for 30 minutes.

Give the dough another two turns, as explained above.

Refrigerate for 30 minutes and give the dough two final turns.

Refrigerate for 30 minutes.

Roll the dough into a 12- x 8-inch (30 x 20 cm) rectangle, then prick the dough. Place the puff pastry on a baking sheet lined with parchment paper. Place another sheet of parchment paper and then a baking sheet on top. Bake at 350 °F (180 °C) for 15 minutes.

Remove top baking sheet, sprinkle with unrefined cane sugar and bake for another 5 minutes, or until caramelized.

VANILLA PASTRY CREAM

In a saucepan, heat plant-based beverage with honey and seeds scraped from the vanilla bean.

In a small bowl, whisk together egg yolks and starch. Add a small amount of the liquid to the yolk mixture and stir. Add this mixture to the contents of the saucepan and bring to a boil, stirring constantly.

Take off the heat and add coconut oil and turmeric powder.

Store in the fridge.

BUCKWHEAT PRALINE

In the oven, toast buckwheat and almonds on a baking sheet at 325 °F (160 °C) for 12 minutes.

When the mixture is cool, combine with syrup and fleur de sel.

ASSEMBLY

Using a serrated knife, cut out identical rectangles of puff pastry.

Pipe the vanilla pastry cream between each layer of puff pastry and on top.

Decorate with the buckwheat praline.

Almond croissants

ᐧᐧᐧ

MAKES 10 PASTRIES

CROISSANT DOUGH • ¾ cup + 4 tsp (200 g) **water** • 1 oz (30 g) **fresh compressed yeast** (or 1 tbsp + ¾ tsp/14 g instant dry yeast) • 1 cup (150 g) **brown rice flour** • 1 cup (140 g) **buckwheat flour** • ⅔ cup (80 g) **tapioca starch** • 7 tbsp (80 g) **potato starch** • 1 tsp (5 g) **psyllium husk powder** • 2 tsp (5 g) **guar gum** • 3 tbsp (60 g) **honey** • 2¼ tsp (10 g) **gray salt** • 5 tsp (25 g) soft **homemade margarine*** (1) • ¾ cup + 4 tsp (200 g) **homemade margarine*** (2), chilled

ALMOND FILLING • ½ cup + 5 tsp (60 g) **ground almonds** • 4 tsp (20 g) soft **homemade margarine*** • 2 tbsp (30 g) **almond butter** • 2 tbsp + 1 tsp (30 g) **coconut sugar** • 2 tbsp (30 g) **water**

GLAZE • 1 pinch **turmeric powder** • 3 tbsp + 1 tsp (50 g) **plant-based beverage** • ¾ cup (100 g) **sliced almonds**

*recipe on page 160

In the bowl of a stand mixer fitted with the dough hook, in order, add water, yeast, flours, starches, psyllium and guar gum on top.

Add honey, salt and margarine (1).

Mix on low speed for 2 minutes, then 2 minutes at medium speed.

Remove the dough from the bowl. Make a ball, folding in all the sides toward the center. Place the ball in a bowl and cover with a tea towel.

Let dough rest in the fridge for 1 hour.

ALMOND FILLING

Meanwhile, combine almonds, margarine, almond butter, sugar and water; cover and refrigerate.

Using a rolling pin, shape the cold margarine (2) into a rectangle. Roll out the dough into a rectangle, double the size of the margarine rectangle. Place the margarine in the middle of the dough and fold over the remaining dough on both sides.

Roll out the dough to make an even rectangle. Fold this long rectangle in three: fold the first third to the middle of the dough and the last third up and over the first fold. Turn the dough a quarter turn so the fold is on your right.

Repeat this process a second time. Let the dough rest for 30 minutes in the fridge, covered with parchment paper.

Repeat the process a third time.

Roll out into a 16 x 24-inch (40 x 60 cm) rectangle. Cut the dough in half lengthwise. Cut the pieces of dough into even triangles to get the same size of croissants.

Cut a notch in the middle of the base of a triangle. Pull lightly on the croissant without tearing it.

Pipe the almond filling into the middle of the triangle.

Roll up the dough to make the croissant shape.

Place the croissants on parchment paper on a baking sheet. Let rise 2 hours in a humid area at 77 °F (25 °C).

GLAZE

Mix turmeric powder with plant-based beverage and, using a brush, glaze the croissants.

Pipe some almond filling on the top and sprinkle with sliced almonds.

Bake for 20 minutes at 350 °F (180 °C).

Coffee, raw cocoa and argan oil éclat

˙·

MAKES 10 PASTRIES

COFFEE SWEET TART CRUST • ¼ cup (60 g) **vegan margarine** • ¼ cup (50 g) **unrefined cane sugar** • ½ cup (80 g) **brown rice flour** • 7 tbsp (70 g) **all-purpose flour** • 5 tsp (25 g) **water** • ¼ tsp (1 g) **fleur de sel** • 1 tbsp (6 g) **instant coffee**

GENOA CAKE • ½ cup (140 g) **almond paste** • 1 **egg** • 4 tbsp (30 g) **chestnut flour**

DARK CHOCOLATE-ALMOND CRUNCH • ½ cup (80 g) **dark chocolate, 70%** • 3 tbsp (25 g) **cocoa nibs** • ½ cup (50 g) **chopped almonds** • ¼ cup (65 g) **almond butter** • 2 tbsp (30 g) **argan oil**

COFFEE SYRUP • ¾ cup + 4 tsp (200 g) **water** • ¼ cup + 2 tsp (20 g) **instant coffee** • ¼ cup (30 g) **yacon syrup or maple syrup**

COFFEE–MILK CHOCOLATE CREAM • 6 tbsp + 2 tsp (100 g) **cream or plant-based cream** • 6 tbsp + 2 tsp (100 g) **milk or plant-based beverage** • ⅛ tsp (0,5 g) **agar agar** • 1 **egg yolk** • ½ cup (80 g) **chopped milk chocolate, 33%** • 1 tbsp + 2 tsp (25 g) **argan oil** • 1 tsp (5 g) **ground coffee**

VANILLA MOUSSE • ⅓ cup (75 g) **cream or plant-based cream** (1) • 1 **vanilla bean** • 1 tbsp + 1 tsp (20 g) **brown sugar** • ¼ tsp (1 g) **agar agar** • ⅔ cup + 2 tbsp (175 g) **cream or plant-based cream** (2)

CHOCOLATE GLAZE • 3 tbsp + 1 tsp (50 g) **water** • 3½ sheets (7 g) **gelatin**, rehydrated • 2 tbsp + 1 tsp (50 g) **yacon syrup or maple syrup** • ½ cup (80 g) **dark chocolate, 64%** • ¼ cup + 1 tsp (65 g) **cream or plant-based cream**

CHOCOLATE GLAZE

In a saucepan, bring water and cream to a boil. Remove from heat. Add softened gelatin sheets. Add syrup and pour the mixture over the chocolate. Let rest in the fridge overnight, covered with parchment paper.

VANILLA MOUSSE

In a saucepan, heat cream (1) with vanilla bean seeds and the split bean. Add brown sugar. Bring to a boil and let steep, covered, for 30 minutes. Strain, return to saucepan, add agar agar and bring to a boil. Add cream (2). Emulsify with a hand blender. Refrigerate for at least 3 hours.

COFFEE SWEET TART CRUST

In a bowl, combine margarine with sugar. Add flours, then water, fleur de sel and instant coffee. Roll out to ⅛-inch (2 mm) between two sheets of parchment paper. Using a rectangular cookie cutter 1 x 5-inch (2.5 x 12 cm), cut out 10 bases. Bake at 340 °F (170 °C) for 12 to 15 minutes.

DARK CHOCOLATE-ALMOND CRUNCH

Using a double boiler, melt dark chocolate at 115 °F (45 °C). Crush the raw cocoa nibs. Mix all ingredients and pour into a 11 x 8-inch (28 x 20 cm) pan. Refrigerate until hardened.

GENOA CAKE

Using an electric mixer, combine almond paste and egg until smooth and creamy.

Using a spatula, fold in chestnut flour. Pour the mixture into a 11 x 8-inch (28 x 20 cm) pan and bake at 325 °F (160 °C) for 12 minutes. Let cool and remove from pan.

COFFEE SYRUP

In a saucepan, heat water and instant coffee. Off the heat, add syrup. Place the Genoa cake on top of the dark chocolate-almond crunch and drizzle with coffee syrup.

COFFEE–MILK CHOCOLATE CREAM

In a saucepan, heat cream, milk and agar agar. Bring to a boil and remove from heat. Add egg yolk and whisk vigorously. Pour slowly over the milk chocolate and emulsify. Mix in argan oil and ground coffee. Pour the cream on the Genoa cake. Freeze for 1 hour. Cut out rectangles slightly smaller than the final shape.

ASSEMBLY

Using rectangular 1 x 5-inch (2.5 x 12 cm) silicone molds, add the vanilla mousse and, using an offset spatula, spread the mousse around the whole mold. Add the crunch-Genoa cake-coffee cream layer and smooth, using a spatula. Freeze for 2 hours and unmold onto a rack. In a double boiler, heat the chocolate glaze to 85 °F (30 °C) and glaze the éclat. Place each éclat on a tart base. Whip the vanilla mousse until fluffy. Using a piping bag and a round piping tip #8, pipe the vanilla mousse along the top and garnish with ground coffee and a chocolate decoration, if desired.

Berry and orange blossom cheesecakes

MAKES 10 INDIVIDUAL CHEESECAKES

SWEET TART CRUST • 3 tbsp + 1 tsp (50 g) **butter or margarine** • 3 tbsp (40 g) **brown sugar** • 1 tbsp + 1 tsp (20 g) **water** • ½ cup (66 g) **buckwheat flour** • ½ cup (60 g) **whole wheat flour** • 1 tbsp + 2 tsp (21 g) **fleur de sel**

RECONSTITUTED SWEET TART CRUST • 1 recipe **sweet tart crust** • 3 tbsp (40 g) **cocoa butter** • ¼ tsp (1 g) **fleur de sel** • 1 tbsp (15 g) **buckwheat flakes** • 1 tbsp + 1 tsp (15 g) **sesame seeds** • Zest of ½ **lemon** • **dried flower petals** (optional)

BERRY GELÉE • ¾ tsp (2 g) **food-grade sodium alginate powder** • 1 tsp (3 g) **unrefined cane sugar** • ¼ cup (30 g) **red currants** • 3 tbsp (25 g) **raspberries** • 2½ tbsp (25 g) **sliced strawberries** • Zest and juice of ½ **lemon** • 1½ tsp (7 g) **orange blossom water**

LIME CHEESECAKE • 1 oz (30 g) **celery root**, washed, peeled and quartered • ⅓ cup + 2 tbsp (85 g) **cream cheese** • 2 tbsp (25 g) **coconut oil** • 2 tbsp + 2 tsp (40 g) **almond butter** • 1½ tbsp (30 g) **honey** • Zest and juice of 1 **lime** • 2 tbsp (30 g) **coconut cream**

ORANGE BLOSSOM WHIPPED CREAM • ⅔ cup (150 g) 35% **cream or coconut cream** • ½ tbsp (10 g) **honey** • 1 tsp (5 g) **orange blossom water**

RED SPRAY • ¼ cup + 3 tbsp (100 g) **cocoa butter** • ¼ cup + 1 tbsp (80 g) **cashew butter** • 1 tsp (3 g) **beetroot powder**

SWEET TART CRUST

In the bowl of a stand mixer fitted with the paddle attachment, combine butter or margarine with brown sugar. Add water, flours and fleur de sel and combine.

Roll out between two pieces of parchment paper to ½-inch (1 cm) thick. Bake at 325 °F (160 °C) for 20 minutes.

RECONSTITUTED SWEET TART CRUST

Cut the baked sweet tart crust into ½-inch (1 cm) cubes. Melt cocoa butter and pour over the sweet tart crust cubes. Mix gently. Add buckwheat flakes, sesame seeds, zest and petals. Divide into 10 portions and press down to make thin biscuits that are 2½ inches (6 cm) in diameter.

BERRY GELÉE

In a small bowl, combine alginate with cane sugar. In a tall cup, combine the berries. Add orange blossom water, zest and lemon juice. Add the alginate mixture and, using an immersion blender, purée for 1 minute. Pour into 1½-inch (4-cm) round molds to make discs and freeze.

LIME CHEESECAKE

Steam celery root and, using a blender, purée until smooth. Add cream cheese and blend. Melt coconut oil and add to the mixture. Add almond butter, honey and lime zest and juice. Using an electric mixer, whip coconut cream until fluffy and gently fold it into the mixture. Pour the mixture into semi-circular molds that are 2½ inches (6 cm) in diameter, inserting the berry gelée discs in the center of the cheesecake mixture. Freeze for 2 hours.

ORANGE BLOSSOM WHIPPED CREAM

Whip the cream until thick; whisk in the honey and orange blossom water.

RED SPRAY

In the microwave, melt cocoa butter. Pour it over the cashew butter in a tall cup. Add beetroot powder and using an immersion blender, emulsify. Strain and refrigerate until ready to use.

ASSEMBLY

Unmold the lime cheesecakes.

Heat the red spray in a saucepan to 105 °F (40 °C) and, using a wooden skewer, dip the cheesecake in the spray. Place on the reconstituted sweet tart crust. Using a piping bag with a round tip #8, pipe the orange blossom whipped cream on top. Decorate with berries and micro greens.

Strawberry shortcake
with dried rose petals

∿

SERVES 6

SWEET TART CRUST • 2 tbsp (30 g) **homemade margarine** (p. 160) • 2 tbsp (25 g) **palm sugar** • ¼ cup (40 g) **brown rice flour** • ¼ cup (35 g) **whole wheat flour** • 2½ tsp (12 g) **water** • ¼ tsp (1 g) **fleur de sel** • **dried rose petals**, slivered

SOFT SPONGE CAKE 1 TSP (5 G) NEUTRAL OIL • 1 **egg** and 1 **egg yolk** • 2 tbsp + 1 tsp (30 g) **unrefined cane sugar** • ⅓ cup (40 g) **ground almonds** • 2 tbsp (10 g) **einkorn** • ¼ tsp (1 g) **psyllium husk powder** • 1 **egg white**

ROSE AND STRAWBERRY JAM • 1 tsp (3 g) **alginate** • 1 tsp (5 g) **unrefined cane sugar** • ½ cup (100 g) **strawberries** • Juice and zest of ½ **lemon** • 1 tbsp + 2 tsp (25 g) **rose water**

LIGHT VANILLA PASTRY CREAM • 1 cup (250 g) **plant-based beverage** • 1 tbsp (15 g) **brown sugar** • 1 tbsp + 1 tsp (10 g) **arrowroot starch** • ½ **vanilla bean** • 2 tbsp (30 g) **coconut oil** • pinch **turmeric** • 6 tbsp + 2 tsp (100 g) **coconut cream**, whipped

STRAWBERRY AND ROSE WATER JELLY • ¼ cup + 2 tsp (70 g) **water** • ¼ cup (20 g) **strawberries** • 2½ tsp (10 g) **palm sugar** • ¼ tsp (0.7 g) **agar agar** • 2 tsp (10 g) **rose water** • **beetroot powder**

ROSE CREAM • 25 g **cream** (1) • ½ **vanilla bean** • 1 tbsp (7 g) **yacon syrup or maple syrup** • 6 tbsp + 2 tsp (100 g) **cream** (2), cold • 1 tsp (5 g) **rose water**

CHOCOLATE DECORATIONS • 6 tbsp (100 g) **chopped white chocolate** • 1 tbsp (2 g) **ground dried strawberries**

ASSEMBLY • 1 cup (200 g) **strawberries**, chopped + ¼ cup (50 g) **strawberries** for decoration

SWEET TART CRUST

Using an electric mixer, combine margarine with sugar. Add flours, then water, fleur de sel and rose petals. Roll out to ⅛-inch (2 mm) between two sheets of parchment paper.

Use a 7-inch (18 cm) springform pan and shape into a disc. Bake at 340 °F (170 °C) for 12 to 15 minutes.

ROSE CREAM

Heat cream (1) with seeds scraped from the vanilla bean and the bean itself. Let steep for 1 hour, covered. Strain and add syrup, cream (2) and rose water. Using an electric mixer, beat into a creamy texture and refrigerate for at least 3 hours.

SOFT SPONGE CAKE

Preheat convection oven to 325 °F (160 °C). Grease a 6-inch (16 cm) springform or round pan with neutral oil. Whisk together egg and egg yolk with cane sugar. Add almonds, then einkorn and psyllium.

Using an electric mixer, beat the egg white until it forms soft peaks. Using a spatula, gently fold the beaten egg white into the mixture.

Bake at 340 °F (170 °C) for 16 minutes. Let cool before removing from the pan.

ROSE AND STRAWBERRY JAM

In a small bowl, combine alginate and cane sugar. In a tall cup, combine strawberries, lemon juice and zest, and rose water. Pour in alginate mixture. Using an immersion blender, blend for 1 minute.

LIGHT VANILLA PASTRY CREAM

In a saucepan, heat plant-based beverage with brown sugar. Add a small amount of the liquid to the arrowroot starch and stir. Return starch and liquid to the saucepan and add seeds from the vanilla bean. Bring to a boil for about 30 seconds, stirring. Remove from heat. Add coconut oil and ground turmeric and refrigerate. Once cooled, add whipped coconut cream.

STRAWBERRY AND ROSE WATER JELLY

In a saucepan, combine water, strawberries, palm sugar and agar agar. Bring to a boil and add rose water and beetroot powder. Stir until combined and use right away.

ASSEMBLY

Prepare a springform pan 7-inch (18 cm) in diameter and 1.4-inch (3.5 cm) high with a sheet of plastic pastry film covering the inside ring of the pan.

Place the sweet tart crust in the pan, then the soft sponge cake layer. Add ⅔ of the light vanilla pastry cream, then the rose and strawberry jam and 1 cup (200 g) strawberries. Cover with the rest of the pastry cream. Smooth, using an offset spatula. Pour on the jelly and refrigerate for 1 hour. Remove the plastic pastry film. **Chocolate decorations:** In a double boiler, melt white chocolate with dried strawberries. Heat to 115 °F (45 °C), then cool to 78 °F (26 °C) and heat again to 82 °F (28 °C).

Using an offset spatula, spread a fine layer of chocolate on plastic pastry film and instantly apply around the shortcake.

Whip the rose cream and, using a piping bag with a ½-inch (1 cm) tip, pipe it around the edge. Add a few sliced strawberries on top.

Apricot, lavender and buttermilk mousse tart

᠊ᢟ᠊

MAKES 10 INDIVIDUAL TARTS

SWEET TART CRUST • 3 tbsp (40 g) **unrefined cane sugar** • ¼ cup (40 g) **brown rice flour** • 7 tbsp (70 g) **spelt flour** • 6 tbsp (40 g) **almond flour** • 1 tbsp (15 g) **water** • ¼ tsp (1 g) **fleur de sel** • 3 tbsp + 2 tsp (50 g) **butter**, softened • 1 tsp (2 g) **dried lavender**

LAVENDER JELLY • 7 tbsp (105 g) **water** • ¾ tsp (3 g) **agar agar** • ½ tbsp (10 g) **honey** • 1 tbsp (7.5 g) **dried lavender**

APRICOT-LAVENDER FILLING • 1 recipe **lavender jelly** • 5 tbsp (60 g) diced **apricots**

BUTTERMILK MOUSSE • 3 tbsp + 1 tsp (50 g) **35% cream (1)** • ¾ tsp (3 g) **agar agar** • 2 tsp (10 g) **date sugar** • 3 tbsp + 1 tsp (50 g) **buttermilk** • 6 tbsp + 2 tsp (100 g) **35% cold cream (2)**

APRICOT GLAZE • 6 tbsp + 2 tsp (100 g) **plant-based beverage** • 4 tsp (10 g) **arrowroot starch** • ½ tbsp (10 g) **honey** • 3 tbsp + 1 tsp (50 g) **apricot purée**

BUTTERMILK MOUSSE

Combine cream (1) with agar agar and date sugar. Pour over the buttermilk and combine. Refrigerate the mixture for 2 hours. Whip cream (2) and add it to the buttermilk mixture.

LAVENDER JELLY

In a saucepan, bring water and agar agar to a boil. Off the heat, add honey and lavender. Mix, strain and store in the fridge.

APRICOT-LAVENDER FILLING

In a bowl, combine lavender jelly with apricots. Pour into discs 1½ inches (4 cm) in diameter to set.

SWEET TART CRUST

In a bowl, combine cane sugar with flours. Add water, fleur de sel, soft butter and lavender. Roll out to ⅛ inch (2 mm) between two sheets of parchment paper. Cut out petal shapes that are 2½ inches (6 cm) in diameter. Bake on a non-stick baking sheet at 325 °F (160 °C) for 12 minutes.

APRICOT GLAZE

In a saucepan, heat plant-based beverage with arrowroot starch and honey. Whisk until thickened. Off the heat, add apricot purée and cool to 95 °F (35 °C).

ASSEMBLY

In a pebble-shaped silicone mold with a 2½-inch (6 cm) diameter, pipe the buttermilk mousse to fill half the mold. Using an offset spatula, spread the mousse into the mold. Add the apricot-lavender filling and freeze for 3 hours. Remove from mold and glaze with apricot glaze. Place on a sweet tart crust petal. Finish by piping drops of buttermilk mousse on top. If desired, decorate with slices of dried apricot and lavender flowers.

Vanilla, mango and ginger
Tahitian pearl
⋆

SERVES 6

SHORTCRUST PASTRY • 2 tbsp (25 g) **coconut sugar** • 2½ tsp (12 g) **coconut oil** • 1½ tbsp (25 g) **applesauce** • 1½ tsp (7 g) **water** • ¼ tsp (1 g) **gray salt** or **fleur de sel** • ⅓ cup (40 g) **rice flour** • 2½ tbsp (22 g) **buckwheat flour** • ¼ tsp (1 g) **baking soda**

RECONSTITUTED SHORTCRUST PASTRY • 1 recipe **shortcrust pastry** • 4 tsp (20 g) **cocoa butter** • ¼ tsp (1 g) **fleur de sel**

SOFT GINGER BISCUIT • 1 tsp (5 g) **neutral oil** • 1 **egg** and 1 **egg yolk** • 2 tbsp + 1½ tsp (30 g) **coconut sugar** • 1¼ tsp (5 g) **gingerroot** • 6 tbsp (40 g) **ground almonds** • 1½ tsp (10 g) **whole spelt flour** • ¼ tsp (1 g) **psyllium husk powder** • 1 **egg white**

MANGO GINGER PRESERVES • 2½ tsp (10 g) **coconut sugar** • ¾ tsp (2 g) **food-grade sodium alginate powder** • 7 tbsp (75 g) **chopped mango** (1) • 1¼ tsp (5 g) **grated fresh gingerroot** • 2 tbsp + 1 tsp (25 g) **diced mango** (2)

VANILLA-COCONUT CREAM • ⅓ cup (100 g) **coconut cream** • 1 **vanilla bean**, split • 1 tbsp (20 g) **honey** • ¾ cup + 4 tsp (200 g) cold **35% cream**

VANILLA-COCONUT CREAM

Heat coconut cream with vanilla bean and seeds. Off the heat, let steep for 1 hour, covered. Strain, then add honey and cold cream. Mix and refrigerate for at least 3 hours.

MANGO GINGER PRESERVES

Combine coconut sugar and alginate. In a blender, puree mango (1) with the alginate mixture and grated gingerroot for 1 minute.

Add mango (2). Pipe into silicone half-sphere molds that are 1½ inch (4 cm) in diameter. Freeze for 1 hour. Unmold and, using a hair dryer for a few seconds, assemble the half-spheres to make a mango pearl ball. Freeze until it's time to assemble.

SHORTCRUST PASTRY

Using an electric mixer, combine coconut sugar and coconut oil. Add applesauce and water. Blend. Gradually add salt, flours and baking soda. Roll out between two pieces of parchment paper to ½ inch (1 cm) thick. Bake at 340 °F (170 °C) for 20 minutes.

RECONSTITUTED SHORTCRUST PASTRY

Once the shortcrust pastry is baked, cut it into ½-inch (1 cm) cubes. Melt cocoa butter and pour it over the cubes. Mix gently. Add fleur de sel. Make biscuits 1½ inches (4 cm) in diameter using 2 tsp (10 g) of reconstituted shortcrust pastry. Press down.

SOFT GINGER BISCUIT

Preheat convection oven to 320 °F (160 °C). Grease a 6-inch (16 cm) springform pan or round pan with neutral oil. Using an electric mixer, beat egg and egg yolk with coconut sugar and grated gingerroot. Add the ground almonds, spelt flour and psyllium.

Separately, using clean beaters, whip the egg white. The texture should be fluffy and form soft peaks. Using a spatula, gently fold the whipped egg white into the mixture. Pour the mixture into the pan and bake for 10 minutes at 320 °F (160 °C). Let cool before removing from pan. Cut out discs that are 1½ inches (4 cm) in diameter.

ASSEMBLY

Whip the vanilla coconut cream. Pipe the cream into the bottom half of a 3-inch (8 cm) half-sphere silicone mold, leaving room to add a soft ginger biscuit, then the mango pearl. Pipe more vanilla-coconut cream into the second half-sphere and place together to make a ball shape. Make a wave out of tempered white chocolate (see chocolate decoration instructions on p. 235, use without dried strawberries) and attach it to the reconstituted shortcrust pastry. Place the pearl inside the wave.

Vanilla, lemon caviar and black tea
baba

ᴖ

MAKES 10 INDIVIDUAL BABAS

SWEET TART CRUST • 3 tbsp (40 g) **unrefined cane sugar** • ¼ cup (40 g) **brown rice flour** • 7 tbsp (70 g) **spelt flour** • 6 tbsp (40 g) **almond flour** • 1 tbsp (15 g) **water** • ¼ tsp (1 g) **fleur de sel** • 3 tbsp + 2 tsp (50 g) **butter**, softened • 2½ tsp (5 g) **black tea**, powdered

BABA DOUGH • 0.3 oz (8 g) **fresh compressed yeast** (or 1 tsp/3.6 g instant dry yeast) • 2 tsp (10 g) **water** • 1 tsp (6 g) **honey** • ¾ cup (125 g) **rice flour** • 3 tbsp (25 g) **tigernut flour** • 3 tbsp (25 g) **cornstarch** • ¼ tsp (1 g) **salt** • 3 tbsp + 2 tsp (50 g) **butter** • 4 **eggs**, beaten

VANILLA LEMON SYRUP • 6 tbsp + 2 tsp (100 g) **water** • 1 tbsp + 1 tsp (15 g) **coconut sugar** • Juice and zest of 1 **lemon** • ¼ tsp (1 g) **agar agar**

LEMON CAVIAR PRESERVES • 1 tbsp (16 g) **water** • Juice and zest of 1 **lemon** • 1½ tsp (6 g) **unrefined cane sugar** • ½ tsp (2 g) **agar agar** • segments from 1 **lemon** • 2 tbsp + 2 tsp (40 g) **preserved lemons** • 15 g **"lemon caviar" pearls** from finger lime

VANILLA JELLY • 3 tbsp (45 g) **water** • 2 tbsp (45 g) **yacon syrup or maple syrup** • seeds of 1 **vanilla bean**, scraped • 0.5 g **capsules activated charcoal** (3 capsules) • ½ tsp (1 g) **food-grade sodium alginate powder**

VANILLA BLACK TEA WHIPPED CREAM • 3 tbsp + 1 tsp (50 g) **35% cream** (1) • ½ **vanilla bean** • 1½ tsp (3 g) **Earl Grey tea** • 1 tbsp (20 g) **honey** • 1 cup (221 g) **35% cream** (2)

YELLOW COATING • 3 tbsp + 1 tsp (50 g) **cocoa butter** • ½ cup (100 g) **white chocolate** • pinch **turmeric** • 3 tbsp + 1 tsp (50 g) **neutral oil**

LEMON CAVIAR PRESERVES

In a saucepan, make a jelly with water, lemon zest and juice, cane sugar and agar agar. Bring to a boil. Let set in the fridge for 30 minutes.

Cut preserved lemons in ¼-inch (0.5 cm) cubes and mix quickly with the agar agar jelly. The mixture shouldn't be smooth: there should be pieces of preserved lemons. Add fresh lemon segments and lemon caviar pearls to the jelly and mix. Pipe 1 tbsp (8 g) into each 2½-inch (6 cm) mold. Freeze for 1 hour.

VANILLA JELLY

In a measuring jug, combine water, syrup, vanilla bean seeds, charcoal and alginate and mix for 1 minute. Pour 3 tsp (8 g) of vanilla jelly on top of each mold with lemon caviar preserves and freeze for 1 hour.

VANILLA BLACK TEA WHIPPED CREAM

Heat cream (1) with the scraped seeds and pod of the vanilla bean, tea and honey. Steep for 30 minutes. Strain. Add cream (2) and, using an electric mixer, beat into a cream. Store in the fridge.

SWEET TART CRUST

In a bowl, combine cane sugar with flours. Add water, fleur de sel, butter and black tea powder. Roll out to ⅛-inch (2 mm) thickness between two sheets of parchment paper.

Cut out petal shapes 2½ inches (6 cm) in diameter. Bake on a non-stick baking sheet at 325 °F (160 °C) for 12 minutes.

BABA DOUGH

In the bowl of a stand mixer fitted with the paddle attachment, combine yeast, water and honey. Add flours, cornstarch, salt, butter and ⅔ of the eggs. Knead on low speed until the dough is smooth, glossy and pulls away from the bowl. Add the rest of the eggs and knead until the dough is elastic and pulls away from the bowl. Lightly grease the pebble-shaped silicone molds that are 2½ inches (6 cm) in diameter and add one-tenth of dough per mold. Let rise 1 hour at 82 to 85 °F (28 to 30 °C), then bake for 10 minutes at 350 °F (180 °C). Remove from molds.

VANILLA LEMON SYRUP

In a saucepan, bring all ingredients to a boil. Soak the babas for 30 seconds when the syrup has cooled to 95 °F (35 °C).

YELLOW COATING

In a double boiler, melt cocoa butter with white chocolate, turmeric and neutral oil. Mix if needed and strain before using immediately.

ASSEMBLY

Whip the black tea cream and pipe to fill ⅓ of a 4-inch (10 cm) diameter mold. Using an icing spatula, spread the whipped cream in the mold. Place the lemon caviar-vanilla filling on top, then the soaked baba. Smooth with an offset spatula and place in the freezer.

Remove from mold and, using a wooden skewer, dip in the yellow coating. Pipe small drops of vanilla black tea whipped cream on top.

Pineapple, coriander and lemon balm Pavlovas

MAKES 10 INDIVIDUAL PAVLOVAS

MERINGUE • 5 tbsp (70 g) **packed brown sugar** • ¼ tsp (1 g) **agar agar** • 6 tbsp + 2 tsp (100 g) **aquafaba** • 2 tbsp + 2 tsp (20 g) **arrowroot starch** or ¼ cup (30 g) cornstarch, sifted • ½ tsp (2 g) **psyllium husk powder**

CORIANDER JELLY • 6 tbsp + 2 tsp (100 g) **water** • 2½ tsp (10 g) **unrefined cane sugar** • ¼ tsp (1 g) **agar agar** • ½ tsp (1 g) **coriander seeds**, ground

PINEAPPLE FILLING • 1 cup (250 g) **cubed pineapple** • 1 recipe **coriander jelly**

VEGAN GELATINE • 6 tbsp + 2 tsp (100 g) **water** • 2½ tsp (10 g) **unrefined cane sugar** • ¾ tsp (3 g) **agar agar**

LEMON BALM WHIPPED CREAM • ¾ cup + 4 tsp (200 g) **35% cream** (1) • 5 sprigs **fresh lemon balm** • 2 tsp (15 g) **honey** • ¾ cup + 4 tsp (200 g) **35% cream** (2)

LEMON BALM WHIPPED CREAM

Steep cream (1) with lemon balm in the fridge for 24 hours. Strain and add honey and cream (2). In a standard mixer fitted with a whisk, whip until you get the texture of whipped cream.

MERINGUE

In a small bowl, combine brown sugar with agar agar and pour into a saucepan that contains the aquafaba. Heat the mixture, then bring to a boil. Transfer the mixture to a stand mixer fitted with the whisk attachment and whip into a meringue.

Using a spatula, fold in starch and psyllium. Pipe meringue balls and thin meringue leaves on a baking sheet lined with a silicone mat and dry in the oven at 190 °F (90 °C) for at least 3 hours.

CORIANDER JELLY

In a saucepan, combine water, cane sugar and agar agar. Bring to a boil.

Off the heat, add coriander and refrigerate for 1 hour.

PINEAPPLE FILLING

Combine pineapple with coriander jelly. Keep ⅔ in the fridge and purée the rest in a blender. Pipe 10 small mounds of 1⅛ inch (3 cm) in diameter onto a baking sheet lined with parchment paper and freeze for 30 minutes.

VEGAN GELATINE

In a saucepan, combine water, sugar and agar agar. Bring to a boil. Refrigerate. To use the jelly, heat to 82 °F (28 °C) and, using a wooden skewer, dip the frozen pineapple ball to coat.

ASSEMBLY

Gently break the crust of the meringue and fill with the refrigerated pineapple filling. Pipe the lemon balm whipped cream and place the frozen pineapple portion on top. Decorate with thin meringue leaves.

Babas
with citrus fruit and lemongrass infusion
·¡·

SERVES 10

INFUSION • ½ cup (125) g **water** • 6 tbsp + 2 tsp (100 g) **orange juice** • 2 tbsp (30 g) **lime juice** • ¼ cup (80 g) **honey** • ½ bunch **verbena** • ½ bunch **lemon balm** • 2 tbsp (25 g) **grated gingerroot** • 1 stalk **lemongrass**

KUMQUAT PRESERVES • ½ cup (125 g) **kumquats** • 1¼ cup (300 g) **orange juice** • 7 tbsp (150 g) **honey**

LEMON BALM OIL • 1 bunch **lemon balm** • 6 tbsp + 2 tsp (100 g) **neutral oil**

BABAS • 0.3 oz (8 g) **fresh compressed yeast** (or 1 tsp/3.6 g instant dry yeast) • 2 tsp (9 g) **water** • 1 tsp (6 g) **honey** • 1½ cup (180 g) **whole wheat pastry flour** • ¼ cup (60 g) **margarine** • ¼ tsp (1 g) **salt** • 4 **eggs**, beaten

WHIPPED COCONUT CREAM • 2 tsp (15 g) **honey** • ⅔ cup (150 g) **coconut cream**

INFUSION

In a saucepan, heat the water and juices with honey, then add verbena, lemon balm, ginger and lemongrass. Bring to a boil, steep for 1 hour, then strain. Keep cool.

Dry the herbs and spices in a dehydrator or in the oven at 105 °F (40 °C). Stir and set aside for decoration.

KUMQUAT PRESERVES

Cut kumquats into thin slices, then preserve them in orange juice mixed with honey.

LEMON BALM OIL

In a large saucepan, add lemon balm and cover with cold water. Bring the mixture to a boil. Drain and mix with neutral oil. Strain and store in a glass bottle with a dropper.

BABAS

In a small bowl, combine yeast, water and honey. Transfer to a standard mixer fitted with the paddle attachment. Add flour, margarine, salt and ⅔ of the eggs. Knead on low speed until the dough is smooth, glossy and pulls away from the bowl. Add the rest of the eggs and knead until the dough is elastic and pulls away from the bowl. Lightly grease 1½-inch (4 cm) diameter silicone molds and fill ⅔ with the dough. Let rise for around 35 minutes at 82 °F (28 °C) in a humid space, then bake for 15 to 25 minutes at 350 °F (180 °C). Remove from molds, then soak in the infusion at 140 °F (60 °C).

WHIPPED COCONUT CREAM

Using an electric mixer, beat honey with the coconut cream until you get the texture of whipped cream.

ASSEMBLY

Place babas in a bowl and top with preserved kumquat slices. Pipe coconut cream on top and pour the infusion, hot or cold, all around. Finalize by adding a few drops of lemon balm oil.

Chestnut, pear and vanilla
velouté

∕

SERVES 10

VELOUTÉ • ½ cup (125 g) **whole chestnuts**, peeled • 2 tsp (12.5 g) **honey** • ½ cup (125 g) **almond beverage** • ½ cup (125 g) **pear purée** • ½ cup (125 g) **water** • 1 **vanilla bean**, split • 2 tsp (10 g) **grated fresh gingerroot**

FLAX SEED CRISP • 1 tbsp (10 g) **ground flax seeds** • 1 tbsp (15 g) **boiling water** (1) • 1 tbsp (10 g) **buckwheat flour** • 2 tsp (10 g) **margarine** • 1 tbsp (15 g) **water**, cold (2) • 2½ tsp (10 g) **fleur de sel** • 6 tbsp (80 g) **unrefined cane sugar**

QUICK-COOKED PEAR • 1 **pear** • 2 tsp (10 g) **olive oil** • 1 tbsp (15 g) **maple syrup**

VELOUTÉ

In a blender, purée chestnuts, honey, almond beverage, pear purée and water.

Transfer to a saucepan and heat gently to reduce until the mixture coats the back of a spoon. Stir in vanilla bean seeds and ginger.

FLAX SEED CRISP

In a bowl, combine ground flax seeds with boiling water. Sift in buckwheat flour. In a saucepan, bring margarine, cold water, fleur de sel and cane sugar to a simmer. Pour over the flour and moistened flax seeds. Stir until smooth. Pour onto a non-stick baking sheet, then bake at 340 °F (170 °C) for 24 minutes. Cut and freefold lightly, then let set. Store in a dry place.

QUICK-COOKED PEAR

Peel the pear, then shape the flesh into small balls. Add any pear scraps to the velouté. In a saucepan, add olive oil and quickly cook the balls, browning them on each side. Avoid cooking too much so they keep their shape and a crisp edge. Place on a baking sheet, then brush with maple syrup to make them shiny.

ASSEMBLY

In a saucepan, heat velouté heated to 140 °F (60 °C) maximum. Pour into serving bowls and add the pear balls. Decorate with a large piece of flax seed crisp.

Rhubarb, hibiscus and verbena
with raspberry sauce

SERVES 10

RASPBERRY WATER • 2 cups (400 g) **fresh raspberries** • 2½ tsp (10 g) **unrefined cane sugar** • ½ **cinnamon stick**

RASPBERRY SAUCE • ¾ cup + 4 tsp (200 g) **raspberry water** • 6 tbsp + 2 tsp (100 g) **coconut milk** • 10 **dried hibiscus petals** • 5 sprigs **fresh lemon verbena**

POACHED RHUBARB • 4 cups (400 g) **rhubarb** • 2 tsp (10 g) **raspberry water**

VERBENA WHIPPED CREAM • ⅔ cup (150 g) **35% cream** • 2 tsp (15 g) **honey** • 5 sprigs **fresh lemon verbena**, stems removed, leaves chopped

DECORATION • 5 **raspberries**

VERBENA WHIPPED CREAM

In a bowl, add cream and verbena, leave to infuse overnight in the fridge. Strain, add honey and, using an electric mixer, beat until fluffy.

RASPBERRY WATER

In a bowl, combine raspberries, sugar and cinnamon, then heat, covered, in a double boiler over low heat for 30 minutes. Strain and set aside the liquid. Dry the leftover raspberry pulp in the oven at 200 °F (100 °C) for 2 hours or overnight in a dehydrator. Grind in a blender to make a powder.

RASPBERRY SAUCE

Heat raspberry water and coconut milk to 122 °F (50 °C), then add hibiscus and lemon verbena and steep for 1 hour, off the heat. Strain and store in the fridge.

POACHED RHUBARB

Peel the rhubarb and cut into pieces. Heat raspberry water to 140 °F (60 °C) and add the rhubarb pieces, cooking until creamy. Drain, then let cool before serving.

ASSEMBLY

In a small bowl, place a large spoonful of verbena whipped cream. Add 3 pieces of poached rhubarb and one raspberry, halved. Sprinkle with dried raspberry powder and pour the sauce over top.

Pineapple, lime and olive oil dumplings
with ginger coconut galangal sauce

⁀

GINGER COCONUT GALANGAL SAUCE • 6 tbsp + 2 tsp (100 g) **water** • ¾ cup + 4 tsp (200 g) **coconut milk** • 1 tbsp + 2 tsp (20 g) **grated galangal** • 1 tsp (5 g) **grated gingerroot** • 2 tsp (10 g) lime juice • Zest of ½ **lime** • Zest of ¼ **wild lime** • 4 **wild lime leaves** • 1½ inch (4 cm) **lemongrass** • 1 tbsp (3 g) **fresh Thai coriander or cilantro leaves** • 1 tbsp (3 g) fresh **Thai basil leaves** • 2 tbsp (40 g) **honey** • ½ **bird's eye chili**

DICED PINEAPPLE • ⅓ cup (75 g) **diced pineapple** • Zest and juice of 2 **limes** • 3 tbsp + 1 tsp (10 g) **chopped fresh Thai coriander or cilantro** • 1 tbsp (15 g) **olive oil**

DUMPLING DOUGH • ½ cup + 2 tbsp (75 g) **tapioca starch** • 6 tbsp (50 g) **all-purpose flour** • ½ cup (75 g) **brown rice flour** • ¼ tsp (1 g) **fine salt** • ½ cup (125 g) **water** • 1 tsp (5 g) **neutral oil**

CILANTRO OIL • 2 tbsp (30 g) **olive oil** • 3 tbsp + 1 tsp (10 g) **Thai coriander or cilantro leaves**

DECORATION • **sesame seeds** • **flower petals**

GINGER COCONUT GALANGAL SAUCE

In a saucepan, heat water and coconut milk to 122 °F (50 °C). Add the remaining ingredients, then steep for 1 hour.

Strain, return to saucepan and reduce over low heat until the mixture coats the back of a spoon.

DICED PINEAPPLE

In bowl, combine pineapple, lime zest and juice, coriander and olive oil.

DUMPLING DOUGH

In a bowl, sift starch and all flours together, then add salt. Boil the water, then pour it gradually over the flour mixture and add neutral oil. Form into dough and refrigerate for 1 hour before using.

Make small balls, then, using a rolling pin, roll out to 4 inches (10 cm) and ¹⁄₁₆-inch (1 mm) thick. Add the diced pineapple mixture in the center of each circle and fold the edges together. In a large pot of boiling water, cook dumplings for 6 minutes like a pasta. Remove with a slotted spoon.

CILANTRO OIL

In a bowl, mix oil with cilantro leaves.

ASSEMBLY

Place the pineapple dumplings in a bowl. Pour the hot ginger coconut galangal sauce over top and sprinkle with sesame seeds and drops of cilantro oil. Decorate with tiny flower petals.

ACKNOWLEDGMENTS

There is always something magical about looking back at the moments and people who left their mark at a turning point in your life.

If I were to begin at the beginning, I would start by thanking the journalist (whose name I've forgotten) who made it possible for me to introduce this vision of healthy French pastries in 2016.

Next, there was a wonderful encounter with **Nicole Couturier**, a Chinese medicine expert, who offered me a personalized introduction to the world of Yin and Yang. I spent many hours with her studying the approach of this ancient and powerful medicine, and I understood that this complementary pathway would be a long learning experience. THANK YOU for giving me this time and this valuable knowledge.

Some of my most fantastic encounters were those with **Adélaïde d'Aboville**, a dietitian-nutritionist, and **Caroline Gayet**, a dietitian and herbalist. Our conversations led me to imagine with them workshops on healthy eating and promoting beauty through diet. Although this project did not see the light of day because of Covid, THANK YOU for your beautiful energy and for all the fascinating discussions.

The path continued with **Mélanie Frechon**. While she was a student, she signed up for a six-month internship at my workshop. I saw a passion for nutrition in this young woman. Her office was already up and running; she worked with, among others, athletes on their diet. When the book project came into view, I suggested that she join me in this adventure. THANKS to you for the long hours of work and for your feedback when I needed it. This became a year-long undertaking where you were fully invested.

Anne Serroy came into my life at a photo shoot for the book *Biscornu* (by Olivier Tran). After the shoot, she asked me, "Have you ever thought of writing a book?" As luck would have it, a few days later, I summoned my teams to talk to them about this new project. Anne has had an extraordinary career in publishing. After more than 20 years at La Martinière and publishing the top pastry cookbooks, she became an independent editorial director. Huge THANKS to you for being with me since day one of this adventure. From the meeting with Flammarion, through all the conversations we had about the writing of the book, we are now finally holding it in our hands.

Romain Roussel was one of my amazing encounters at the workshop, where he turned up one day, without warning, offering to set up the farmers' network La Ruche qui dit oui [The hive that says yes] in Neuilly. I soon discovered his track record in publishing and his boundless creativity. It seemed obvious that I should involve you in this book to enhance it with your ideas and give it an educational and, at times, slightly quirky aspect. THANK YOU for your support, your helpful rereading of the book and your constructive ideas.

At the workshop, the excitement of the first recipe testing took place under the guidance of **Thibault Lefebvre**. A flurry of activity and hundreds of tests later, the first recipes were approved. Heartfelt THANKS to you, Thibault, for opening your mind, adapting when needed and looking for new possibilities for flavors and textures with new constraints.

I would also like to thank from the bottom of my heart our young interns throughout 2023 for their very active participation in the recipe and ingredient testing: **Marine Londero, Faustyne L'Hostis, Valentine Boitelle, Alberic Behagel, Chaîma Lemoine, Julie Agullo, Aliénor Cohet, Abi Despagne** and **Margot Billeau**.

Special thanks for another incredible encounter: **Katia Elmalek**, who shared with me her vision of low-GI and healthy pastries. As someone who is passionate about nutrition, she shared with us her in-depth knowledge of this subject.

The project as a whole caught the eye of **Jessica Da Silva**, my fabulous community manager. She was able, as she always does, to capture in photos and videos each instant of these precious moments. A big THANKS to you for your professionalism and the quality of your work every day.

One of my greatest sources of pride regarding this book is having called upon two absolutely essential gems, without whom the book would not be what it is. We have worked together for many years, and here we had the opportunity to put our stamp on a most successful collaborative effort: a big, an immense, a gigantic THANK YOU, therefore, to **Nicolas Bouriette**, an exceptional photographer, and to **Coralie Chaffanjon**, a high-caliber designer, for being by my side as we developed this book, which was a project close to my heart for many years. Nicolas, the quality of the book is so closely tied to your stunning photos, to ingredients taken from every angle, to stolen moments in my garden or at the workshop. Hours of shooting, waiting, retouching, going from Paris to Biarritz and back... That's it: we won't change another thing!

Coralie, such amazing work! You dove into the project with so much precision that you managed to portray its essence through a vision that is both informative and elegant on every page. The layout of the book is phenomenal, and although I want to congratulate you for your outstanding work, I cannot help but mention your human qualities, your wholehearted commitment and your energy, which are unshakably positive.

Huge THANKS to the entire Flammarion team: to **Ronite Tubiana**, editorial director of the Art de vivre department, and editor **Élise Bigot**, who supported me through all the key stages of the book. Élise, you trusted me at every step, with much kindness, and you brought a keen eye to the text and to the final layout. Bravo for your support.

I would like to warmly thank the publishing house Robert Rose for its support for the English edition, as well as to the entire Canadian team who accompanied me: **Kevin Cockburn, Meredith Dees, Merel Elsinga, Jennifer MacKenzie** and **Anne Louise Mahoney**. A very special thanks to **Bob Dees** who, with a lot of humor, embraced this project from the beginning.

Thanks to **Hélène Clastres** from the Flammarion team for supporting the discussions with Robert Rose with great commitment and trust.

Finally, after a year of work, I understand deeply that this book could not have come to be without the trust and never-ending encouragement of the one who walks with me every day in all my wildest projects. An enormous MERCI to you, **François Daubinet**, for offering me your support, a listening ear and such valuable advice.

In you and in our two daughters, Lara and Hailie, I found the strength to bring this project to fruition.

Index

pineapple (continued)
Pineapple Coconut Sorbet, 186
pineapple sage, 144, 148
pine nuts, 120
pistachios, 120
plums, 101
pomegranates, 102
poppy flower, 144
poppy seed oil, 76
poppy seeds, 122
potato starch, 32
psyllium, 153
Puff Pastry, Quick, 226
pumpkin seeds, 122

Q

quark (fromage blanc), 63
quinces, 102
quinoa beverage, 62
quinoa flour, 28

R

rapadura (panela), 45
raspberries, 102
Raspberry, Lychee and Galangal
Sorbet, 187
Rhubarb, Hibiscus and Verbena,
248
rice beverage, 62
rice flour, 28
rice starch, 32
rice syrup, 48
rosemary, 145, 148
roses, 135, 144
rye flour, 28

S

sacha (Inca) inchi oil, 76
safflower oil, 77

saffron, 135
St. John's wort, 145
salts, 136–37
seeds, 121–22, 123. See also specific
seeds
sesame oil, 77
sesame seeds, 121, 122
shea butter, 82
Shortcrust Pastry, 166
Snickers Bars, Healthy, 222
sodium alginate, 153
sorrel, 148
soy beverage, 62
soy flour, 28
spelt beverage, 62, 161
spelt flour, 29
spices, 124–37. See also specific spices
Sponge Cake, Soft Almond, 172
Sponge Cake Roll, 170
squash, 109, 110
star anise, 133
starches, 31–32
stevia leaf powder, 48–49
strawberries, 103, 104
Strawberry Shortcake with Dried
Rose Petals, 234
sumac, 133
sunflower oil, 77
sunflower seeds, 122
Sweet Dough, 164
sweeteners, 36–55. See also specific
sugars and syrups
sweet potatoes, 109
sweet potato flour, 29

T

tapioca, 32
tarragon, 148
tea, 161
teff flour, 30
thickeners, 151–53

thyme, 145, 148
tigernut flour, 29
tofu (silken), 64
tonka beans, 128, 134
trans fats, 72
turmeric, 130

V

vanilla, 133, 161
Vanilla, Lemon Caviar and Black Tea
Baba, 240
Vanilla, Mango and Ginger Tahitian
Pearl, 238
Vanilla–Orange Blossom Ice Cream,
185
vegetables, 92, 106, 112–13. See also
greens; specific vegetables
verbena, 148
violets, 145
vitamins, 154–55

W

Waffles, 192
walnuts, 120
walnut oil, 79
watermelon, 103
wheat flour, 15, 30

X

xylitol, 49

Y

yacon syrup, 49
yogurts, 63–64

Z

zucchini, 110